# DISPUTE RESOLUTION

**Amanda Powell**

Published by
The University of Law,
2 Bunhill Row
London EC1Y 8HQ

British Library Cataloguing in Publication Data

A catalogue record for this book is available from the British Library.

ISBN 978 1 914219 01 6

# Contents

# Table of Cases

# Table of Statutes

# 1 Different Options for Dispute Resolution

## SQE1 syllabus

By the end of this chapter you will be able to apply relevant core legal principles and rules appropriately and effectively, at the level of a competent newly qualified solicitor in practice, to realistic client-based and ethical problems and situations in relation to the **different options for dispute resolution** as follows:

- mediation
- arbitration
- litigation

Note that for SQE1, candidates are not usually required to recall specific case names, or cite statutory or regulatory authorities and these are provided for illustrative purposes only.

## Learning outcomes

The learning outcomes for this chapter are:

- To understand the characteristics of arbitration, mediation and litigation which make them an appropriate mechanism to resolve a dispute.
- To appreciate how alternative dispute resolution differs from arbitration and litigation.
- To explain the advantages and disadvantages of alternative dispute resolution.

## 1.1 Introduction

Whilst the public perception of litigation as slow and expensive, with cases argued by pompous barristers and presided over by elderly and out of touch judges may not have changed, the reality certainly has. Indeed, civil litigation disputes are more likely to be 'fought' in the tranquil surroundings of lawyers' offices or even a hotel boardroom than the courtroom, as the popularity of alternative dispute resolution increases. Even if the case does proceed through the courts, many claims are dealt with online – a development which is set to continue in the future. To facilitate this, the courts' system is in the throes of a £1 billion reform programme aimed at reducing reliance on buildings, face to face hearings and paper to allow for and promote the use of technology in resolving disputes.

There are several alternatives to court proceedings which may produce the remedy the client wants and, as part of the government's commitment to reducing the costs of litigation, alternative dispute resolution is actively encouraged. Arbitration, mediation and negotiation are now important aspects of civil litigation with most cases being settled well before the trial. These alternative procedures should always be considered at the first interview with the client and reviewed regularly thereafter.

This chapter will provide an overview of the civil litigation process and of some of the more common types of alternative dispute resolution.

## 1.2 Alternative dispute resolution

Litigation is considered the last resort and sanctions may be imposed on those clients who refuse to consider other options. Alternative dispute resolution (ADR) is a collective term which refers to any means of settling disputes outside of the traditional litigation process. Negotiation, in which the parties and the lawyers discuss possible solutions whether in formal meetings or by correspondence, is a form of ADR which is used routinely throughout the litigation process. In practice, the vast majority of claims are settled and negotiation is usually a key element in achieving this outcome. Although there are a number of other different types of ADR, most of these are outside the scope of this manual and this chapter will concentrate on just two – arbitration and mediation.

### 1.2.1 The nature of ADR

ADR, such as mediation, is a means of resolving disputes with the assistance of an independent third party who may help the parties to reach their own solution but who cannot impose a solution. It is voluntary and confidential or 'without prejudice'. This means that if it fails and court proceedings are taken, the court will not be made aware of the ADR until after the judge has dealt with the issues of liability and the award of damages. The parties choose the process and can withdraw at any time before a settlement is reached. If either party does not like the proposed solution, they do not have to accept it.

Arbitration is also voluntary, but only in the sense that the parties either voluntarily entered into an arbitration agreement or agreed to decide the matter in this way once a dispute arose. If the former, the effect is that one party may force the other to arbitrate against their will provided the original contractual agreement to arbitrate is valid.

In contrast, litigation is not voluntary (save that the claimant chooses to issue a claim in the first place). Once the case is started, usually, neither party can withdraw without paying the opponent's costs. If the parties are unable to negotiate a settlement or otherwise resolve their differences through ADR, the court will impose its own solution which may be enforced by the party who obtains judgment.

## 1.2.2 Failure to engage with ADR

When a dispute arises, a solicitor should discuss with the client the availability of ADR. If the client is willing (or has already agreed) to participate in ADR, it should be used unless:

- it is obviously inappropriate, for example because an injunction is required;
- the other party is unlikely to co-operate in the process; or
- the other party cannot be trusted to comply with an award.

Although actively promoted by the courts, there is no point in proceeding with ADR if it will inevitably fail. Nevertheless, a party who decides not to engage in ADR must be made aware that penalties may well be imposed for this failure, unless they can justify their stance to the court. The litigation process is subject to rules, one of which specifically requires the parties to consider the use of alternative dispute procedures, if appropriate. As a consequence, parties who choose to litigate may well receive judicial encouragement (and sometimes a degree of pressure) to attempt ADR although they cannot be ordered by a court to pursue this route.

Set out below is the wording of a direction which would commonly appear in a court order detailing what the parties are required to do to progress the matter.

### Alternative Dispute Resolution

At all stages the parties must consider settling this litigation by any means of Alternative Dispute Resolution (including Mediation); any party not engaging in any such means proposed by another must serve a witness statement giving reasons within 21 days of that proposal; such witness statement must not be shown to the trial judge until questions of costs arise.

The importance the court attaches to proposals for ADR is evidenced by the provisions of the Civil Procedure Rules 1998 which dictate how a case is litigated; and a failure to respond to a reasonable proposal to attempt settlement by ADR may have a significant impact on any subsequent order for costs.

 *In the leading case of* Halsey v Milton Keynes General NHS Trust *[2004] EWCA Civ 576, the Court of Appeal held that the court may impose a costs sanction on a party if they unreasonably refuse to take part in ADR. The court listed a number of factors which may be taken into account when determining this question:*

*(a) the nature of the dispute;*

*(b) the merits of the case;*

*(c) the extent to which other settlement methods have been attempted;*

*(d) whether the costs of the ADR would be disproportionately high;*

*(e) whether any delay in setting up and attending the ADR would have been prejudicial; and*

*(f) whether the ADR had a reasonable prospect of success.*

The burden is on the other party to show that the refusal is unreasonable with the court rejecting any presumption in favour of mediation.

 *The hard line the courts adopt was also apparent in the case of* Laporte v Commissioner of Police for the Metropolis *[2015] EWHC 371, in which two protesters alleged they had*

*been assaulted by the police and falsely imprisoned. The claim failed in every way, thus confirming the Police Commissioner's view that it was entirely without merit. Despite this, the court penalised the defendant by ordering that the claimants only pay two thirds of the defendant's costs as the defendant had failed, without adequate justification, to engage in ADR.*

*However, Gore v Naheed and Ahmed [2017] EWCA Civ 369 demonstrates that sanctions will not always apply where the parties refuse to take part in ADR. The case involved a dispute about a right of way for vehicle access. Although the court stressed that silence in the face of an invitation to participate in ADR would, as a general rule, be regarded as unreasonable, this was not automatic. In this particular instance, the judge did not penalise the successful claimant for their failure to consider ADR because he concluded that mediation had no reasonable prospect of success, would only add to costs and the matter raised complex questions of law that made it unsuitable for mediation.*

During the course of the court proceedings the parties complete what is known as a directions questionnaire and, to ensure that clients are fully aware of the importance and implications of ADR, solicitors are required to confirm they have explained to their client:

(a) the need to try to settle;

(b) the options available; and

(c) the possibility of costs sanctions if they refuse to attempt to settle.

The message is clear – clients should always consider ADR and engage in the process unless there are convincing reasons not to do so; and even then, they should be prepared to justify their decision before a sceptical judge if necessary.

### 1.2.3 The independent third party

The independence of the third party is an essential feature of ADR, as is the fact that (with the exception of arbitration) they cannot impose a solution. Because of this, the parties are more likely to be open in their discussions and less likely to be aggressive towards each other. As a consequence, the prospects of reaching a settlement are higher. A further advantage is that the independent third party will not only be trained to act as a neutral, but they also should have the appropriate industry or commercial knowledge required to understand the dispute. This may allow them to come up with ideas the parties may not have thought of and which solve the problem without either side losing face.

## 1.3 Mediation

Mediation is becoming increasingly popular as a form of ADR. At an early stage, the availability of mediation as an option should be discussed with the client. If the client is open to the suggestion, mediation should be proposed, usually by letter, to the opponent.

### 1.3.1 Procedure

In a typical mediation, the parties will agree an independent third person or body who will act as a 'go-between' known as a mediator. The mediator will be sent written statements from both parties and, thereafter, will discuss the case with them on a 'without prejudice' basis. Because any future judge in the proceedings will not be made aware of the discussions, the parties should feel free to engage in frank exchanges with both the mediator and each other. These conversations will also assist the mediator in identifying the real areas of disagreement and the points that are most important to the respective parties, with the aim being to move the parties towards constructive solutions to the problem.

In most cases, the mediator and the parties will meet in the same building. This enables any issues to be dealt with quickly because, if necessary, the parties can meet face to face to resolve their differences. There are, however, other forms of mediation in which the dispute is dealt with by correspondence, telephone conversations or online with the use of technology.

### 1.3.2 Advantages

Apart from the fact that an independent third party may find it easier to lead the parties to a settlement, mediation has many other attractions.

*Cost and speed*

Mediation can be significantly cheaper than both arbitration and litigation, primarily because the process is quicker. A skilled neutral can often help the parties to resolve their dispute in a relatively short period of time.

Nevertheless, clients should not be given the impression that mediation comes at 'bargain basement' prices. The parties have to pay the third party for their services and, in addition, lawyers will usually be instructed. However, if the mediation is successful, there will be a significant reduction in the amount of time the lawyers would have spent in preparing and presenting the case and this, in itself, will save costs.

*Flexibility*

Mediation is also very flexible, because the parties may choose the procedure to be followed. There are no legal requirements and thus no need to comply with any statutes, rules of court or even case law.

*Privacy*

Mediation takes place in private so that clients, customers and the public are unaware of the circumstances or the outcome of the dispute. This may be important where the party's reputation is an issue or where there may be possible future claims from other litigants.

*Preserving a business relationship*

Mediation is also ideal for cases where the parties to the dispute will need to continue to deal with each other. The fact they have chosen a non-confrontational method of solving their problem makes it much easier for them to continue their relationship, since the solution is theirs and has not been imposed upon them.

*Commercial reality*

A third party unconnected with the dispute may be able to assist the parties to arrive at realistic and workable terms of settlement. This could include arrangements that a court could not order, such as discounts on future orders. In contrast, litigation with its final court judgment will be decisive but the process carries inherent risk and uncertainty.

*Ability to withdraw*

If the client is unhappy with the progress, mediation allows them to withdraw at any time.

### 1.3.3 Disadvantages

There are occasions where mediation is simply not appropriate, such as where the client needs a ruling on a point of law or if an injunction is required. Matters involving allegations of fraud or other commercially disreputable conduct are also generally unsuitable for mediation. However, although in most other cases the advantages of mediation will usually outweigh the disadvantages, these must also be considered.

*Disclosure*

Because there are no formal procedures for disclosure of documents and evidence, there is a risk the parties may resolve the dispute without knowing all the facts. This may lead to a decision that is subsequently found to be unjust. However, many business clients take the view that a quick decision, even if it is not completely accurate, is better than wasting time and money on a protracted dispute in order to get a (potentially) more correct outcome.

*Privacy*

If the client requires public vindication – perhaps to ensure that any damage to their reputation is repaired – privacy is a disadvantage as they will lose the opportunity to demonstrate they were not at fault.

*Ability to withdraw*

As a general principle, no one can be forced to engage in mediation against their wishes. Furthermore, even if the parties have started to resolve a dispute by mediation, they may withdraw at any stage before a solution has been agreed despite objections from the other party. It will then usually be necessary to resort to litigation.

As with privacy, the ability to withdraw is both an advantage and a disadvantage. A party who decides to walk away from the mediation process will be pleased they can do so, whereas the other party is likely to be unhappy at the time and money expended without a resolution.

## 1.3.4 Enforcement

Even if an agreement is reached, it is not automatically binding as the client cannot enforce this like a court judgment. However, if the parties do agree to terms suggested as a result of mediation, they have entered into a contract. If one of the parties does not carry out that contract, they may be sued for the breach.

## 1.3.5 Summary

Set out below is a summary of the advantages and disadvantages of mediation over litigation as well as two factors that could be viewed either way.

**Table 1.1** Advantages and disadvantages of mediation over litigation

| Advantage | May be either | Disadvantage |
| --- | --- | --- |
| • involvement of an independent third party<br>• cost<br>• speed<br>• flexibility<br>• preserving business relationship<br>• commercial reality | • privacy<br>• ability to withdraw | • limited disclosure<br>• enforcement is not automatic |

# 1.4 Arbitration

Some cases proceed entirely separately from the civil justice system – in a 'parallel' dispute resolution process known as arbitration. It is a substitute for litigation and, once a party has agreed to be subject to it, they cannot take advantage of the normal court processes.

Arbitration may arise in two ways:

(a) The parties may be contractually bound to use arbitration and many business contracts contain a clause requiring the parties to submit to arbitration in the event of a dispute. It is common in certain industries such as construction and shipping, for example.

Such a clause would be:

> Any dispute arising out of or in connection with this contract, including any question regarding its existence, validity or termination, shall be referred to and resolved by arbitration under the XXX Rules.
>
> The number of arbitrators shall be [one/three].
>
> The language of the arbitration will be English.
>
> The governing law of the contract shall be the substantive law of England and Wales.

(b) In the absence of such a clause, the parties may agree to arbitration once a dispute has arisen and may choose their own arbitrator with the relevant expertise.

### 1.4.1 Legal authority

Arbitration is largely governed by statute, namely the Arbitration Act 1996, although this only applies if the agreement to arbitrate is in writing.

### 1.4.2 Procedure

The dispute is referred to an independent arbitrator. The person, professional or trade body may be specified in the original contract; alternatively, the parties may choose their own arbitrator with the relevant experience. An arbitration process will be adopted but this will be less formal than the court procedure. Once the third party has reached their decision, this is binding on both parties to the dispute.

### 1.4.3 Advantages

Many of the advantages of the parties agreeing to arbitration rather than litigation are similar to those of mediation. The main ones are:

(a) arbitration is likely to be quicker than going to court and may be cheaper although there will be costs implications in retaining the services of an arbitrator, who may be a highly qualified and experienced expert in their field;

(b) the procedures are less formal;

(c) the decision is made by an impartial third party with expertise in the matter;

(d) arbitration takes place in private thus retaining confidentiality – particularly important if the parties wish to preserve a business relationship or to ensure that customers or competitors are unaware of the dispute or the outcome;

(e) the solutions reached are often more practical than those a court has the power to order; and

(f) the decision is binding on the parties.

The binding nature of the outcome is the most important distinction with mediation.

### 1.4.4 Disadvantages

The main disadvantages are:

(a) the dispute may not receive the depth of investigation it would receive in the courts (depending upon the procedures adopted); and

(b) certain remedies such as injunctions are not available.

Furthermore, arbitration is unlikely to be a cheap alternative as the arbitration expert or panel will need to be paid and parties often want to be represented by lawyers, particularly if the amounts in dispute are significant.

One disadvantage mirrors an advantage: the decision is binding with very limited rights of appeal.

### 1.4.5 Enforcement

Once a decision has been reached, the winning party to an arbitration can apply to the High Court under s 66 of the Arbitration Act 1996 for permission to enforce the arbitration award as if it were a court judgment.

### 1.4.6 Summary

Below is a summary of the advantages and disadvantages of arbitration over litigation as well as three factors that could be viewed either way.

**Table 1.2** Advantages and disadvantages of arbitration over litigation

| Advantage | May be either | Disadvantage |
|---|---|---|
| • cost<br>• speed<br>• less formal<br>• involvement of an expert to determine the issue<br>• preservation of business relationship<br>• commercial reality | • privacy<br>• the decision of the arbitrator is binding<br>• enforcement is available through the courts | • limited disclosure<br>• some remedies are not available |

## ✪ Examples

*You are a solicitor acting for ULaws LLP. You have been asked to advise on the most appropriate way forward for a number of clients.*

*(a) Maria booked a holiday to Costa Rica for April 2020. Her trip was cancelled due to the Covid19 pandemic and her travel agent is only prepared to offer her a credit note for the cost of the flight. Maria wants a refund. Because her holiday contract contains an arbitration clause requiring her to submit to arbitration at ABTA (Association of British Travel Agents), she must refer her dispute to this body.*

*(b) Natalie is an international sprinter. She has failed a drugs test and wants to contest the findings. She agrees to submit to arbitration at the Court of Arbitration for Sport in Switzerland after the dispute has arisen.*

*(c) Pembroke Windows Ltd (Pembroke) supply double glazing to a large company, National Homes Plc (NHP), which specialises in building housing developments. A dispute has arisen in relation to the installation of windows at one particular site. Pembroke need the payment as they are experiencing cash flow problems but are*

*anxious not to lose their customer as the contracts with NHP are vital to the success of the company. Given the importance of maintaining its business relationship with NHP, Pembroke are keen to reach an early settlement and agree to mediation. The involvement of an independent third party enables the parties to reach an agreement with which both are satisfied.*

(d) *Oliver owns a hotel near to a farm. Guests have been complaining about the smell from the chickens that are housed in a barn in the field next to the hotel. ADR would not be appropriate in this instance because Oliver needs an injunction to stop the legal nuisance. Mediation might, however, assist once any injunction had been granted.*

## 1.5 Litigation

If the parties either cannot or will not engage in ADR, they will be left with no alternative but to proceed by way of litigation through the courts. Once they have done so, neither party can withdraw without paying the opponent's costs. If the parties are unable to negotiate a settlement, the court will impose its own solution that may be enforced by the successful party. Indeed, this is the main advantage of litigation as it breaks the deadlock between the parties, albeit at a cost.

Most civil disputes are between individuals and/or companies and they may arise in many different contexts. The most common types are contractual disputes, perhaps involving the sale of unsatisfactory goods, and negligence claims in relation to, for example, road traffic accidents, injuries at work or inadequate professional advice.

### 1.5.1 The Civil Procedure Rules

Civil litigation is governed by the Civil Procedure Rules 1998 (CPR), which dictate the procedure that must be adopted when pursuing a claim through the courts. These are regularly updated and details of updates and amendments may be accessed at www.justice.gov.uk

- The CPR consist of 89 Parts each of which deal with one aspect of civil procedure.
- Additional information on how the rules work is set out in linked Practice Directions bearing the same reference number. Thus, Part 36, which concerns offers to settle, is supplemented by Practice Direction 36 (PD 36), which provides detail on, for example, the formalities required for such offers.

The aim of the CPR is to provide a more 'user-friendly' system of resolving such disputes. This has become increasingly important due to the increase in litigants in person (those individuals who represent themselves) who are unlikely to have the degree of legal knowledge of a lawyer. To ensure that the process proceeds at a reasonable pace, with the consequent reduction in cost, the courts have control over the conduct of the matter. This includes making appropriate directions, setting strict timetables and ensuring the parties comply with them, backed up by a system of sanctions that the court can impose.

### 1.5.2 The civil courts

In England and Wales, most civil disputes are dealt with either by the County Court or the High Court. These are discussed in **Chapter 3** when determining where to start proceedings.

### 1.5.3 Terminology

Proceedings may be brought by individuals, organisations or companies. In all cases, the person or body who issues the claim is referred to as the claimant. The party against whom proceedings are issued is called the defendant.

There may be more than one claimant or defendant.

### 1.5.4   Court personnel

To ensure the civil system operates effectively, the courts are supported by various personnel.

*Judges*

Much of the County Court and High Court work is dealt with by district judges, although for matters proceeding in the Central Office in London they are referred to as masters. These judges deal with the majority of interim applications (which are considered later in this manual) and also have jurisdiction to hear trials where the amount involved does not exceed £25,000. Trials for amounts in excess of this figure are heard by circuit judges in the County Court and by High Court judges in the High Court.

*Court manager*

The court manager is the senior civil servant in charge of the court office, although they are supported by a team of administrative staff. Formal documents that are sent to the court, such as claim forms and defences, are addressed to the court manager.

*Ushers*

When the court is sitting, ushers are in attendance. Their role is to assist in the smooth running of the courts including ensuring the lists of cases are dealt with efficiently.

*Enforcement officers*

Finally, bailiffs and High Court Enforcement Officers serve court documents and enforce court orders and judgments, so that claimants receive their money.

## 1.6   An overview of a civil claim

Before moving on to consider the detail of how to start and progress a civil litigation claim, it is important to have an understanding of the overall picture. The flowchart in **Figure 1.1** shows the structure of a case and how it proceeds from the pre-action steps right through to a trial, and the matters that may arise thereafter. For the purposes of this manual, these are referred to as the five stages of litigation.

### 1.6.1   Stage 1: pre-commencement of proceedings

There are a number of steps to take before issuing proceedings and the starting point is the client – what are their objectives, both legal and commercial? Having established this, evidence must be gathered to confirm the viability of the claim and the prospects of success. Costs will be at the forefront of the client's mind and should be addressed; and serious consideration must be given to ADR.

Pre-action protocols govern the steps the parties should take before commencing a court case. The parties must establish what issues are in dispute, share information that is available to them concerning these matters and endeavour to resolve the issues. Failure to follow a protocol step or its spirit, without good reason, will usually incur a sanction such as a reduction in the costs recovered by that party if litigation proves successful.

Immediately after collecting sufficient evidence to substantiate a realistic claim, the potential claimant should send to the proposed defendant a letter detailing the claim; and the defendant is expected to send a letter in response.

Only after these steps have been completed should litigation be started.

**Figure 1.1**  An overview of civil litigation

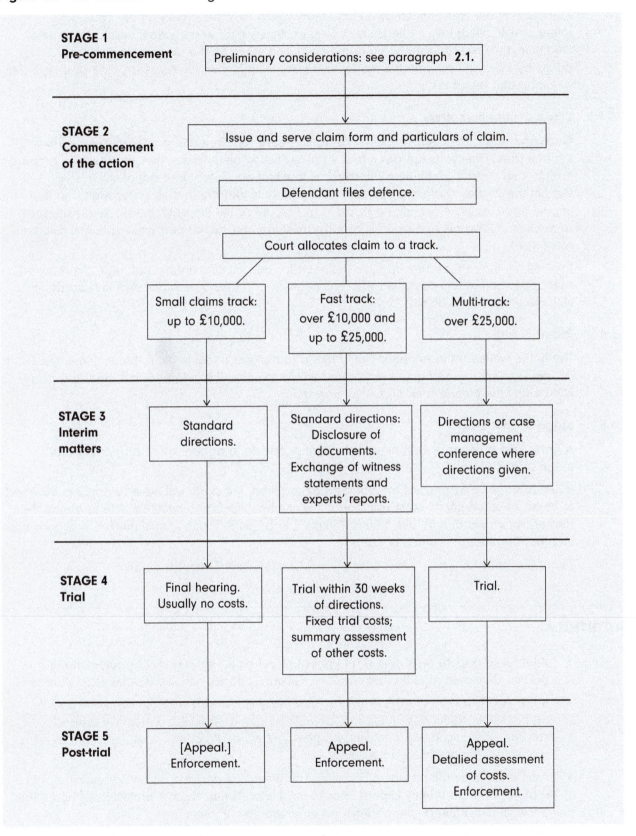

### 1.6.2 Stage 2: commencement of the claim

Proceedings are commenced by a claim form, which must be served on the defendant together with full details of the claim, called particulars. If the defendant wishes to contest the claim, they are required to file at the court and serve on the claimant a defence. At this point, the court will allocate the matter to a track, with higher value cases being given greater attention and resources.

### 1.6.3 Stage 3: interim matters

Once on a track, the court carefully manages a case to ensure the matter progresses towards the trial date. Directions are given to the parties listing all the steps they must take to prepare for trial and a strict timetable is imposed as to when each step must be taken. This will include the parties disclosing any relevant documents that are in their possession and that impact upon the case (whether they assist or not). Evidence the parties wish to rely on, such as witness statements and experts' reports, must then be exchanged; and costs will also be scrutinised.

In addition, the parties may apply to the court for any specific orders that might be required, perhaps to compel an opponent who has neglected to take a required step in accordance with the timetable to do so.

### 1.6.4 Stage 4: trial

The judge will hear the evidence at the trial and make a decision as to the outcome, resolving all issues of liability and quantum (damages). As to costs, the judge will decide if any party should pay the other's costs and, if so, how much.

### 1.6.5 Stage 5: post-trial

A party who is unhappy with the judgment may decide to appeal all or part of the trial judge's decision.

If the damages and/or costs are not paid as required, the party will have to apply to the court to enforce the judgment. Most commonly, this involves instructing court officials to attend the debtor's premises and to take their belongings to be sold at public auction. The proceeds are then paid to the appropriate party.

During this manual, each of these stages will be considered in more detail.

---

## Summary

- Alternative dispute resolution is an important option for solving civil disputes and the parties should engage if at all possible. Failure to do so may result in financial sanctions.

- Mediation is a type of ADR. A neutral third party is involved who discusses the dispute and possible solutions with the parties with the aim of reaching a mutually agreed solution. The outcome is a voluntary agreement which, if not met, must be enforced as a breach of contract through the courts.

- Arbitration is an alternative to litigation. The dispute is decided by a single arbitrator or a panel who are usually experts chosen from a particular field or professional body. The decision is binding on the parties and enforceable in the courts.

- Negotiation, either face to face or by correspondence, is another important means of achieving settlement and should be considered throughout the litigation process.

- There are five stages to litigation: pre-commencement, issuing of proceedings, interim matters, trial and appeal and/or enforcement.

- The main civil courts are the County Court and the High Court. They deal with disputes that arise between individuals and companies, such as breach of contract or negligence.

- The Civil Procedure Rules dictate the procedure that must be followed by the courts. They are regularly updated and amended. The CPR are divided into Parts, most of which are supplemented by a Practice Direction providing additional detail.

## Sample questions

### Question 1

A client purchases a software package to assist in the ordering and distribution of stock for their manufacturing process. The system does not comply with the client's requirements and they instruct their solicitors to issue proceedings for breach of contract.

**What is the best advice the solicitor can give their client concerning alternative dispute resolution (ADR)?**

A   There is no need for the client to engage in ADR unless they choose to do so.

B   The client may decide not to engage in ADR but should be prepared to justify this decision to a judge.

C   If the client fails to engage in ADR, the court will impose costs sanctions.

D   The only options of ADR that are available to the client are mediation and arbitration.

E   In ADR, a third party selected by the claimant will assist the parties to resolve their disputes.

### Answer

Option B is correct. Although the client may choose whether to engage in ADR, there are consequences if they do not and so the advice in option A is incomplete. Option C is wrong as the courts have discretion as to whether to impose sanctions; whilst D is wrong as there are other forms of ADR available to the client, although this chapter has concentrated on mediation and arbitration. Option E is wrong as the third party is independent and should be agreed between the parties, rather than being selected by the claimant.

### Question 2

A client runs a business providing educational software to colleges of further education to improve their assessment processes. However, complaints have been received from one college that the assessments are not being correctly recorded and the principal has indicated that they will not be renewing the contract. It becomes apparent to the client there may be errors in the system. The client has a number of other colleges that are considering using the system.

**Which of the following statements describes the client's best option for resolving the matter and why?**

A   Mediation because it is a cheaper and faster option than litigation.

B   Mediation because it takes place in private and will ensure that other colleges do not become aware of the dispute.

C   Mediation because it is more likely that the parties will preserve their business relationship.

D   Arbitration because the decision is binding on both parties.

E   Arbitration because an expert on information technology can determine the dispute.

**Answer**

Option B is correct as the client has a number of other colleges that are considering using the system and it is unlikely they will do so if they become aware of the problems with the software. Although speed and cost are advantages of mediation over litigation, they are not the most important issues here, so option A is not the best answer. Option C is wrong because the college are not looking to renew the contract, so maintaining the business relationship is immaterial in this instance. The statement in D is correct but the binding nature of any decision is both an advantage and a disadvantage. Option E is also not the best answer for the reasons already stated, although it is an advantage of arbitration as a means of resolving the dispute.

**Question 3**

A company is owed a significant amount of money by a partnership in relation to an alleged failure to comply with a contract to supply goods. The partners are adamant they do not owe the money, arguing that the company is in breach of contract of an implied term as to quality. Negotiations to resolve the matter have failed, as has mediation, and the company has not received the outstanding monies.

**What advice should the solicitor give to the company before issuing proceedings?**

A   As it has not been possible to resolve the dispute, there is no alternative but to resort to litigation and issue proceedings.

B   Civil litigation is governed by the Civil Process Rules, which dictate the procedure that must be adopted when pursuing a claim through the courts.

C   The only advantage of litigation is that a final decision will be made by the judge but the disadvantage is the increased cost.

D   Once a judgment has been given, the parties must write to the High Court for permission to enforce the judgment.

E   Once a claim has entered the litigation process, it must follow all five stages up to and beyond the trial.

**Answer**

Option A sets out the best advice as litigation is the only means of resolving the dispute in the absence of agreement. Option B is wrong as the procedure is governed by the Civil Procedure Rules and not the Civil Process Rules. Option C is not the best advice as there are other advantages to litigation over ADR including the availability of full disclosure of documents. Option D is wrong as the successful party does not have to write to the High Court for permission to enforce the judgment – this is the procedure required to enforce a decision in arbitration. Option E is wrong as most claims are settled well before a trial.

# 2 Resolving a Dispute Through a Civil Claim

## SQE1 syllabus

By the end of this chapter you will be able to apply relevant core legal principles and rules appropriately and effectively, at the level of a competent newly qualified solicitor in practice, to realistic client-based and ethical problems and situations in relation to **resolving a dispute through a civil claim** as follows:

- preliminary considerations: limitation, pre-action protocols
- parties and causes of action
- calculating limitation periods for claims in contract and tort
- Practice Direction on Pre-Action Conduct and Protocols
- principles and purpose of pre-action protocols governing particular claims and consequences of failure to follow their terms
- applicable law: mechanisms to determine which country's laws apply to a contractual or tortious claim issued in the courts of England and Wales
- jurisdiction: mechanisms to determine jurisdiction over an international contractual or tortious claim.

Note that for SQE1, candidates are not usually required to recall specific case names, or cite statutory or regulatory authorities. These are provided for illustrative purposes only and the case analysis is included for the same reason.

## Learning outcomes

The learning outcomes for this chapter are:

- To understand the preliminary matters that must be considered before litigation is commenced.
- To be able to explain and apply the Practice Direction on Pre-Action Conduct and the pre-action protocols.
- To understand the jurisdiction requirements for a civil claim.

When considering these issues, this manual concentrates on claims involving the recovery of money as opposed to, for example, claims for the recovery of land or judicial review.

## 2.1    Introduction

In **Chapter 1**, the five stages of a civil claim were outlined, the first of which is pre-commencement matters. Dealing effectively with these is key to a successful outcome. Indeed, much of the work in civil litigation is carried out by solicitors before matters reach the court and most cases never do. Those claims that are intrinsically weak or where the evidence is lacking should be weeded out at this early stage to avoid the client losing even more money. Efforts can then be concentrated on settling the matter without commencing proceedings – a course of action that is generally in the parties' interests.

However, for reasons other than the merits of the case, it may not be possible to pursue a claim to a successful conclusion. This may be because the client has left it too long to take action or due to a lack of funding or even because the defendant is simply not worth suing.

Thus, before issuing proceedings, there are a number of factors to be considered:

(a)  Can the claim be brought at all?

(b)  Who are the parties?

(c)  Does the defendant have the means to pay a judgment?

(d)  What are the merits of the case?

(e)  What steps must be taken before proceedings are issued?

This chapter focuses on the answers to these questions. However, a solicitor should always be mindful of professional conduct issues and, before taking any action, consider whether they can act for the client at all.

### ✪ *Example*

*A firm of solicitors already acts for a client in negotiating with publishers for the publication of the client's novel. The firm is now asked to act for a new client who alleges that the novel is plagiarised and breaches their copyright. As this is a related matter, there is a conflict of interest and the firm cannot represent the new client.*

## 2.2    Limitation

Before issuing proceedings, the solicitor must ensure that the client is not precluded from making a claim at all. The Limitation Act (LA) 1980 prescribes strict time limits with which the claimant must comply. If these are missed, unless there are exceptional circumstances, that is the end of the matter as the claim will be 'statute barred'. The rationale behind imposing these deadlines is to prevent a potential defendant remaining under constant threat of litigation for events that happened many years before; and to recognise that the passage of time results in evidence being lost and witness accounts becoming less reliable.

From the outset, a solicitor must ascertain when the limitation period began and when it will expire. These dates should be diarised to remind the lawyer that time is marching on, particularly if the expiration of the relevant period is drawing near. It is vital that proceedings are issued before the limitation period expires, otherwise the solicitor is likely to face a claim in negligence.

### 2.2.1    Effect of limitation

If a party has missed the limitation period, the defendant will have a technical defence to the claim. This means that, if the court agrees the claim is statute barred, the claimant will not succeed in the litigation.

### 2.2.2 What are the limitation periods?

For claims founded on contract or tort, the time limits are set out in ss 2 and 5 of the LA 1980. The basic rule is that the claimant has six years from the date of the cause of action to commence their proceedings, with the limitation period starting from the day after.

- In contract, the cause of action accrues as soon as the breach of contract occurs. This will be a question of fact to be determined by the court.

- In tort, the cause of action accrues when the tort is committed. In negligence, this will be when damage occurs as a result of a breach of duty.

In contrast, the limitation period for personal injury matters is three years. This runs from the date of the cause of action or the date of knowledge of the person injured, except for children where the time limit does not start to run until their 18th birthday.

Furthermore, in a claim based on negligence where the damage is latent (hidden) at the date when the cause of action accrued, s 14A of the LA 1980 provides that the limitation period expires either:

- six years from the date of the cause of action; or

- three years from the date of knowledge of the damage, whichever is later; but

- no later than 15 years after the date of the negligent act or omission.

⭐ *Examples*

(a) *Freshfruit Ltd supply a consignment of strawberries to Supermarket Plc on 10 September 2020. The strawberries are inspected immediately and found to be rotten; consequently, they cannot be sold. The breach of contract occurs on the date of delivery and Supermarket Plc has six years in which to issue proceedings, so until 10 September 2026.*

(b) *Hamish is aware that the tree in his garden is rotten and needs to be cut down. During a storm on 5 January 2021, the tree is uprooted and smashes into his neighbour's conservatory causing extensive damage. The limitation period for the neighbour to issue proceedings for the tort of negligence does not expire until 5 January 2027.*

(c) *Anne purchased a property from a building company on 17 October 2016. Four years later, on 26 November 2020, the property begins to subside due to inadequate foundations having been built. Because the damage is latent, Anne has until 26 November 2023 to commence proceedings.*

These basic rules are summarised in **Table 2.1**.

**Table 2.1**  Limitation periods

| Nature of action | Starting point | Length of period |
|---|---|---|
| **Simple contract** | The date of breach of contract. | 6 years |
| **Tort** other than:<br>• personal injury<br>• actions under the Consumer Protection Act 1987<br>• latent damage | The date the damage occurs. | 6 years |

*(continued)*

**Table 2.1** (*continued*)

| Nature of action | Starting point | Length of period |
|---|---|---|
| **Latent damage** (in the tort of negligence) | Later of:<br>(a) the date when the damage occurred; or<br>(b) the date on which the claimant first had the knowledge required to bring an action. | (a) 6 years<br>(b) 3 years<br>Overriding time limit: 15 years from the date of the negligence |

### 2.2.2.1 Contractual limitation

In a contract case, it is very important to check whether a different limitation period is specified in the contract. This is because any such provision is usually shorter than the statutory limitation periods referred to above, and the claim should therefore be commenced within the contractually specified period.

### 2.2.3 Can the limitation period be extended?

The general rule is that actions commenced outside the limitation period where the defendant has raised the issue as a defence will not be allowed to proceed, although extensions may be available in exceptional circumstances.

 *The case of* A v Hoare *[2008] UKHL 6 illustrates this, albeit in a different context. The claimant issued proceedings against the defendant, Hoare, who had been convicted in 1989 for a serious sexual assault against her. In 2004, while still serving his sentence of imprisonment, Hoare won £7 million on the national lottery. The appeal court granted the claimant permission to pursue her claim for damages against the defendant despite being well outside the limitation period.*

### 2.2.4 Summary of limitation

To assist, set out below is an overview of the rules that apply to limitation.

**Table 2.2** Limitation

| | |
|---|---|
| **What is limitation?** | The strict time limit imposed on a claimant that determines the last date on which they can issue proceedings against a defendant in relation to a cause of action. |
| **What is the effect?** | A claimant may still commence their claim but the defendant will have a complete defence. |
| **General rule** | If the defendant establishes that the claim is statute barred, the court will not allow actions commenced outside the limitation period to proceed. |
| **Limitation periods** | These vary depending upon the type of claim. The statutory time limits apply unless those stipulated in the contract are shorter. |
| **Extending limitation** | The court has discretion to extend the deadline but will only do so in exceptional circumstances. |

## 2.3 Parties to a claim

The claimant is the party who starts the case whilst the party against whom proceedings are brought is the defendant. In all cases, it is vital to check the correct spelling and title of the party concerned.

### 2.3.1 Who is the defendant?

All potential defendants should be identified at this early stage to avoid incurring costs later on, for example, to amend court documents. Often this will be straightforward as usually there will only be one potential defendant, but there are occasions when it is less so.

- If an employee commits a tort when acting in the course of their employment, both the employee and the employer should be sued, as the latter is vicariously liable for the former.

- A consumer may have a cause of action against both the retailer and the manufacturer of a defective product.

There are special safeguards in place for children (a person under 18) and protected parties (a person who is incapable of managing their own affairs because of a mental disorder as defined by the Mental Capacity Act 2005). Because these individuals are considered in law to be unable to make the decisions required of a party to court proceedings, they must have a litigation friend to act on their behalf. For children, this will usually be a parent or guardian.

A litigation friend must be able to fairly and competently conduct proceedings on behalf of the party and have no adverse interest.

### ✪ *Example*

*Sufia, aged 12 years, is injured in a road traffic collision caused by her father's negligent driving. In this instance, her father cannot be Sufia's litigation friend because he would be the defendant in her claim and, thus, has an adverse interest.*

A further safeguard is provided to these parties by the requirement that any settlement reached involving a child or a protected party will only be valid if approved by the court.

### 2.3.2 Where is the defendant?

Clearly, the defendant needs to be traceable and their whereabouts known in order to communicate the claim and, if necessary, serve proceedings. An inquiry agent may be able to assist if this is an issue.

### 2.3.3 How should defendants be sued?

Prospective defendants must be sued in their correct capacity and it is important to check this as a person may have entered into a contract in one of a number of different ways. Equally, a tort may have been committed or suffered by different legal entities.

The solicitor should check whether the defendant is:

- an individual;
- a sole trader;
- a partnership;
- a limited liability partnership (LLP); or
- a limited company.

*Example*

> *You are contacted by a client, Chantelle White, who entered into a contract with Arjun Bajwa to purchase a consignment of jumpers that she intended to sell at her shop. She was unable to do so as the items were poorly made and she wants her money back. Before taking the matter further, you must establish in what capacity Arjun acted.*
>
> *(a) As an individual on his own behalf?*
>
> *(b) As a representative of a partnership or LLP?*
>
> *(c) As a director of a limited company?*
>
> *The answer to these questions will determine the defendant against whom Chantelle will bring proceedings. If Arjun is an individual, his correct name must be ascertained. If he is a partner in a firm, the defendant would be (for example) Bajwa & Co (a firm), whereas if he contracted on behalf of a LLP or company, the LLP or company itself would be the defendant.*

### 2.3.4 Is the defendant worth suing?

Suing a defendant who is on the verge of either bankruptcy or liquidation is a pointless exercise as enforcement of any judgment obtained would be impossible. If the client has any concerns about the prospective defendant's ability to pay, further enquiries should be made. These could include:

- a search at Companies House to ascertain information about the financial position of a company;
- a bankruptcy search of an individual;
- instructing an inquiry agent (although the costs of this must be considered); and
- the use of various internet search engines to see if there is any relevant information there.

If the outcome of these investigations is that the defendant is struggling financially, although making a claim is possible, it would not be viable.

### 2.3.5 Types of claims

When pursuing litigation, the claimant must be aware of the type of claim they are issuing as this impacts upon how certain court documents are drafted and also the procedure.

#### 2.3.5.1 Specified claims

A claim is specified if it is for a fixed amount of money; usually, it is a claim for a debt owed. Because the amount is known already (perhaps from an invoice), the figure owed can be calculated by mere mathematics. Examples would include the price of goods sold and commission due under express contractual terms.

#### 2.3.5.2 Unspecified claims

If the court will have to conduct an investigation to determine the amount of money payable, the claim is an unspecified one even if the claimant puts forward some figures. Thus, damages claims are usually unspecified.

 *Example*

> *The claimant, Merlin Events Ltd (Merlin), instructs ULaws LLP to start proceedings against an entertainer, Janice Star, for breach of contract. Janice refused to perform at a concert in accordance with her agreement with Merlin resulting in the cancellation of the event, and Merlin is claiming for loss of profits. This is an unspecified claim because the amount of lost profits is not fixed and will require the court to decide on an appropriate figure.*

*What if Merlin also claims the return of the fee paid to Janice (a specified sum)? In circumstances where the claim is a mixture of specified and unspecified amounts, the entire claim will be treated as unspecified.*

## 2.4 Case analysis

A lawyer will not be acting in the best interests of their client if they encourage them to pursue a case that is hopeless from the outset or with only limited prospects of success. Taking full instructions at the first interview with the client will assist in this regard. The client will be anxious that the solicitor appreciates their problem and will want to be assured that there is a satisfactory solution, achievable at a reasonable cost. At the same time, the solicitor needs to be able to extract relevant information from the client in order to give preliminary advice on such issues as liability and quantum.

### 2.4.1 Causes of action

A cause of action is the legal basis of a claim, such as breach of contract or negligence. To determine whether a client has a cause of action and the likelihood of success, it is essential at the outset that a solicitor analyses all the available evidence, whether given orally by the client and any witnesses or contained in documentation.

**Table 2.3** contains examples of the most common types of causes of action that are likely to arise in civil litigation.

**Table 2.3**  Causes of action

| Types of dispute | Legal definition | Possible claims | Purpose of damages |
|---|---|---|---|
| Contract | A party enters into an agreement with another, one or more of the terms are breached and this causes the other party to suffer a loss. | Breach of express terms, for example: <br>• non-payment of monies due (debt claim); or <br>• failure to deliver a consignment on time. <br>Breach of statutory implied terms such as: <br>• the goods supplied were not of satisfactory quality, contrary to s 14(2) Sale of Goods Act 1979. | To put the claimant in the position they would have been in had the contract been properly performed. |
| Tort (Negligence) | A duty of care is owed by one party to another, the duty is breached and this causes the other party to suffer loss (financial and/or otherwise). | Negligence including: <br>• a road traffic collision where a motorist breaches their duty of care to another road user by failing to brake in time; or <br>• medical negligence where a doctor misdiagnoses a patient. <br>Negligent mis-statement such as where: <br>• a financial adviser gives inadequate investment advice to a client. | To put the claimant in the position they would have been in had the negligent act not occurred. |

*(continued)*

21

**Table 2.3** (*continued*)

| Types of dispute | Legal definition | Possible claims | Purpose of damages |
|---|---|---|---|
| Tort (Nuisance) | Where use or enjoyment of land is unreasonably interfered with by another landowner. | Examples are:<br>• excessive noise from a neighbour;<br>• tree roots causing damage to an adjoining property;<br>• water flooding from another's property. | To put the claimant in the position they would have been in had the nuisance not occurred. |
| Misrepresentation | An untrue or misleading statement of fact by Party A that induces Party B to enter into a contract with Party A and that causes loss to Party B. | An example is:<br>• a car salesman who induces a customer to purchase a vehicle by falsely representing that it has not been involved in any road traffic collisions when this is untrue. | To put the claimant back to the position they were in before the contract was entered into. |

### 2.4.2 Case study of breach of contract

Although it is important to identify the relevant cause of action, it is equally vital to understand how this impacts upon the progression of the matter. The legal elements form the basis of the statements of case (the documents that outline the parties' positions) and the substantive law provides the structure upon which the evidence will be draped. Take a claim for breach of contract as an example.

(a) Existence of contract

First, it must be established that there was a contract although, in practice, this will rarely be disputed.

(b) Terms relied on (express and/or implied)

Next, the lawyer should establish the terms. If the dispute concerns what express terms were agreed in a contract, a written agreement will assist. Where the contract was made orally, the situation is more complex as often the only evidence available is from the parties who made the contract and who are now locked in dispute. In addition, where a contract is entered into in the course of business, there may be implied terms that are imposed by statute. These apply to both written and oral contracts.

(c) Breach of those terms

Thereafter, the solicitor must consider how the client will prove there was a breach that resulted in recoverable losses. What does the client say the opponent did (or failed to do) that amounts to a breach of the contract? This is a question of fact, and the solicitor must assess the evidence the client has to prove the claim.

(d) Consequences

Once a breach has been established, the factual consequences of that breach should be identified.

(e) Damage and loss

Finally, each item of loss claimed will have to be proved.

Analysing a case study demonstrates how this works in practice.

⭐ *Example*

*ULaws LLP are consulted by Factory Goods (Midlands) Limited (FG) who wish to bring a claim against Cool Systems Limited (CSL).*

*FG must first establish that a contract existed, although this is unlikely to be disputed. FG provide a copy of a written contract in which CSL agreed, on 29 November [last year], to supply and install at FG's factory a new air conditioning system. In addition to the express terms, such as the particular system required and the date of installation, the law provides that certain terms are implied into the contract. In this instance, that the air conditioning system would be of satisfactory quality and installed exercising reasonable care and skill in accordance with s 4(2) and s 13 of the Supply of Goods and Services Act 1982.*

*FG's case is that the system is not of satisfactory quality and, furthermore, it was installed without reasonable care and skill being taken. In particular, the system:*

- *does not start automatically; and*

- *fails to achieve the required temperature settings.*

*Evidence would be required to prove the breach of contract. The client provides the solicitor with a report from the head of FG's factory maintenance team identifying faults in the system and its installation and a daily record of when these arose. However, a report from an expert confirming FG's allegation would need to be obtained to provide independent evidence for the court.*

*The next element of the claim to be established is that the client suffered consequences as a result of the breach. The client explains that:*

- *portable air conditioning units had to be hired;*

- *the factory had to close in excessively hot weather causing a loss of profit; and*

- *the system needs upgrading or replacing.*

*The available evidence is written complaints by FG's staff about extremes of temperatures since installation and a daily record of factory temperatures kept by their employee responsible for health and safety. In addition to taking a detailed proof of evidence from the individuals concerned, the solicitor may commission a report from an independent expert confirming these allegations.*

*Finally, proof of damage and loss must be obtained. The items that FG will be claiming are:*

*(1) The cost of upgrading the system supplied or replacement by a suitable system. A report from an expert would be required to cover this.*

*(2) Loss of profit due to the time the factory had to close because of the excessively hot working conditions. The client has records supplied by FG's head of human resources detailing the occasions when the factory was shut; whilst FG's profit and loss accounts and production records would assist in establishing this aspect of the damages. However, it is likely that an independent accountant's report would also be required.*

*Furthermore, the client is required to mitigate their loss, namely to show they have taken reasonable steps to minimise the amount of loss suffered. FG can demonstrate this as they hired portable air conditioning units, although these proved insufficient. Receipted invoices would be useful in this regard.*

Although an initial case analysis would be conducted, as the case develops, the solicitor should continually review which issues remain in dispute and how these are to be proved.

## 2.5 Pre-action procedure

Before issuing court proceedings, the parties are required to comply with various pre-action rules, known as pre-action protocols. These are annexed to the CPR and, over time, a number have been developed, for example in relation to:

- debt claims
- personal injury
- construction and engineering
- professional negligence.

In addition, if no relevant protocol exists, there is a Practice Direction on Pre-Action Conduct and Protocols (PDPAC), which contains general guidance to be followed in such cases. Many of the provisions mirror those of the protocols so that, effectively, all civil cases are dealt with in a similar way.

### 2.5.1 The Practice Direction and the pre-action protocols

The PDPAC and the protocols are important elements of civil litigation, and solicitors must ensure they understand the content and are able to apply the provisions effectively.

*Purpose*

The objective of the PDPAC and the protocols is to initiate and increase pre-action contact between the parties. In particular, to encourage better and earlier exchange of information so the parties are in a position where they may be able to settle cases fairly and early without litigation, and to enable proceedings to run to the court's timetable and efficiently if litigation does become necessary.

These aims are consistent with the overriding objective of the CPR.

### 2.5.2 Principles

There are elements of the PDPAC and the protocols that are common to all.

(1) Litigation should be a last resort. The parties should consider whether negotiation or some other form of alternative dispute resolution (ADR) might enable them to settle their dispute without commencing proceedings.

(2) The parties should exchange sufficient information in order to:

(a) understand each other's position;

(b) make decisions about how to proceed;

(c) try to settle the issues without proceedings;

(d) consider a form of ADR to assist with settlement;

(e) support the efficient management of those proceedings; and

(f) reduce the costs of resolving the dispute.

(3) The steps taken should usually include:

(a) the claimant writing to the defendant with concise details of the claim;

(b) the defendant responding within a reasonable time; and

(c) the parties disclosing key documents relevant to the issues in dispute.

(4) Only reasonable and proportionate steps should be taken by the parties to identify, narrow and resolve the legal, factual and/or expert issues.

(5) Where a dispute has not been resolved after the parties have followed the Practice Direction, they should review their respective positions to see if proceedings can be

avoided and at least seek to narrow the issues in dispute before the claimant issues proceedings.

(6) If a dispute proceeds to litigation, the court will expect the parties to have complied with the Practice Direction. A party may be sanctioned for failing to do so.

Early disclosure of the substance of the claim and supporting evidence, particularly relevant documents, will assist the parties in making an informed decision on the merits of the case at a preliminary stage. This, combined with the active encouragement of ADR, should lead to a greater number of settlements without the need for court proceedings. The volume of pre-action work means that, even if proceedings prove unavoidable, the costs of the litigation should be reduced. It is for these reasons that there are penalties for non-compliance.

Although the purpose and principles of the PDPAC and the protocols are similar, in recognition of the differences between types of claims, a variety of protocols are specifically tailored to their individual requirements. Any claims that fall outside the protocols must proceed in accordance with the PDPAC.

### 2.5.3 Practice Direction on Pre-Action Conduct and Protocols

The PDPAC provides a safety net ensuring that no civil claim escapes the requirement to follow the pre-action procedures.

#### 2.5.3.1 Steps

The Practice Direction is clear that, before commencing proceedings, the parties must exchange information so they can understand the issues, consider ADR and attempt to settle the dispute without litigation.

The importance of ADR is recognised specifically in paragraph 8 of the PDPAC, which instructs the parties to give consideration to it. If proceedings occur, both the claimant and defendant will normally be required by the court to provide evidence that they reflected upon alternative means of resolving the dispute. The courts take the view that litigation should be a last resort, and that claims should not be issued prematurely when a settlement is still actively being explored. Parties are warned that if this provision is not followed then the court must have regard to such conduct when determining costs.

The PDPAC expressly states that only reasonable and proportionate steps should be taken by the parties to try and resolve the matter and costs incurred should also be proportionate. This will include the claimant writing to the defendant with concise details of the claim, including a summary of the facts, the sum due and how the amount is calculated. Thereafter, the defendant must provide a response within a reasonable time – 14 days in a straightforward claim and three months maximum in a complex case – to include confirmation of whether all or part of the claim is accepted, and if not the reasons why, together with details of any counterclaim. Key documents relevant to the issues in dispute should also be disclosed.

### 2.5.4 Consequences for failure to follow the terms

A failure to comply with both the Practice Direction and the substance of any approved protocol that applies to the dispute may lead to sanctions later on. Where non-compliance has led to proceedings that might otherwise not have been commenced, or has led to unnecessary costs being incurred, the court may impose penalties. These can include an order:

(a) that the party at fault pays some or all of their opponent's costs (perhaps on the penalty, indemnity basis);

(b) depriving a claimant who is at fault of some or all of the interest they may subsequently be awarded on any damages recovered; or

(c) requiring a defendant who is at fault to pay interest on any damages awarded to the claimant at a rate of up to 10% per annum above the base rate.

The CPR also include a provision that a person who knowingly makes a false statement in a pre-action protocol letter or other document prepared in anticipation of legal proceedings may be subject to proceedings for contempt of court.

### 2.5.5 Summary

The Practice Direction requires the parties to complete a number of steps and the flowchart in **Figure 2.1** summarises the main provisions.

**Figure 2.1** Practice Direction on Pre-Action Conduct and Protocols

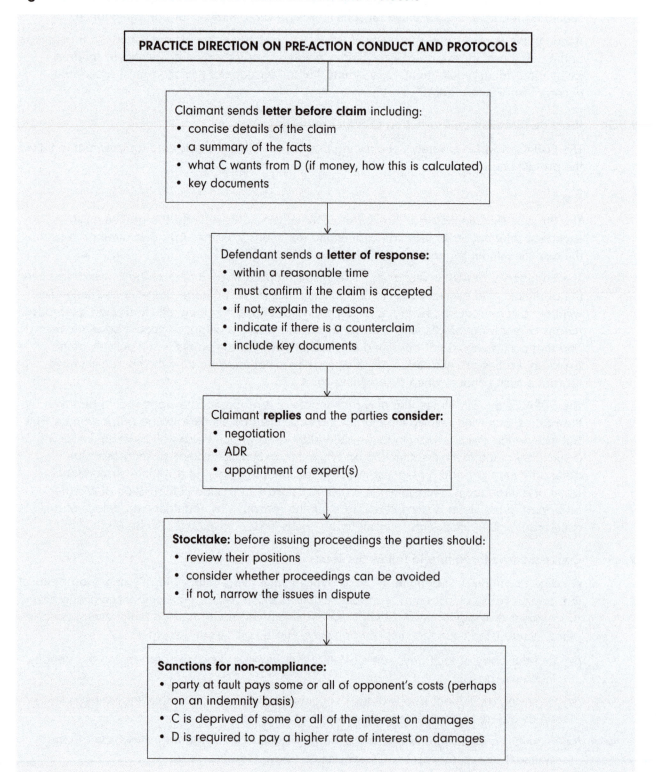

### 2.5.6 Pre-Action Protocol for Debt Claims

To assist in an understanding of the purpose and principles of the various pre-action protocols, two specific examples are examined in this chapter.

The vast majority of claims issued each year are for straightforward debt matters such as unpaid invoices for goods sold and delivered or for services provided, for example, construction works. The claim may also arise because money has been borrowed and not repaid. Because the amounts involved are often relatively small, firms handling large numbers of debt claims will often utilise specialist case management software to ensure the monies can be recovered efficiently and economically.

Debt claims are covered by the Pre-Action Protocol for Debt Claims (PPDC).

- This applies to any business including sole traders and public bodies (the creditor) that brings a claim against a debtor who is either an individual or a sole trader (the debtor).

- It does *not* apply to business to business debts (unless the debtor is a sole trader).

Because the PPDC is specifically aimed at debt claims, the focus is slightly different. The potential claimant must give full information on the debt owed, including an up-to-date statement of account with details of interest and charges, and how the debt can be paid. The standard Reply Form, Information Sheet and Financial Statement forms that are annexed to the protocol should also be included. This is to encourage settlement, perhaps by way of agreeing repayment plans.

Recognising that most debtors will be individuals, they are given a little longer to respond – 30 days – and court proceedings cannot be issued before this deadline. The creditor should also allow extra time if necessary for the debtor to seek legal or debt advice or in order to pay.

### 2.5.7 Pre-Action Protocol for Professional Negligence

At the other end of the spectrum, the Pre-Action Protocol for Professional Negligence applies when a claimant wishes to make a claim against most types of professionals as a result of alleged negligence.

As with all protocols, the primary aim is to set out a code of good practice, achieved by listing the steps the parties should follow before commencing court proceedings. Although many are the same as for the Practice Direction on Pre-Action Conduct, there are some differences.

The first additional requirement is that a party is encouraged to notify the professional in writing of any intended claim. This letter (the Preliminary Notice) contains information about the claimant, a brief outline of the claimant's grievance against the professional and, if possible, a general indication of the financial value of the potential claim. The professional should be instructed to inform their insurers immediately and to acknowledge the notice in writing within 21 days of receipt.

Next, the claimant should write a Letter of Claim giving full details of the issues and attaching key documents. The professional must acknowledge this in writing within 21 days of receipt. Thereafter, they have three months to investigate and to respond.

The Letter of Response sets out whether the professional admits the allegations and if not why not, with accompanying documents. Alternatively, or as well as the Letter of Response, a Letter of Settlement may be sent if the professional intends to make proposals for settlement of all or part of the claim.

If the Letter of Response denies the claim in its entirety and there is no Letter of Settlement, it is open to the claimant to start court proceedings. In any other circumstance, the professional and the claimant should instigate negotiations with the aim of resolving the claim within six months of the date of the Letter of Acknowledgment. If matters cannot be resolved, there must be a final Stocktake in which the parties review their positions, or at least narrow down the issues, before court action is taken.

As with all the protocols and the Practice Direction, the parties must consider ADR.

A summary of the steps is set out in the flowchart in **Figure 2.2**.

**Figure 2.2**  Pre-Action Protocol for Professional Negligence

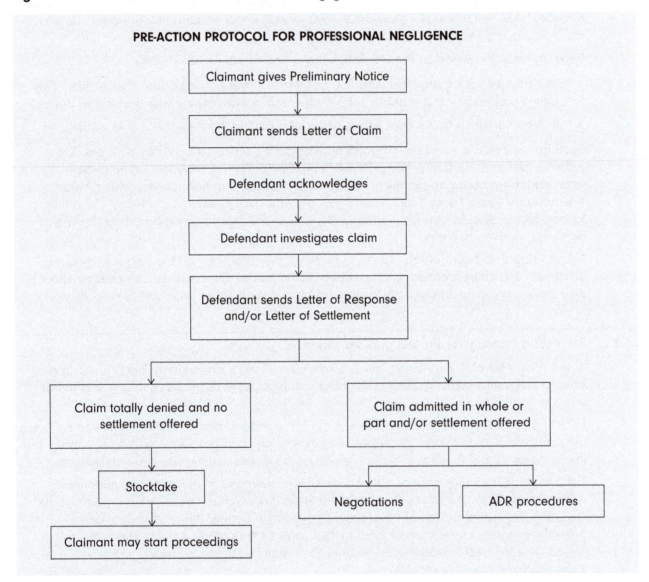

### 2.5.8 Summary

- Most civil actions are now governed by pre-action protocols, for example, professional negligence and debt claims. These dictate the stages that must be followed before proceedings may be issued, with the aim of settling the matter without the necessity of litigation.

- If the type of case has no pre-action protocol, such as debt claims between two companies or claims for breach of contract, the parties must comply with the Practice Direction on Pre-Action Conduct and Protocols. The steps that must be taken are similar to those outlined in the pre-action protocols.

## 2.6 Foreign element and choice of forum

In the modern world with its global economy, business and trade are international. As a consequence, to ensure that disputes which take place outside the confines of England and Wales may be litigated, mechanisms are in place to determine both the applicable law and the jurisdiction of international contractual and tortious claims. These are likely to change, potentially significantly, due to the UK's withdrawal from the European Union (EU) and after the end of the Transition Period, which is currently 31 December 2020. However, as yet, the way forward is unclear.

### 2.6.1 Which country's laws apply? *See update*

The starting point for a contractual or tortious claim with international implications is to decide which country's laws apply.

#### 2.6.1.1 Choice of law

All contracts should have a clearly worded clause stating what law will govern the contract to avoid uncertainty in the event of a dispute arising. Usually, the parties will be able to nominate the governing law of their choice although there are some exceptions, for example, the Unfair Contract Terms Act 1977 contains requirements that apply to the contract regardless of any agreement to the contrary. If agreement has been reached in advance as to which country's laws apply to the claim, the case will usually proceed on that basis.

#### 2.6.1.2 Other mechanisms

In situations where no governing law has been chosen, various default provisions come into play. At this point, the parties no longer have a choice over the law that is applicable to their dispute.

**Disputes located within the European Union**

Rules are in place to determine the applicable law to ensure, as far as possible, consistency across the EU.

- Contract cases

Contractual disputes are covered by Regulation 593/2008, which provides that the contract will be governed by the law with which it is most closely connected. It also sets out specific rules that must be applied and these may be found in Article 4(1) to the Regulation as outlined in the table below.

**Table 2.4** Contractual disputes within the EU

| Type of contract | Which country's laws apply in the absence of agreement? |
| --- | --- |
| Sale of goods | The country where the seller has their habitual residence. |
| Supply of services | The country where the supplier has their habitual residence. |
| Rights in land and tenancies | The country where the property is situated. |

If any of the above do not apply, or more than one does, the applicable law will be the country where the 'characteristic performer' of the contract has their habitual residence.

- Tort cases

Regulation 864/2007 deals with tortious disputes. The general rule is that, where there is no agreement between the parties, the law of the country in which the damage occurs or is likely to occur will apply. However, there are exceptions to this, such as if the tort is 'manifestly more closely connected with another country' or where the dispute involves, for example, product liability.

It is unclear how the situation will change once the UK exits the EU, although the Government's stated aim is to incorporate the existing provisions into domestic law so the current position would remain the same.

### Disputes outside the European Union

If the court that is determining the dispute is located outside the EU, the procedure will vary depending upon the local courts. Thus, there is a real possibility of becoming embroiled in contentious litigation even before the proceedings have properly commenced because establishing the applicable law would need to be decided as a preliminary matter. In such situations, it is even more important to agree a governing law clause if at all possible.

### 2.6.2 Jurisdiction – where can proceedings be commenced?   *See update*

If a solicitor is instructed by a client who is based abroad, or is instructed to take proceedings against a party based abroad, the question of jurisdiction must always be considered – in which country's courts can proceedings be commenced?

#### 2.6.2.1 Cases within the European Union

If the defendant is located in the EU, or the parties have agreed to litigate the dispute in the courts of any EU Member State, then Council Regulation 1215/2012 (the Regulation) is applied when assessing which EU Member State may have jurisdiction. Norway, Switzerland and Iceland are governed by a similar provision called the Lugano Convention. These rules are incorporated into the UK by virtue of the Civil Jurisdiction and Judgments Act 1982.

At the time of writing, the European Union (Withdrawal) Act 2018 preserves and incorporates into domestic law all EU-derived legislation so that it retains the same effect after exit as before. However, this may change at the end of the Transition Period and the applicability of the Regulation will depend upon whether the UK enters a bespoke agreement to that effect with the EU.

Currently, to determine which courts of a Member State have jurisdiction, the following approach should be adopted.

- Exclusive jurisdiction (Article 24)

In some cases, such as disputes over land, the Regulation confers jurisdiction on the courts of one State and proceedings must be taken there.

- Exclusive jurisdiction by agreement (Article 25)

If the parties have agreed that the courts of a particular Member State are to have jurisdiction to settle any disputes, proceedings must be taken in those courts. Thus, a clause in a contract giving the courts of England and Wales exclusive jurisdiction over any disputes is effective even if none of the parties are domiciled in a Member State.

If these options do not apply, the next stage is to consider the special rules that relate to those defendants who are domiciled in a Member State.

- The basic rule (Article 4)

The basic rule is that the defendant must be sued in their local courts. For an individual, this means the place where they are domiciled whilst for a company this is, for example, the registered office address in the United Kingdom. Hence if a client wants to sue someone domiciled in France, they must do so in the French courts.

However, for contract and tort cases, the Regulation provides an alternative to suing the defendant where they are domiciled.

- Contract cases (Article 7(1))

Contract cases may be dealt with by the courts of the State where the contract was to be performed. In a sale of goods case, this would be where the goods were delivered; whereas in a contract for the provision of services, this is the State where the services were provided.

- Tort cases (Article 7(2))

The Regulation confers jurisdiction in tort cases on the courts of the State where the harm caused by the tort occurred. So, if a German driver causes a road traffic collision in England, they can be sued in Germany (where they are domiciled) but also in England as this is where the accident occurred.

2.6.2.2 **Cases outside the European Union**

Cases may also involve defendants who live beyond the EU; and there are mechanisms in place to determine jurisdiction of such claims if issued in the courts of England and Wales.

Even if a claimant does not have any real connection with this country, they may still issue proceedings here and it is possible (albeit unlikely) that a claim could reach trial and be enforced without the claimant ever setting foot in England or Wales.

- Service within England and Wales

The courts of England and Wales can hear any proceedings if the claim form was served on the defendant while they were present in these countries (no matter how briefly). This is because service of court papers itself establishes the English courts' jurisdiction over the defendant. The rationale behind this principle is that the mere presence of the defendant indicates their acceptance of the nation's jurisdiction.

The defendant could, however, object to the proceedings continuing in England and Wales on the ground that the English courts are not the most appropriate for resolving the dispute.

⭐ *Example*

*An Englishwoman is involved in an accident in New York caused by the negligence of a local New York taxi driver. She is able to serve the defendant with a claim form while he is in England on holiday. The defendant could object to the proceedings continuing in England on the basis that New York State was a more convenient forum.*

- Service outside England and Wales

If proceedings are issued and a non-EU defendant cannot be served with the documents in England and Wales, the permission of the court must be obtained to serve them outside the jurisdiction. This may be granted in the following circumstances.

(a) The contract was made or breached in England or Wales, is governed by English law, or contains an agreement conferring jurisdiction on the English courts.

(b) In a tort claim, the act causing the damage was committed in England and Wales, or the loss was sustained here.

Although the rules in relation to jurisdiction are complex, they give reassurance to those who interact and trade internationally that the courts are willing and able to step in and provide a remedy to wrongs committed anywhere in the world.

### 2.6.3 Scotland and Northern Ireland

A reference to 'English law' covers England and Wales but not Scotland or Northern Ireland, which have their own legal systems. Although many of the laws made by the UK Parliament at Westminster do apply or are very similar, this is not always the case. As above, whenever possible, the parties should agree which law is applicable and the jurisdiction to avoid incurring costs in establishing this and in enforcing any judgment.

## Summary of pre-action steps

A significant amount of work is completed by the lawyer before proceedings reach the court, if they ever do. Set out below is a summary of the most important pre-action steps.

- The client's objectives must be established and, before issuing proceedings, all potential parties should be identified and located.

- The financial viability of the defendant should be checked to determine whether they have the means to pay any judgment and costs, and what assets are available for enforcement.

- There are strict time limits within which proceedings must be issued and these run from the date of the cause of action. For most tort and contract claims, the limitation period is six years.

- A case analysis should be completed to identify all potential causes of action and the likely disputed issues for each element, to ensure evidence is collected and preserved and to consider the realistic prospects of success.

- The parties are required to comply with the pre-action protocols or the Practice Direction on Pre-Action Conduct and Protocols as relevant. These list the steps that must be taken before issuing proceedings, with the aim of avoiding litigation by agreeing a settlement.

- Jurisdiction should be considered in cases where there is a foreign element. In particular, the question of which country's laws are applicable to the dispute and where proceedings should be issued must be decided. If no prior agreement has been reached, different mechanisms come into play depending upon whether the party is based inside the EU or beyond.

## Sample questions

### Question 1

A man, who owns a florist business, entered into an oral contract on 16 January with a company that grows and sells flowers. He submits that the contract contained an express term the flowers would be delivered on 8 February with time being of the essence. The reason for this provision was that the flowers were required for the lucrative Valentine's Day market on 14 February. The flowers failed to arrive until 17 February and most remained unsold. The company disputes such a term was agreed and neither party has a written note that time was of the essence.

**Which of the following statements best describes the advice the solicitor should give to the man concerning the commencement of proceedings?**

A There is no hurry to issue proceedings as the limitation period does not expire for three years from 16 January.

B    The limitation period runs from the date of breach of the contract, this being the date of delivery of the flowers on 17 February.

C    When issuing proceedings, it does not matter whether the defendant is sued in their company name or as individual directors.

D    There is no need to look into the defendant's finances until judgment has been obtained.

E    The prospects of the man succeeding in his claim are likely to be affected by his failure to record in writing that a specified delivery date was agreed and that time was of the essence.

**Answer**

Option E is correct. To succeed in a breach of contract claim, the man must establish that a contract existed, a term was breached and this caused his losses. The crucial issue will be whether a delivery date was specified and whether time was of the essence in relation to the delivery of the flowers. The lack of written evidence to support the man means that the court will have to decide this based upon conflicting oral evidence.

Option A is wrong because, as this is a contract claim, the man has six years from the date when the cause of action accrued to commence proceedings. Option B is also wrong as the limitation period runs from the day after the breach of contract which, in this case, is 8 February when delivery was not made in accordance with the terms of the contract; it does not run from the date of the actual delivery on 17 February.

Option C is wrong because proceedings must be issued in the correct name of the defendant and, in this instance, the company is a separate legal entity to the individual directors. Option D is not the best advice to give a client as there is little point in winning a claim only to discover that the defendant is insolvent or otherwise cannot pay the damages and costs awarded.

**Question 2**

A company client seeks advice in relation to a contract for the sale of a carpet to a hotel. The customer strongly disputes payment on the basis that the carpet supplied did not match the sample provided. The client instructs their solicitor to issue proceedings against the customer.

**Which of the following best describes the approach that should be taken by the client?**

A    The client may issue proceedings against the customer immediately with confidence that sanctions will not be imposed.

B    As the only purpose of the pre-action protocols is to assist the parties in settling cases without litigation, the client need not comply as agreement is unlikely.

C    Unless the limitation period is about to expire, the client should write to the customer with concise details of the claim and disclose key documents.

D    The client may choose whether to follow a pre-action protocol or whether to rely upon the Practice Direction for Pre-Action Conduct.

E    When trying to resolve matters, all possible steps should be taken by the client to effect this but only proportionate costs need be incurred.

### Answer

Option C is correct. According to the Practice Direction on Pre-Action Conduct and Protocols, these are the steps with which the claimant should usually comply before issuing a claim. Option A is wrong as there are a number of sanctions that the court could impose if a party fails to comply with the Practice Direction or a relevant pre-action protocol. These include penalties relating to costs and interest. Option B is wrong as assisting the parties in settling cases without litigation is not the 'only' purpose of the protocols and the parties should comply even if agreement seems unlikely.

Option D is wrong as the client cannot choose which route to take. The PDPAC only applies if there is no specific protocol in relation to the particular dispute. Option E is also wrong as the client is required to take 'reasonable and proportionate steps' to try and resolve the matter, not 'all' steps, although it is correct that the costs incurred in doing so should be proportionate.

### Question 3

A claimant (an English company) enters into a contract with an Italian company for the purchase of 500 bicycles. As required by the agreement, the claimant pays in full for the bicycles on 14 March and they are delivered to England on 27 March ready for sale at a cycling festival scheduled to take place in London. When the bicycles arrive at the claimant's premises in England, the claimant inspects them and finds that a faulty gear mechanism has been installed on all the bicycles. As a consequence, the claimant wishes to reject the goods and claim the return of the monies paid. The claimant requests advice on issuing proceedings.

**Which of the following statements best explains how the claimant should proceed?**

A   The claimant has complete choice as to jurisdiction and so should issue proceedings in the English courts as this would be more convenient.

B   The claimant should check the contract to see if there is a term agreeing which country's laws apply and whether the courts of England and Wales or Italy have jurisdiction to hear the dispute.

C   In the absence of prior agreement, in a contract case such as this, a defendant must always be sued in their local courts so the Italian courts would have jurisdiction in this dispute.

D   In the absence of prior agreement, as this is a contract for sale of goods, the Italian company must be sued in the Italian courts as this is where the goods were despatched from.

E   In the absence of prior agreement, the dispute will be determined by English law as it is a sale of goods contract and the applicable law is that of the country where the buyer has their habitual residence.

### Answer

Option B is correct. This is because, although there are mechanisms in place to determine the applicable law and the appropriate jurisdiction in cases with a foreign element, these only apply if the parties have not reached agreement on these issues. Hence, the claimant should check the contract before proceeding further.

Option A is wrong because there may be a jurisdiction clause in the contract and, even if not, the claimant does not have complete choice due to the 'default' mechanisms under Articles 4 and 7, which come into effect in the absence of agreement. Option C is wrong as the defendant may also be sued in the country where the contract was to be performed.

Option D is wrong as, in a sale of goods case, the country that has jurisdiction is the one where the goods were delivered (England), and not the country from which they were despatched. Option E is wrong because the applicable law for sale of goods cases is that of the country where the *seller* has their habitual residence (in this instance, Italy) and not that of the buyer. Hence, English law would not apply on this basis.

# 3 Commencing Proceedings

## SQE1 syllabus

By the end of this chapter you will be able to apply relevant core legal principles and rules appropriately and effectively, at the level of a competent newly qualified solicitor in practice, to realistic client-based and ethical problems and situations in relation to:

**Where to start proceedings:**

- allocation of business between the High Court and the County Court
- jurisdiction of the specialist courts

**Issuing and serving proceedings:**

- issuing a claim form
- adding, removing or substituting parties
- service of a claim form within the jurisdiction
- procedure for service of a claim form outside the jurisdiction (with or without the court's permission) and mechanisms for effecting valid service in another jurisdiction
- deemed dates of service and time limits for serving proceedings
- service by an alternative method

Note that for SQE1, candidates are not usually required to recall specific case names, or cite statutory or regulatory authorities and these are provided for illustrative purposes only. Furthermore, the sample claim form included in this chapter is to assist in understanding the requirements as candidates are not required to draft these forms for SQE1.

## Learning outcomes

The learning outcomes for this chapter are:

*   To appreciate which court to use and why.
*   To understand how to issue and serve a claim form both inside and outside the jurisdiction.
*   To comprehend and apply the procedure for changing the parties.
*   To understand how service is effected and to be able to calculate this accurately.

## 3.1 Introduction

If the matter cannot be resolved, either due to the attitude of one or more of the parties or simply because, despite their best efforts, there is insufficient common ground between them, proceedings will have to be commenced to break the deadlock. Action must be taken before the limitation period (see **Chapter 2**) expires to avoid the defendant having a complete defence to the claim.

The starting point for any litigation is the court and, in this chapter, the different types and work allocation will be considered. Having determined the most appropriate forum for the particular case, how to issue and serve proceedings will be outlined including the practical steps required to initiate such litigation.

## 3.2 The civil courts

In England and Wales, civil disputes are dealt with either by the County Court or the High Court. It is important to ensure that cases are issued in the correct court to avoid the delay and expense of a subsequent transfer; but also so that the claim proceeds in the court to which the matter is best suited in terms of the specialism of the judge and the procedure.

### 3.2.1 Which court?

In some cases, the client will be able to select the court in which to start proceedings. However, the most important element in determining venue is likely to be the amount in dispute.

*   If the value of the claim is £100,000 or less, it *must* be started in the County Court.
*   If the value of the case exceeds £100,000, it *may* be commenced in the High Court.

Note that different rules apply to proceedings that include a claim for damages in respect of personal injuries; these cannot be started in the High Court unless the value of the claim is £50,000 or more.

As a consequence, for claims in excess of £100,000 (or £50,000, as appropriate), the claimant has a choice of which court to use. To assist lawyers in determining the appropriate venue, further guidance is provided by the CPR. These indicate that, in addition to the value of the claim, the High Court may also be used if there are other factors present, in particular:

*   the claim is complex either in relation to the facts, the legal issues, the remedy or the procedures; or
*   the outcome is important to the public in general.

Even if a claim is issued in the High Court, the judge may decide to transfer the matter to the County Court at a later date.

 *Example*

*Northern Finance Ltd (Northern) instructs ULaws LLP to issue against Technology and Co Ltd (TCL) for breach of contract in relation to the installation of a computer system. The purpose of the software was to increase the speed and efficiency of Northern's dealings with customers. However, the system kept crashing and data was lost causing Northern to suffer losses of £124,000. As the amount in dispute is more than £100,000, Northern can issue their claim in the High Court and may decide to do so due to the technical nature of the dispute and the likely complexity of the facts.*

### 3.2.2  The County Court

The County Court generally deals with the more straightforward cases including claims for money only where the value of the claim is £100,000 or less (unless damages are sought for personal injuries). These may consist of:

- specified claims, namely those for a specific sum of money (debt claims); or
- unspecified claims for damages, where the amount in dispute will need to be quantified by the court.

There is a single national County Court, served by named County Court hearing centres across the country. There are also two County Court Business Centres, which issue most civil claims and retain those that are undefended. Because details of what should be included in the claim form are set out in Part 7 of the CPR, they are sometimes referred to as Part 7 claims.

Where and how to issue proceedings depends upon the type of claim.

- All money-only claims made on paper, including both specified and unspecified claims, must be sent to the County Court Money Claims Centre (CCMCC), which is based in Salford. If a hearing is required, usually in contested cases, the matter will be transferred to the County Court hearing centre local to the defendant.

 *Example*

*Northern Finance Ltd also require proceedings to be started against Harris Tools Ltd for an unpaid invoice of £67,000. The value of the claim means that it must be started in the County Court and, as a money-only claim, it should be issued in the CCMCC.*

- The County Court Business Centre at Northampton deals with online claims for specified sums of money (debt claims) for amounts of up to £100,000. These are made via the website Money Claim Online (MCOL), which allows individuals, businesses and solicitors to issue proceedings, check the status of the claim, request judgment and enforce it over the internet.

    This court also provides a service for bulk users, such as utility providers and credit card companies, that file large volumes of claims for money.

- For all other County Court claims, the claimant can usually issue proceedings in any of the County Court hearing centres situated throughout England and Wales. In such circumstances most claimants will choose to start proceedings in the court closest to their home or business.

### 3.2.3  The High Court

The High Court is made up of three divisions.

(a) The Queen's Bench Division, which has a workload consisting primarily of actions in contract and tort.

(b) The Chancery Division, which is used for disputes arising over land, trusts, contentious inheritance matters, partnership claims and company law.

(c) The Family Division, where family disputes such as defended divorces and adoption are resolved.

The Central Office of the High Court is located inside the Royal Courts of Justice in London, but a party may also issue their action in a number of regional District Registries such as in Birmingham and Leeds. Most claimants will choose to start proceedings in the court closest to their home or business.

### 3.2.3.1 The Business and Property Courts

The Business and Property Courts is an umbrella term for a number of courts that decide specialist business and other civil disputes, both national and international. Amongst these are:

- the Commercial Court, which deals with complex cases arising out of business disputes over contracts, insurance, banking and finance; and

- the Technology and Construction Court, which handles claims about buildings, engineering and surveying.

Cases that are suitable for hearing in these courts would be outside the norm of most civil disputes and, as a consequence, the (different) procedure is not covered in this chapter.

## 3.3 Issuing proceedings

Proceedings commence when the claimant or their solicitor send a claim form and other relevant documents to the appropriate court to be 'issued'; effectively, a file is opened.

The documents are:

- a claim form (form N1);

- particulars of claim (which may be drafted as part of the claim form or sent separately); and

- documents that are required to be annexed by the CPR such as a copy of any contract.

Many claims are now dealt with online but, if not, sufficient copies for the defendant and any other parties should be sent, together with a covering letter indicating whether the court or the claimant is to serve proceedings and the court issue fee.

Once the claim form has been issued by the court, proceedings are formally started. Although this rarely arises in practice, a claim is 'brought' for limitation purposes (and so time stops running) when the claim form is *received* in the court office.

### 3.3.1 Completing the claim form  *See update*

The claim form is the point of departure for the litigation and blank forms are accessible on the Ministry of Justice website. It summarises the most important aspects of the claim, both the substantive law that underpins the case and the facts in support. The content should be sufficiently detailed so that the court and the other parties understand the claimant's case without being a full recitation of all the evidence in support. The key word is 'summary'.

**Figure 3.1** sets out an example of a claim form to assist in understanding the content and to illustrate the points that are listed subsequently (not for drafting purposes). The letters in the headings below cross-refer to the relevant part of the form.

**Figure 3.1** Example of claim form in a County Court debt action

| | |
|---|---|
| **Claim Form** | **In the** County Court Money Claims Centre **[A]** |
| | Fee Account no. |
| | Help with Fees - Ref no. (if applicable) **H W F** - ☐☐☐ - ☐☐☐ |
| | *For court use only* |
| | Claim no. |
| | Issue date |

You may be able to issue your claim online which may save time and money. Go to www.moneyclaim.gov.uk to find out more.

**Claimant(s) name(s) and address(es) including postcode**

Brewsters Limited
Unit 12, Brownside Industrial Estate
Reading
RG2 6DS
Tel: 0118 598 3990          **[B]**

SEAL

**Defendant(s) name and address(es) including postcode**

Gates Launderettes Limited
73 Cider Street, Slough SL1 1PP
Tel: 01753 547790

**Brief details of claim**

The claim is for an unpaid debt of £63,450 in respect of 3 industrial drycleaners and 6 industrial washing machines supplied by the Claimant to the Defendant.

**[C]**

**Value**

The claim is for a specified sum of £63,450 plus accrued interest of £1,965.74 and compensation of £100.

**[D]**

**You must indicate your preferred County Court Hearing Centre for hearings here** *(see notes for guidance)*

Reading          **[E]**

| Defendant's name and address for service including postcode | Gates Launderettes Limited 73 Cider Street Slough SL1 1PP **[F]** | **[G]** | £ |
|---|---|---|---|
| | | Amount claimed | 65515.74 |
| | | Court fee | 3275.78 |
| | | Legal representative's costs | 100.00 |
| | | **Total amount** | **68891.52** |

For further details of the courts www.gov.uk/find-court-tribunal.
When corresponding with the Court, please address forms or letters to the Manager and always quote the claim number.

N1 Claim form (CPR Part 7) (06.16)          © Crown Copyright 2016

*(continued)*

**Figure 3.1** (*continued*)

| Claim No. | |
|---|---|

Does, or will, your claim include any issues under the Human Rights Act 1998?  ☐ Yes  ☑ No

**[H]**

Particulars of Claim

**[I]**

1. By clause 1 of a written agreement (the 'Agreement') dated 5 March 2020 the Claimant agreed to sell the Defendant machinery, namely 3 Chloridal dry cleaning machines and 6 Isadal washing machines for an agreed price of £63,450.00. A copy of the Agreement is attached.
2. By clause 4 of the Agreement payment of the agreed price was due within 7 days of delivery.
3. In pursuance of clause 6 of the Agreement the machinery was delivered to the Defendant's premises at 6, Station Rd, Reading on 19 March 2020.
4. In breach of the Agreement the Defendant has failed to pay the agreed price or any part thereof.
5. The Claimant claims the sum of £63,450.00.
6. The Claimant claims interest on the sum of £63,450.00 and compensation under the Late Payment of Commercial Debts (Interest) Act 1998.

AND THE CLAIMANT CLAIMS

1. The sum of £63,450.00.
2. Interest pursuant to the Late Payment of Commercial Debts (Interest) Act 1998. For the purposes of the Act, both parties acted in the course of business. The statutory interest rate began to run from and including 27 March 2020 (the 8th day after delivery) at 8% over the reference rate of 0.5% then in force, totalling 8.5% per annum. Interest due to the date of issue is £1,965.74 (27 March 2020 to 6 August 2020 inclusive being 133 days) and is continuing until judgment or sooner payment date at the daily rate of £14.78.
3. Compensation for late payment pursuant to the Late Payment of Commercial Debts (Interest) Act 1998 in the sum of £100.

DATED: 6 August 2020

**Statement of Truth**  **[J]**  Note that the wording of the statement of truth on the form is incomplete as the Ministry of Justice website is out of date.

*(I believe)(The Claimant believes) that the facts stated in these particulars of claim are true.
* I am duly authorised by the claimant to sign this statement

Full name  Brian Charlton

Name of claimant's legal representative's firm  Collaws

signed _____  position or office held  Managing Director

　　　*(Claimant)　　　　　　　　　　　　　(if signing on behalf of firm or company)

*delete as appropriate*

Collaws  **[K]**
14 Ship Street
Weyford
Guildshire WE1 8HQ
Ref: BM/ABC/Brewsters
DX 1599 Weyford
Fax: 01904 876554

Claimant's or claimant's legal representative's address to which documents or payments should be sent if different from overleaf including (if appropriate) details of DX, fax or e-mail.

### 3.3.1.1 Heading (A)

In the top right hand corner of the claim form, details of the relevant court must be inserted. This will be:

- the County Court Money Claims Centre for money-only claims; or

- the appropriate County Court in other instances; or

- the relevant High Court division and local District Registry for High Court matters, for example:

  The High Court of Justice
  Queen's Bench Division
  Birmingham District Registry

Details of the solicitors' fee account must be added so the court fee may be paid.

The court will assign a claim number when the claim form is issued, which must be included on all subsequent court documents and correspondence with the court. The date of issue will also be inserted.

### 3.3.1.2 Details of the parties (B)

The parties' names and status must be described accurately with the full address and postcode. Failure to do so could result in the proceedings being struck out, particularly if the mis-spelling means the wrong defendant is sued. Further details on how the parties should be described is set out below.

**Table 3.1** Parties to proceedings

| Party | General rule | Illustration |
|---|---|---|
| Individual | Individuals must be described using their full unabbreviated names and title. | Mrs Rehana Waheed |
| Sole traders | Individuals who engage in business are referred to as sole traders. If they use a business name, this should also be included. | An example of a business name is: Antony Tucker T/A Marble Designs Note: T/A is an acceptable abbreviation of 'trading as'. |
| Partnerships | A partnership is a formal arrangement by which two or more parties manage and operate a business and share its profits. They should sue and be sued in the name of the firm rather than by naming individual partners. | Justice & Co (a firm) |
| Companies | For limited liability companies, the correct registered name and address must be stated and this should be checked by carrying out a company search. | Arrow Engineering Ltd Note: check minor points such as whether the word used is 'Ltd' or 'Limited'. |

What if a defendant is an individual who has died before proceedings are commenced? In such circumstances, the claim should be made against the executors or administrators if appointed; or 'the personal representatives of [name] deceased' if not.

3.3.1.3    Brief details of claim (C)

The claim form must contain a concise statement of the nature of the claim and specify the remedy that the claimant is seeking. The sample claim form (**Figure 3.1** above) is for a breach of contract claim. However, the wording will change depending upon the relevant cause of action, as demonstrated below.

**Brief details of a claim relating to professional negligence:**

By a written contract dated [date] the Defendant agreed to manage the Claimant's portfolio of investments. The Defendant was in breach of its obligations and negligent in this management by failing to invest the Claimant's investments in accordance with his stated aim of conservative growth, choosing instead to invest in high-risk investments, causing the Claimant damage and loss. The claimant seeks damages estimated at £500,000.

3.3.1.4    Statement of value (D)

Where the claim is for money, the estimated or actual value of the claim must be inserted.

(a)  Specified claims

For specified (debt) claims: the precise figure should be calculated including the interest that has accrued – see **Figure 3.1**.

(b)  Unspecified claims

For unspecified claims, such as an action for damages for breach of contract, in the High Court the claimant need only put: 'The Claimant expects to recover more than £100,000'. This provides confirmation that the matter has been issued in the correct court. Where damages are claimed for personal injury, the relevant figure is £50,000.

However, in the County Court, the claimant must state:

- whether they expect to recover:
    - not more than £10,000; or
    - more than £10,000 but not more than £25,000; or
    - more than £25,000; or
- they cannot say how much they expect to recover.

When calculating this figure, the following should be disregarded:

- possible awards of interest or costs;
- contributory negligence; and
- counterclaims.

Note that:

- In a claim for personal injuries, the claimant must also state whether the amount that the claimant expects to recover as general damages for pain, suffering and loss of amenity is not more than £1,000 or more than £1,000.

- If a claim is for both damages and a non-monetary remedy such as an injunction to prevent a private nuisance, a statement of value must be given in respect of the damages claimed.

The reason for requesting this information is to assist the County Court in allocating the case to an appropriate 'track'. There are three different procedural routes that a claim may take depending upon the value and these are discussed later in this manual.

In addition, the amount claimed impacts upon the size of the court fee.

### 3.3.1.5 Preferred County Court hearing centre (E)

If a claim is for money only, it must be issued in the County Court Money Claims Centre where it will remain unless the claim is defended or a hearing is required. To assist the parties, the claim will then be transferred to:

- the defendant's home County Court; or to
- the claimant's preferred hearing centre as stated on the claim form.

Thus, to avoid increased costs, the claimant should always include a named court that is most convenient to them.

### 3.3.1.6 Defendant's name and address for service (F)

The defendant's name and address for service should be described accurately in the box on the bottom left hand side of the form; or alternatively, the solicitors' details, provided either the defendant or their legal representatives have confirmed in writing that the latter have been instructed to accept service of the court proceedings on their client's behalf.

### 3.3.1.7 Financial summary of the claim (G)

The last piece of information on the front of the form is a financial summary.

- The amount claimed must be stated. For specified claims, an exact figure should be given, including the interest that has accrued to the date of issue of the proceedings. For unspecified claims, an estimate of what the claimant genuinely expects to recover should be stated.
- The court fee payable on issue is based upon the statement of value and the maximum fee payable is £10,000 – a hefty sum.
- The legal representative's costs are fixed under Part 45 of the CPR for specified money claims. For all other claims, the words 'to be assessed' should be inserted, as any costs awarded will be assessed by the court at the conclusion of the proceedings.

### 3.3.1.8 Human rights (H)

The claimant must indicate whether the claim includes any issues under the Human Rights Act 1998 (this would be rare).

### 3.3.1.9 Particulars of claim (I)

The details of the claim, known as the particulars of claim, must be set out either on the claim form itself or in a separate document. If the claim is for a debt, there is usually sufficient space on the form to outline the relevant details (see **Figure 3.1**). However, more complex cases will be dealt with by way of a separate particulars of claim and the form should be amended accordingly.

3.3.1.10  Statement of truth (J)

CPR Part 22 requires that various documents, including the claim form, are verified by a statement of truth, which must be in the witness's own language, signed and dated. If the particulars of claim are served separately, they must also be verified in this way. The wording is as follows:

> [I believe] [The party believes] that the facts stated in this [name of the document] are true. I understand that proceedings for contempt of court may be brought against anyone who makes, or causes to be made, a false statement in a document verified by a statement of truth without an honest belief in its truth.

As to who can sign the statement of truth, this may be either the party or their legal representative. If the claimant is an individual, this will be straightforward. If not:

- any of the partners or a person having the control or management of the business may sign for a partnership; and
- a person holding a senior position such as a director, secretary, chief executive or the treasurer may sign on behalf of a company.

Where an individual signs on behalf of a party, the following should be added to the statement of truth:

> I am duly authorised by the [party] to sign this statement.

Where a legal representative signs a statement of truth, this will be taken as their statement that:

(a)  the client has authorised them to do so;

(b)  they have explained to the client that in signing the statement of truth the solicitor is confirming the *client's* belief that the facts stated in the document are true; and

(c)  the client was warned of the possible consequences if it should subsequently transpire that the client did not have an honest belief in the truth of those facts; specifically, the client may be prosecuted for contempt of court.

A legal representative who signs a statement of truth must sign in their own name and not that of their firm or employer, but should state the capacity in which they sign and add the name of their firm where appropriate.

Failure to include a statement of truth means that the court may strike out the document and, even if not, the claimant is precluded from relying upon its contents.

3.3.1.11  Address for service (K)

An address for service within the jurisdiction must be given and this will usually be the claimant's own address or their solicitors' address (thereby nominating those solicitors to accept service of proceedings on the claimant's behalf).

3.3.2  **Adding, removing or substituting the parties**

On occasion, it will be necessary for another party to be added to a claim or for one party to be removed or replaced by another.

 *Example*

> *Petra issues proceedings against Barry for negligence after he swerved across the road and collided with her vehicle, causing significant damage. She subsequently discovers that he acted to avoid a pedestrian who had stepped into the road without looking. Petra may want to add the pedestrian to the proceedings as a second defendant.*

The relevant provisions are contained within CPR 19 and are summarised below.

**Figure 3.2**   Adding, substituting or removing a party

```
                    ┌─────────────────────────────┐
                    │  ADDING, SUBSTITUTING OR    │
                    │      REMOVING A PARTY        │
                    └─────────────────────────────┘
        ┌────────────────────┬─────────────────────┬──────────────────┐
        ▼                    ▼                     ▼
┌──────────────┐    ┌──────────────┐       ┌──────────────┐
│ Who can make │    │Is permission │       │  Grounds?    │
│an application?│   │  required?   │       │              │
└──────────────┘    └──────────────┘       └──────────────┘
```

| Who can make an application? | Is permission required? | Grounds? | |
|---|---|---|---|
| An existing party or a person who wants to become a party | Yes unless the claim form has **not** been served | Application made **within** the limitation period | Application made **outside** the limitation period |

**but**

No-one may be added or substituted as a **claimant** unless their consent in writing has been filed at court

It is desirable:
- to **add** a new party to resolve matters in dispute; or
- to **remove** a party; or
- to **substitute** a party where the existing party's interest or liability has passed to them.

A party may only be **added** or **substituted** if the limitation period was current when proceedings were started

**and**

- the original party was named by mistake; or
- the original party has died/is subject to a bankruptcy order and their interest or liability has passed to the new party; or
- the claim cannot properly be carried on without the new party.

Although the law is clear, it is important to consider how this applies to the facts of each particular case.

## ⭐ *Example*

*During the course of the proceedings, Petra dies. An application is made to the court to order that the personal representatives of Petra's estate are substituted as the claimant in her place in the litigation. The judge makes the order after being satisfied that Petra's interest has passed to the personal representatives and their consent in writing has been filed at court.*

## 3.4   Service of the claim form

Once a claim form has been issued, it must be served on the other parties within four months. This means that it must be sent to or delivered to the defendant so they are aware of the existence of the proceedings. The rules governing service of documents are set out in CPR Part 6.

A claim form can only be served on a firm of solicitors if the defendant has nominated them in writing and this should not be presumed just because that firm has represented the defendant in pre-action negotiations. Once nominated, all court documents are served on the lawyers unless (exceptionally) the document must be served personally on the party, such as an injunction.

### 3.4.1 Methods of service

The following methods of service are permitted under CPR, r 6.3:

(a) personal service;

(b) first class post or document exchange;

(c) leaving the claim form at a specified place;

(d) fax or other means of electronic communication; or

(e) any other method authorised by the court.

#### 3.4.1.1 Personal service

The arrangements for personal service will depend upon the status of the defendant.

- A claim form is served personally on an individual by simply handing it to them. If they refuse to accept the document, it may be left with or near them.

- If the defendant is a partnership, the form may be left either with a partner or with a person who has the control or management of the partnership at its principal place of business.

- Personal service is effected on a company by leaving the documents with a person who holds a senior position such as a director, treasurer, secretary or chief executive.

#### 3.4.1.2 First class post or document exchange

Only first class post will satisfy the requirements of the CPR for service. Alternatively, where a document exchange (DX) number is provided on the letter heading, this may be used unless otherwise stated. DX is a system used by many solicitors and other professionals to transport documents between their offices, arriving the next business day.

#### 3.4.1.3 Leaving the form at a specified place

Here, the claim form is delivered by hand to the address specified by the CPR (see **Table 3.2** below).

#### 3.4.1.4 By fax or other electronic means

Service by fax is waning in popularity as email and similar electronic methods become the normal means of communication. In both instances, the party to be served (or their solicitor) must have expressly confirmed they are willing to accept service in this manner.

- An email address or fax number on the *party's* headed paper is not enough to satisfy this requirement.

- In contrast, the inclusion of a fax number on the *solicitor's* letterhead is sufficient indication they are willing to accept service by fax.

- The same does *not* apply for an email address, where the solicitor must specifically confirm this method may be used for service.

A party or their nominated solicitors may include in a statement of case a fax number, email address or electronic identification for the purpose of service of proceedings.

#### 3.4.1.5 Service by an alternative method

In addition to the specific ways listed in Part 6 above, the court can authorise other methods or places of service, such as sending a text message or leaving a voicemail on a particular telephone number.

The court may also sanction service by a contractually agreed method, or on the agent of an overseas principal. Furthermore, where the party to be served is a limited company, s 1139(1) of the Companies Act 2006 provides that documents may be left at or posted to the registered office of the company.

 *Example*

*ULaws LLP are acting on behalf of Burton Carpets Ltd in a breach of contract claim. It has proved impossible to serve the defendant with the court documents and so the solicitors make an application to the court to serve by an alternative method. They obtain information that the defendant regularly sees his partner at a different address to his own and apply for permission to serve the documents by delivering them to his girlfriend's property. The application must be supported by evidence that the document is likely to be brought to the attention of the defendant. In this instance, the solicitors rely upon a report from an enquiry agent confirming the defendant stays at the property three nights each week.*

## 3.5 Where to serve?

Where no solicitor is authorised to accept service and the defendant has not given an address for service, the default position of the most common defendants is as set out in **Table 3.2**.

**Table 3.2** Service at a specified place

| Nature of defendant to be served | Place of service |
| --- | --- |
| Individual | Usual or last known residence. |
| Individual being sued in the name of a business (sole trader) | Usual or last known residence of the individual; or principal or last known place of business. |
| Individual being sued in the name of a partnership | Usual or last known residence of the individual; or principal or last known place of business of the partnership. |
| Limited liability partnership | Principal office of the partnership; or any place of business of the partnership within the jurisdiction that has a real connection with the claim. |
| Company registered in England and Wales | Principal office of the company; or any place of business of the company within the jurisdiction that has a real connection with the claim. |

## 3.6 When to serve?

Once a claim form has been issued, the claimant has four calendar months in which to serve it on the defendant.

 *Example*

*A claim form is issued on 20 January to be served on the defendant who is living in Bristol. The claimant must complete the step required by the CPR, in relation to the particular method of service chosen, before 12.00 midnight on 20 May.*

It would be unusual for the claimant to wait before serving the document because this imposes an unnecessary deadline upon the solicitor. However, if the limitation period is running out, the claimant may be forced to issue proceedings and, if difficulties arise in relation to tracing the defendant, this four month window gives a little more breathing space.

Whether or not the time limit is met depends upon the method of service used; so the period ends on the date:

- personal service was effected or delivery was made at the relevant place; or
- the letter was posted or left with the DX provider; or
- the transmission of the fax was completed or the email was sent.

Once this has been done, the claimant has completed the 'step required' for service of the claim form.

## 3.7 Deemed service

The potential problem with any method of service, apart from personal service, is that the claimant cannot know precisely when the defendant receives the claim form and this information is essential in order to determine the next stage in the proceedings. To avoid disputes about whether and when documents are served, the CPR adopt the concept of deemed service. This means that a document will be taken to have arrived on a given day regardless of whether it actually did. However, there are different rules for the claim form as opposed to all other court documents.

### 3.7.1 Deemed service of the claim form

Rule 6.14 introduces a simple, indisputable presumption that the claim form is deemed to have been served on the second business day after the step required has occurred. Establishing this requires two pieces of information.

- A 'business day' is any day except Saturday, Sunday, a bank holiday, Good Friday or Christmas Day.
- The 'step required' is, for example, putting the claim form in the post (see **3.4** above).

Thus, a claim form sent by post on Monday will usually be deemed served on Wednesday.

### ⭐ *Example*

(a) *An individual defendant is personally served with a claim form on Friday. It is deemed served on Tuesday, provided Monday and Tuesday are business days.*

(b) *A firm of solicitors authorised to accept service receives the claim form by an email transmitted on Saturday. Sunday will not count. Assume Monday is a bank holiday and so does not count either. Deemed service will be on Wednesday as this is the second business day (Tuesday being the first) after the email was sent.*

If this was the only rule, deemed service would be straightforward but there are different provisions in place for all other documents. Thus, it is important to check what type of document is being sent to determine when it is deemed served.

### 3.7.2 Deemed service of other documents

The rules that apply to all other documents (such as a defence or a Part 36 offer) are somewhat complex and produce a variety of deemed dates of service according to the method used. An important point to remember is that the particulars of claim, if served separately, falls under these rules and *not* those that apply to claim forms.

The requirements are set out in CPR, r 6.26 and can be divided into two sim[...]
those with and without a cut off time of 4.30pm. They are summarised in **Tab**[...]

**Table 3.3** Deemed service of documents other than the claim form

| Method of service | Deemed date of service |
| --- | --- |
| Personal service<br>Delivering the document to a permitted address<br>Fax<br>Email | • If served before 4.30pm on a business day, on that day.<br>• If not, on the next business day. |
| First class post or DX | • The second day after it was posted provided that day is a business day.<br>• If not, on the next business day. |

A key difference is that service by first class post or DX is effected on the *second day* after the document was posted, in contrast with the claim form where it is the second *business* day. This is illogical, not just because it is inconsistent, but because this may fall on a Sunday when there is no postal delivery service. In such cases, the practical effect is that service will 'roll on' to the next business day.

⭐ *Examples*

(a) *A document is personally served at 3.30pm on a Monday. Provided this is a business day, service is deemed to occur that day as it has taken place before 4.30pm.*

(b) *A defence is posted first class on a Tuesday. The day of deemed service is Thursday, the second day after it was posted as it is a business day.*

(c) *The particulars of claim is served after the claim form. It is left in a numbered box at the Document Exchange (DX) on Friday. The day of deemed service is the second day after it is left, provided this is a business day. The second day will be Sunday but, as this is not a business day, the day of deemed service is the next day, Monday.*

(d) *A document is sent by fax on a Saturday and the transmission of that fax is completed by 11.25am. Although this occurs before 4.30pm, Saturday is not a business day and so does not count as the day of deemed service. The next business day will be Monday and this is the date of deemed service.*

### 3.7.3 Service of the particulars of claim

In many cases, such as debt actions, the particulars of claim will be included on the claim form itself. However, for more complex cases, there is unlikely to be sufficient space to detail the legal elements and the facts in support. In such instances, the particulars of claim may be served separately:

• either at the same time as the claim form; or

• within 14 days after service of the claim form (but no later than four months after the date of issue of the claim form).

⭐ *Example*

*ULaws LLP are instructed by a client to issue proceedings. They issue a claim form marked 'particulars of claim to follow' on 5 March. The four month deadline for serving the claim form expires at 12 midnight on 5 July.*

(a) *The solicitors decide to serve the claim form on 10 April. As soon as they do this, the (separate) clock starts ticking for service of the particulars of claim. This must be done within 14 days so by 24 April.*

(b) *In an alternative scenario, having issued the claim form, ULaws LLP have difficulties in tracing the defendant and are unable to serve the claim form until 27 June. In this instance, the solicitors only have until 5 July to serve the particulars of claim, so less than 14 days, because they are approaching the (long stop) deadline of four months.*

Understanding the rules that apply to service is essential to a practising solicitor as missing these important dates may lead to the proceedings being compromised or struck out, with a consequential claim for negligence against the solicitor.

## 3.8 Service out of the jurisdiction   *See update*

If a claim form is to be served outside the jurisdiction of England and Wales, the CPR allow extra time for this to be effected. Instead of four months, the document must be served on the other parties within six months of being issued.

Furthermore, there are special procedures in place for service of a claim form outside the jurisdiction, whether with or without the court's permission, and mechanisms for effecting valid service in another jurisdiction.

- **Service within the European Union**

No special permission is required to serve proceedings in Scotland, Northern Ireland or any EU Member State, provided the English courts have jurisdiction under Council Regulation 1215/2012 (see **Chapter 2**). The claim form must be accompanied by a notice setting out the grounds on which the claimant is entitled to serve it outside the jurisdiction.

However, there are special provisions as to the *methods* of service of the claim form that are acceptable and these are detailed in CPR Part 6.

- **Service outside the European Union**

In cases that are not governed by Regulation 1215/2012, the claimant must obtain permission to serve proceedings out of the jurisdiction. Examples of the grounds that may be relied upon are where the claim is brought to enforce a contract that is governed by English law, or where the breach of contract occurred in England and Wales. The application must be supported by evidence and is made without notice.

If an order permitting service outside the jurisdiction is made, the time limit for responding to the claim will be extended. Service is usually effected through the judicial authorities of the State in question or the British Consul.

## Summary

- The majority of cases are issued in the County Court and only claims in excess of £100,000 (or £50,000 for personal injury claims) may be commenced in the High Court.

- Proceedings are commenced by way of a claim form, which provides a concise statement of the nature of the claim and the remedy sought. It is reinforced by the particulars of claim, which includes details of the cause of action and the facts in support. The particulars of claim is usually included on the claim form itself for straightforward cases, for example a debt action, but is drafted as a separate document for more complex matters.

- The claim form, particulars of claim and any required documents (such as a copy of the contract) are sent to the appropriate court with the court fee to start proceedings. The court will issue the claim by noting the issue date upon the claim form, sealing it and allocating a claim number.

- Thereafter, the claim form will be served upon the defendant by the court, unless the claimant has indicated otherwise, in which case they will arrange for service.

- There are several methods of service that may be used, for example, personal service, first class post or email. How service is effected will depend upon the status of the defendant, whether it be an individual, a sole trader, a partnership or a company. The CPR dictate when the documents are deemed served regardless of when they are actually served and the claim form is treated differently from all other documents in this regard.

- There are special rules in the CPR that detail how claims may be served outside the jurisdiction.

## Sample questions

### Question 1

A claimant wants to issue proceedings for a breach of contract claim arising from the provision of goods that were not of satisfactory quality. This caused the claimant to suffer losses of £43,000 being the price of the goods and £52,000 loss of profits. The defendant is an individual who trades under a business name. The defendant has failed to respond to any correspondence from the claimant. When the contract was negotiated, the defendant instructed solicitors to act on their behalf.

**Which statement describes the best way in which the claimant should issue proceedings?**

A    In the High Court against the defendant in their individual and business names, with the address for service being that of the defendant.

B    In the High Court against the defendant in their business name only, with the address for service being that of the solicitors.

C    In the County Court against the defendant in their personal name only, with the address for service being that of the defendant.

D    In the County Court against the defendant in their business name only, with the address for service being that of the solicitors.

E    In the County Court against the defendant in their individual and business names, with the address for service being that of the defendant.

### Answer

Option E is correct. The claim must be issued in the County Court as the value of the losses claimed is £95,000, so less than £100,000 which is required for High Court proceedings. Both options A and B are wrong for this reason.

The defendant should be sued in their full unabbreviated name together with their full trading name. For this reason, options B, C and D are wrong. Options B and D are also wrong because the defendant has not confirmed that their lawyers are instructed to accept service of court proceedings on their behalf.

## Question 2

A claim form is served by first class post on Friday 2 April. The particulars of claim is delivered to a permitted address at 5pm on the following Thursday 8 April. The next day is Good Friday and the Monday 12 April is also a bank holiday, being Easter Monday.

**Which of the following statements gives the correct days of deemed service?**

A   The claim form is deemed served on Tuesday 6 April; the particulars of claim is deemed served on Tuesday 13 April.

B   The claim form is deemed served on Monday 5 April; the particulars of claim is deemed served on Thursday 8 April.

C   The claim form is deemed served on Tuesday 6 April; the particulars of claim is deemed served on Friday 9 April.

D   The claim form is deemed served on Tuesday 6 April; the particulars of claim is deemed served on Monday 12 April.

E   The claim form is deemed served on Monday 5 April; the particulars of claim is deemed served on Tuesday 13 April.

### Answer

Option A is correct. Under the rules, the claim form is deemed served on the second business day after the step required (here sending by first class post) has occurred. Monday 5 April is a business day, as is Tuesday 6 April so the claim form is deemed served on the Tuesday. However, different rules apply to other documents.

The particulars of claim was delivered to the permitted address at 5pm. Even though Thursday 8 April is a business day, it was delivered after the 'cut-off' time of 4.30pm, so this date is not the day of deemed service. Service will be effected on the next business day, which is Tuesday 13 April because both Friday and Monday are bank holidays. The other options are wrong because one or more of the dates given do not accurately describe the dates of deemed service.

## Question 3

A claimant commences a claim for breach of contract against a company (the defendant). Two years later, the company is sold to another company (the purchasing company), which takes over all the assets and liabilities. The claimant applies, within the limitation period, to substitute the company as a defendant with the purchasing company so that the claim may continue.

**Which statement best describes the court's powers in this situation?**

A   Because the purchasing company has taken over the company's liabilities, the claimant has the right to substitute the purchasing company as a new party.

B   The purchasing company must file their consent in writing with the court before they may be substituted as a defendant.

C   The court can substitute the purchasing company as a defendant as it is desirable to do so given that the company's liabilities have passed to the purchasing company.

D    The court can substitute the purchasing company as a defendant because the claim cannot properly be carried on without the new party.

E    The court cannot substitute the purchasing company as a defendant.

**Answer**

Option C is the correct option as the application was made within the limitation period and the statement correctly describes the legal test to substitute a party.

Option A is wrong because the claimant will require the court's permission to substitute the purchasing company as a new party given that the claim form has been served (two years have passed). Option B is wrong as written consent is only required if the claimant is to be added or substituted as a new party, and here it is the defendant.

Option D is wrong as this provision relates to applications made outside the limitation period, which does not apply in this instance. Option E is wrong as the court does have the power to substitute the purchasing company as a defendant.

# 4 Responding to a Claim

## SQE1 syllabus

By the end of this chapter you will be able to apply relevant core legal principles and rules appropriately and effectively, at the level of a competent newly qualified solicitor in practice, to realistic client-based and ethical problems and situations in relation to **responding to a claim** as follows:

- admitting the claim
- acknowledging service and filing a defence and/or counterclaim
- disputing the court's jurisdiction
- entering and setting aside judgment in default
- discontinuance and settlement
- time limits for responding to a claim

Note that for SQE1, candidates are not usually required to recall specific case names, or cite statutory or regulatory authorities. These are provided for illustrative purposes only and the sample documents are included for the same reason.

## Learning outcomes

The learning outcomes for this chapter are:

- To appreciate the different ways in which a defendant may respond to a claim form.
- To understand when to apply for a judgment in default and how to set this aside to allow the proceedings to continue.
- To evaluate ways in which the litigation may be brought to an early conclusion.
- To raise arguments in relation to jurisdiction.

# 4.1 Introduction

Once proceedings are issued, the defendant is compelled to take action unless they are prepared for the claimant to win outright. Quite when the defendant needs to respond depends upon the approach taken by the claimant in drafting their claim. If the claim form is marked 'particulars of claim to follow', the defendant must await service of these. This is logical as it is the particulars of claim that set out the detail of the case and, without this information, the defendant cannot properly draft their response.

Once the defendant has been served with both the claim form and the particulars of claim (whether separately or together), the defendant must react in some way. To assist, at the same time, the defendant will receive Form N9 – the response pack – which explains how the defendant should respond and the time limits for doing so. There are three options open to the defendant under the CPR, namely:

(a)  to file an admission (Part 14);

(b)  to file an acknowledgment of service (Part 10); or

(c)  to file a defence (Part 15).

There is a fourth choice, which is to ignore the claim entirely, but this does not mean the litigation goes away as the claimant will be able to apply for judgment in default. **Figure 4.1** contains a summary of the defendant's options and the effect of these.

**Figure 4.1**   Defendant's response to proceedings

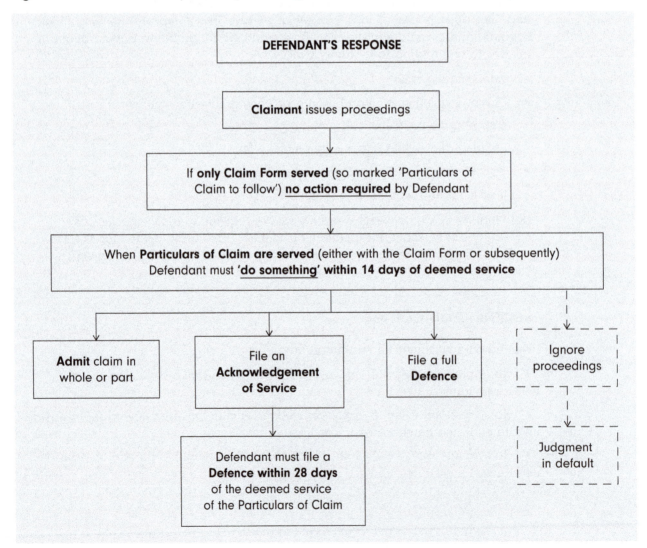

## 4.2 Admissions

If a defendant is aware they owe the money, provided they have the means to pay, it is likely to be in their interests to admit the claim as this will bring the matter to an early conclusion and limit their liability for costs.

A defendant who wishes to admit either the whole or part of the claim should complete the appropriate sections of the response pack. There are two types of admission forms – one for specified (debt) claims and the other for unspecified claims (where damages are sought) and the defendant should ensure they select the correct form.

### 4.2.1 Specified claims

As to what happens next, the procedure will vary depending upon the parties' responses.

#### 4.2.1.1 Admission of entire claim

If a defendant admits the whole claim for a specified amount, they must provide details of their income and expenditure and make an offer of payment, either in full or by way of instalments. Upon receipt of the form, the claimant may then file a request for judgment. If the claimant rejects the defendant's payment terms, the judge will decide the appropriate rate of payment, usually in the absence of a court hearing.

#### 4.2.1.2 Admission of part of the claim

Alternatively, the defendant may admit only part of a claim for a specified amount. In this instance, the claimant has 14 days in which to consider any offers made and to decide on their next course of action as follows:

(a) to accept the part admission in full satisfaction of the claim and request that judgment be entered by the court for that amount;

(b) to accept the part admission but not the defendant's proposals for payment in which case the court will decide on their suitability; or

(c) to reject the offer entirely and proceed with their claim as a defended action.

This decision is likely to be based, primarily, on the defendant's ability to pay.

### 4.2.2 Unspecified claims

Where the defendant admits liability for a claim for an unspecified amount and offers a sum of money, the court will serve a notice on the claimant asking whether or not they accept the figure in satisfaction of the claim.

If the offer is accepted, the claimant may enter judgment for the amount offered and, if the defendant has asked for time to pay, the procedure described above in **4.2.1.1** applies. However, if *either* the claimant does not accept the offer *or* the defendant makes no offer, the claimant will enter judgment for damages to be assessed at a disposal hearing.

## 4.3 Acknowledgment of service

In many cases, the defendant may be sure they want to defend the claim but are not yet in a position to draft a full defence, perhaps because they are still gathering evidence. Filing the acknowledgment of service form buys the defendant time to enable them to do this. The effect is that, instead of having 14 days from service of the particulars of claim to file their defence, they now have 28 days.

*Example*

*ULaws LLP are instructed by Harrison Curtains Ltd (Harrisons) to issue proceedings against Marches Hotels Ltd (Marches). The contract was for the supply and fitting of curtains for a hotel in Hereford. The first instalment was paid by Marches in accordance with the contract, but the second instalment (due within seven days of completion of the contract) has not been received. Harrisons issue proceedings for the outstanding invoice.*

*Marches are served with a claim form and particulars of claim form on 2 November, giving them 14 days in which to respond to the court. Because Marches dispute the claim, they may either:*

*(a)  file a full defence by 16 November; or*

*(b)  file an acknowledgement of service on any day up to and including 16 November. This will have the effect of extending the time for Marches to file their defence until 30 November.*

*If Marches meet either of these deadlines, they will be able to proceed with their defence against Harrisons.*

## 4.4    The defence

The third viable option for the defendant is to respond to the proceedings by filing a full defence. As stated above, this may either be within the initial 14 day limit from service of the particulars of claim or within 28 days if an acknowledgement of service is filed.

The response pack contains forms that the defendant can use and most litigants in person (parties who are not represented by a lawyer) will take advantage of these. Alternatively, a separate document may be prepared and this is the approach a solicitor would generally take. The reason is that a well drafted defence would set out more factual detail than could be included on the form.

Once the defence has been filed, a copy must be served on all other parties. The court will be responsible for this unless the defendant's solicitor has indicated otherwise.

### 4.4.1    Counterclaim

As part of the defendant's response, they may wish to pursue their own claim against the claimant and this is known as a counterclaim.

 *Example*

*Continuing with the claim by Harrisons, ULaws LLP are served with a copy of Marches' defence by the court. Marches assert that the curtains are poorly made and do not hang properly. In their defence, they dispute liability alleging that Harrisons are in breach of the implied terms as the goods are not of satisfactory quality and were not fitted with reasonable care and skill. Marches also attach a counterclaim for the repayment of the first instalment.*

### 4.4.2    Extending the time limit

On occasion, the defendant may not be able to meet the deadline for filing the defence and so, with agreement from the other parties, this can be extended by a maximum of 28 days. The effect is that the defendant has a total of 56 days from the date of service of the particulars of claim. Any further extension would need the court's permission.

## 4.5 Default judgment

Once proceedings have been served upon the defendant, it is common for them to take no action at all. To ensure such defendants cannot evade liability for monies owed by simply doing nothing, the CPR include a mechanism whereby the claimant can force the issue and this is known as a judgment in default (of the defence) or a default judgment – the terms are interchangeable. This means that the claimant obtains a judgment without there being any consideration of the facts involved. The process is a straightforward paper exercise.

### 4.5.1 Procedure

The claimant will make an application under CPR Part 12 and this will require them to complete a request for default judgment. To succeed, they must satisfy the court that:

- the particulars of claim have been served upon the defendant; and
- the defendant has not filed an acknowledgement of service form or a defence within the relevant time period.

⭐ *Example*

*Wessex Insurance Plc (Wessex) issue proceedings against Alpha Motor Services Ltd (Alpha) for non-payment of an insurance premium of £37,000. The claim form and the particulars of claim are issued and served on Tuesday 9 February 2021. Alpha have until close of business on Tuesday 23 February 2021 to take action.*

*(a) If Alpha ignores the claim, Wessex may apply for default judgment on Wednesday 24 February.*

*(b) If Alpha file an acknowledgement of service by Tuesday 23 February, the time to file a defence is extended until Tuesday 9 March 2021, this being 28 days after service of the particulars of claim. However, if this deadline is missed, Wessex may request (and be granted) judgment in default.*

There are limited circumstances where a claimant may not obtain a default judgment, specifically if there is a pending application by the defendant for summary judgment or to have the claimant's statement of case struck out.

### 4.5.2 Types of default judgment

The application for a default judgment is dealt with in different ways depending upon whether it is a debt claim or not.

When applying for judgment in default for a specified sum, the claimant must:

- indicate the date payment was due;
- calculate an up-to-date total for the interest claimed; and
- state a daily rate at which interest accrues.

This will enable the court to enter judgment for the correct figure on any given day. Once final judgment has been entered, the payment will usually be required within 14 days.

However, if the claim is for an unspecified sum, the court will grant the claimant's request for default judgment but the case will need to come back before the court to decide the amount of damages payable (a disposal hearing).

⭐ *Examples*

*(a) Continuing with Wessex's claim against Alpha, the insurance premium should have been paid before 1 January and, under the contract, interest is also due on the sum*

*of £37,000 at a rate of 10% per annum. This gives a daily rate of interest of £10.14 (£37,000 x 10% divided by 365).*

*Wessex may claim the interest from 1 January to 9 February 2021 (the date of issue of proceedings), being 40 days. Multiplying this by the daily interest rate of £10.14 gives a total of £405.60.*

*In addition, Wessex will be entitled to an additional £10.14 for every day that passes up until the date of judgment.*

(b) *In contrast, if Wessex had also claimed for loss of profits, default judgment would have been entered on liability with damages to be decided (assessed) by the court at a later date. This is because where a claim includes both specified and unspecified amounts, the entire claim is treated as unspecified.*

### 4.5.3 Setting aside default judgments

Having initially ignored the proceedings, if the claimant enters default judgment, the defendant will have no choice but to face them. If the defendant accepts that the monies are owed, it is best for them to pay the judgment, if at all possible, to avoid increased costs and interest. If not, the way forward is for the defendant to apply for the judgment to be set aside.

There are two grounds under CPR Part 13 upon which the defendant may rely in their application.

### 4.5.4 The mandatory ground

The court is obliged to set aside a default judgment if it was wrongly entered. This would occur where judgment has been entered too early, before the time for filing an acknowledgment of service or a defence (whichever is applicable) expired; or because the claim has already been paid in full.

### 4.5.5 The discretionary ground

The court also has the power to set aside a default judgment in circumstances where the defendant:

- has a real prospect of successfully defending the claim; or
- there is some other good reason why the defendant should be allowed to defend the claim.

The first of these grounds is clearly linked to the merits of the defence and indeed, there is little point in the defendant being allowed to re-open proceedings in a case where their prospects of success are limited.

With regard to the second ground, good reasons that may satisfy the test could be that the defendant was ill or away on holiday so they could not respond within the time constraints. Excuses such as pressure of work or the documents being misplaced would not be sufficient.

In addition, the court will also take account of the promptness of the defendant's application to set aside. It is therefore essential that the defendant issues their application as soon as they become aware of the default judgment, to comply with the overriding objective of ensuring that cases are dealt with expeditiously and fairly.

 *Example*

*Kanji Okinawan buys a dining room table and chairs from Quality Furniture Ltd (QFL). There is a dispute about the quality of wood used in the construction of the furniture and Kanji refuses to pay for it. While Kanji is away visiting family in Japan, QFL issue and*

*serve proceedings for the price of the goods and then enter default judg
acknowledgement of service or defence is filed. When Kanji returns, he*
*that a judgment has been made against him and instructs ULaws LLP on his* bc.

*Kanji has a good reason for asking the court to set aside the default judgment as he was
out of the country at the relevant time and so was unable to respond to the proceedings
through no fault of his own. In accordance with best practice, ULaws LLP write to QFL and
ask them to agree to the judgment being set aside. When the claimant refuses, they issue
an application to the court on Kanji's behalf.*

*The application will need to be supported by evidence to show Kanji was in Japan and
that he acted promptly when becoming aware of the default judgment. The basis of
Kanji's defence and any evidence in support should also be included to show that he has
a defence with a real prospect of success at trial. This is because whether to grant the
application is a matter of discretion for the court and the judge is more likely to set the
judgment aside and allow the proceedings to continue if the defence has real substance.*

### 4.5.5.1 Procedure

The application is made by filing an application notice (form N244), which is usually supported
by a witness statement outlining the defendant's submissions.

### 4.5.5.2 Orders

In determining the application, there are three possible orders the judge can make:

(a) the defendant succeeds and the judgment is set aside, allowing them to continue to
defend the action;

(b) the claimant wins and the judgment remains in place, so they may proceed to
enforcement; or

(c) a conditional order is made, namely, the judgment is set aside on condition the
defendant pays monies into court, for example, the amount of the claim. This is the least
likely outcome and is used in situations where the court is concerned the defence is being
pursued as a delaying tactic where the defendant does not have the money to pay.

### 4.5.5.3 Costs

Costs of interim applications such as this are dealt with in more detail in **Chapter 6**. Dealing
specifically with an application to set aside a default judgment, the costs order made at the
conclusion of the hearing will depend upon the outcome as follows:

- If the application is granted on a mandatory ground, the claimant will have been at fault
for entering judgment when they should not have done and, therefore, the claimant is
liable to pay the defendant's costs.

- Where the defendant establishes the discretionary ground of a good reason for the
default, as neither side is at fault, costs are usually in the case.

- Where the defendant only establishes the discretionary ground of a defence with a real
prospect of success at trial, the defendant is at fault in failing (initially) to deal with the
proceedings. As a consequence, they normally have to pay the claimant's costs.

- If the application fails, the defendant will pay the claimant's costs of the application.

### 4.5.6 Summary

**Figure 4.2** contains an overview of the process for applying for and setting aside default
judgments.

**Figure 4.2** Setting aside default judgments

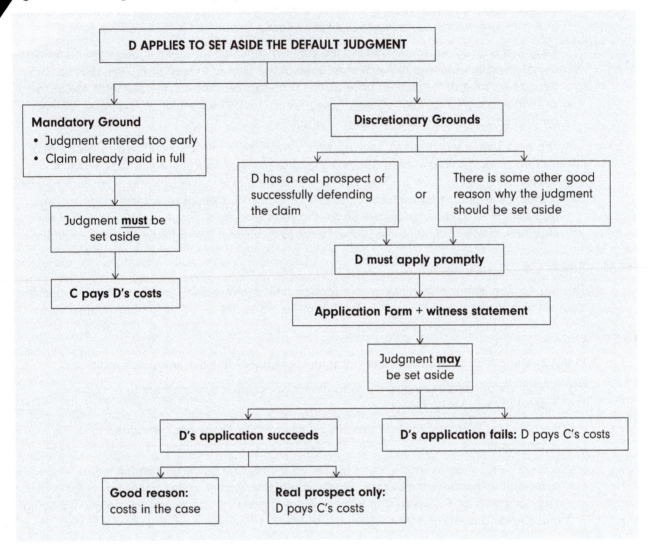

## 4.6 Discontinuance

A claimant may decide not to pursue their claim, even though no settlement has been reached. This may be for a variety of reasons but will usually be because, after further consideration of the evidence, they conclude their prospects of succeeding at trial or of recovering any money from the defendant are so slim that it would be better to cut their losses and discontinue.

- *Can a claimant discontinue all or part of a claim?*

  Yes, at any time during the proceedings.

- *Is permission required?*

  Not usually, but permission must be obtained in certain circumstances such as if the court has granted an interim injunction.

- *What if there is more than one claimant?*

  A claimant may not discontinue unless every other party consents in writing or the court gives permission.

- *What if there is more than one defendant?*

The claimant may discontinue the claim against all or any of the defendants.

- *What is the procedure?*

  The claimant must file and serve a notice of discontinuance on the parties to the proceedings. If consent is required, a copy of this must be attached to the notice.

- *What is the effect?*

  The proceedings are brought to an end against the defendant on the date the notice of discontinuance is served upon them. The claimant will be liable for the costs of the proceedings unless the court orders otherwise and it is vital that the solicitor explains this to the client.

  Because of the costs implications of discontinuance, a claimant should not issue proceedings lightly and should consider carefully their prospects of success before doing so.

## 4.7 Pre-action settlements

Where a settlement is reached prior to the issue of proceedings, the prospective claimant will not be entitled to recover their legal costs unless this has been agreed.

Once settlement terms have been agreed, they must be clearly and accurately recorded in writing, so that the agreement can be enforced if one of the parties defaults. It may be sufficient for the terms to be recorded in an exchange of correspondence, but more complicated settlements should normally be recorded in a formal settlement agreement.

## 4.8 Settlements reached after the issue of proceedings

If a settlement is concluded after proceedings have started, it is preferable for this to be recorded in a court order or judgment. This is so that enforcement proceedings may be commenced to recover any monies due under the settlement (including costs) should the agreement not be honoured.

### 4.8.1 Consent orders

Where none of the parties is a litigant in person, it will often be possible to avoid an application to the court by drawing up a consent order or judgment for sealing by a court officer. Although in theory the court retains the power not to approve the proposed order, in practice, it will only be referred to a judge if it appears to be incorrect or unclear.

The formalities for a consent order are as follows:

(a) the order agreed by the parties must be drawn up in the terms agreed;

(b) it must be expressed as being 'By Consent'; and

(c) signed by the legal representative acting for each of the parties to whom the order relates.

⭐ *Example*

*Returning to the case of Quality Furniture Ltd and Kanji Okinawan, the parties agree that the latter will pay the sum of £12,000 for the dining room table and chairs and a consent order is drawn up.*

**Figure 4.3**  Consent order

IN THE STAFFORD COUNTY COURT

WF-20-1234

BETWEEN

QUALITY FURNITURE LTD                                          Claimant

and

MR KANJI OKINAWAN                                          Defendant

**CONSENT ORDER**

Upon the parties agreeing to settle this matter

AND BY CONSENT

IT IS ORDERED THAT

1.   The Defendant shall pay the Claimant the sum of £12,000 by 2.30 p.m. on 7 May 20XX.

2.   Upon payment, the claim will be stayed.

3.   No order as to costs.

| We consent to the terms of this order. | We consent to the terms of this order. |
|---|---|
| Advocates & Co | ULaws LLP |
| *Advocates & Co* | *ULaws LLP* |
| ———————— | ———————— |
| Dated 19 April 20XX | Dated 20 April 20XX |

*The effect of the Consent Order is that, provided Kanji pays £12,000 to QFL by the stated deadline, the claim will come to an end. However, if the monies are not paid, interest will start to run on the sum and the claimant can take enforcement action. The reference to the claim being stayed means that the proceedings will be 'paused' until the agreement is put into effect, allowing the claimant, Quality Furniture Ltd, to return to court should the defendant fail to meet his commitments. It is also clear, from paragraph 3 of the Consent Order, that each side has agreed to pay their own costs.*

Only terms that are within the powers of the court to order may be agreed, for example the payment of a sum of money. Furthermore, the terms of a consent order are open to public inspection. Thus, if the parties want any terms to be confidential and/or are beyond the powers of a court to order, they should use a special form of consent order known as a Tomlin order.

### 4.8.2 Tomlin orders

A Tomlin order stays the claim on agreed terms that are set out either in a schedule to the order or separately. The key to an effective Tomlin order is to appreciate that certain terms must appear in the order itself, while others can be put in the schedule or a separate document that is normally held by the parties' solicitors.

The provisions that must appear in the order are summarised in **Table 4.1**.

**Table 4.1**   Terms contained within the Tomlin order

| Order | Explanation |
| --- | --- |
| 'By consent' | This term records the fact of there being agreement. |
| Stay of proceedings | Confirms the proceedings are 'paused'. |
| Liberty to apply | This provision allows any party to apply to the court for the stay to be lifted and the court can be asked to enforce the settlement if a party does not perform its part of the agreement. The important effect is that new court proceedings do not have to be commenced to enforce the terms. |
| Payment of costs or detailed assessment of costs | Where one party is to pay another's costs and/or the parties want the amount of those costs to be assessed (checked and calculated) by the court, that direction must go in the order itself. |
| Signed by the parties' solicitors | A formal requirement signifying consent to the agreement. |

Terms that the parties wish to keep confidential or that the court does not have the power to order must be set out in a schedule to the Tomlin order or in a separate document. Often this will be for the payment of a sum of money so that other businesses or customers cannot see how much the matter was settled for. Any other agreed terms should also be recorded, for example that in future dealings one party is to give the other a discount.

An example of a Tomlin order is set out in **Figure 4.4**. The order is made 'By Consent', the proceedings are stayed, there is liberty to apply and the defendant has agreed to pay £40,000 of the claimant's costs. The attached schedule records (at paragraph 1) the settlement payment, the provision for interest on any late payment is contained in paragraph 2, whilst paragraph 3 records the parties' agreement to enter into a particular contract as part of the settlement.

**Figure 4.4**   Example of a Tomlin order

IN THE HIGH COURT OF JUSTICE

QUEEN'S BENCH DIVISION                                                      20XX L 164

MANCHESTER DISTRICT REGISTRY

BETWEEN

LA BOULE PLC                                      Claimant

and

CHRISTALINE LIMITED                                Defendant

ORDER BY CONSENT

UPON the parties having agreed terms of settlement

BY CONSENT IT IS ORDERED THAT:

1.  All further proceedings in this action shall be stayed upon the terms set out in the attached schedule, except for the purpose of carrying such terms into effect.

2.  Each party shall have liberty to apply to the court if the other party does not give effect to the terms set out in the schedule.

3.  The Defendant do pay the Claimant within 28 days the sum of £40,000 in respect of the Claimant's costs.

Dated: ....................................

We consent to the making of an order in the above terms.

................................................

Swallows & Co., Solicitors for the Claimant

................................................

Singleton Trumper & Co., Solicitors for the Defendant

SCHEDULE

1.  The Defendant shall pay or cause to be paid to the Claimant the sum of £500,000 within 28 days of the Order in full and final satisfaction of all claims and counterclaims arising in this action.

2.  In the event of late payment, the Defendant will pay interest on the sum of £500,000 or any part remaining due at a daily rate equal to 10% above the Bank of England base rate as at 1 January 20XX.

3.  The Claimant and the Defendant will on the making of the Order enter into a distribution agreement on terms agreed between the parties and held by the Claimant's solicitors as part of the compromise of this action.

## 4.9    Disputing the court's jurisdiction

If a defendant wishes to dispute the jurisdiction of the court, this must be stated on the acknowledgement of service. The defendant then has 14 days after filing the acknowledgment of service form to make a challenge, failing which they will be treated as having submitted to the jurisdiction. The application to the court to dispute the court's jurisdiction must be supported by evidence as to why England and Wales is not the proper forum for the case.

*   If the court grants the application and finds that the claim should not have been brought in England and Wales, service of the claim form will usually be set aside. As a consequence, the proceedings come to an end.

- If the court refuses the defendant's application, the original acknowledgement of service ceases to have effect and the defendant must file a further acknowledgement within 14 days. The proceedings will then continue in the usual way.

## Summary

- Having received court proceedings, a defendant must respond within 14 days of service of the particulars of claim by filing an admission, an acknowledgment of service or a defence (and perhaps also a counterclaim).

- Filing an acknowledgment of service gives the defendant an extra 14 days in which to file their defence, granting them a total of 28 days from the date of service of the particulars of claim.

- A defendant may admit the whole or part of the claim and either pay the sum or request time to do so. If the claimant does not accept the part admitted in full and final settlement, the case will continue as a defended claim. If the defendant admits an unspecified claim, the amount of damages payable must be determined at a court hearing before the matter may be concluded.

- If a full defence is filed with the court, the litigation will proceed as a contested matter.

- If a defendant does not file an acknowledgement of service or a defence within the required time limits, the claimant may enter judgment in default. On a specified claim, this will be for a final sum of money and the matter will proceed immediately to enforcement. If the claim is for an unspecified amount of money, the judgment is for damages to be assessed by the court at a disposal hearing.

- Default judgments may be set aside either on mandatory grounds; or on discretionary grounds provided the defendant applies promptly.

- A claimant may discontinue the proceedings, usually without needing the permission of the court, but they will be responsible for the costs of doing so.

- A settlement reached before proceedings are issued may be recorded either by letter or in a formal agreement. Once proceedings have commenced, the terms of a settlement must be recorded in a formal court order or, if the parties require confidentiality or the imposition of terms beyond the powers of the court, in a Tomlin order.

- The defendant may dispute the court's jurisdiction to hear the claim and the issue will then be determined by the court.

## Sample questions

### Question 1

A claimant issues proceedings against a travel company for failing to repay the monies that he paid for his holiday, which was cancelled due to civil disorder in the country he was intending to visit. The claim form and the particulars of claim are deemed served on Tuesday 11 May.

**Which of the following answers correctly describes the time limits imposed by the CPR?**

A   The company must file a full defence within 14 days and in any event by Tuesday 25 May.

B   If the company files an acknowledgment of service within 14 days, they have until Tuesday 8 June to file a full defence.

C   If the company files an acknowledgement of service on Thursday 13 May, they have until Thursday 27 May to file a full defence.

D   If the company files an acknowledgment of service on Friday 14 May, the claimant may apply for default judgment 14 days thereafter.

E   If the company fails to respond to the proceedings, the first date on which the claimant could apply for default judgment is Tuesday 25 May.

**Answer**

Option B is the correct answer. The company has 14 days, so until Tuesday 25 May, to file either an acknowledgment of service or a full defence – hence, option A is wrong. If an acknowledgement of service is filed within 14 days, the deadline to file the defence is extended to 28 days from service of the particulars of claim, so until Tuesday 8 June (option B). The effect is not to 'add' 14 days to the date when the acknowledgment of service was filed and this is why option C is wrong. For the same reason, option D is wrong.

The claimant may apply for default judgment after 14 days if the defendant fails to respond at all. However, as the company has until close of business on Tuesday 25 May to do so, the first date on which an application for judgment in default could be made is Wednesday 26 May – explaining why option E is wrong.

**Question 2**

A woman is the managing director of a company. She becomes aware that default judgment has been entered, correctly, for an outstanding invoice. The employee in the accounts department who is responsible has been extremely busy and confesses that he forgot to deal with the invoice. However, he explains to the woman that the reason for the non-payment was because there was a dispute about the quality of the consignment delivered under the contract.

**Which of the following best describes the course of action which the woman should take?**

A   The woman should write to the court on behalf of the company requesting more time to investigate and ask that judgment be set aside in the meantime.

B   The company should apply to the court requesting that the judgment be set aside under the mandatory ground.

C   The company should apply to the court requesting that the judgment be set aside on the discretionary ground that the defendant has a real prospect of successfully defending the claim.

D   The company should apply to the court and rely upon the discretionary ground that there is some other good reason why the judgment be set aside.

E   The woman should advise her fellow directors that if the company succeeds in the application, the claimant will be ordered to pay their costs.

**Answer**

Option C is correct as the facts state there is a dispute about the quality of the consignment and so the company may succeed in their defence. Option A is not the best approach because a formal application must be made to the court to set the judgment aside and a letter will not suffice. Option B is wrong as the mandatory ground is irrelevant here – the company have not paid the invoice in full and default judgment was entered correctly, so not too early. Option D is not an appropriate way forward – pressure of work is not a sufficient 'good reason' to satisfy the court. Option E is wrong as the company may well be ordered to pay the costs of the application even if they succeed. This is because the company is at fault in failing to deal with the claim form in the first place.

**Question 3**

A claimant has issued proceedings against a defendant and the trial date is approaching. The parties enter into negotiations and agree that the defendant will pay half of the outstanding invoice that is in dispute, and the claimant will supply additional materials at no extra cost. The claimant does not want other customers to be aware of this arrangement. Both parties are represented by solicitors.

**Now the parties have agreed a resolution to their dispute, what answer describes the best way forward?**

A    The claimant will agree to discontinue their claim.

B    The parties will record their agreement in an exchange of correspondence.

C    The parties will need to attend a court hearing to confirm their agreement.

D    The parties should sign a formal consent order to be sealed by the court.

E    The parties should sign a Tomlin order.

**Answer**

Option E is correct. Option A does not apply in these circumstances. A notice of discontinuance would be served by the claimant where, for example, they conclude that they are unlikely to succeed at trial and so decide to cut their losses and bring the litigation to a halt. Option B is wrong because proceedings have been issued and, thus, recording the terms of the settlement in correspondence would not be sufficient. Option C is wrong as there is no need for a court hearing to confirm the agreement – it may be ratified in the absence of the parties.

Although the agreement could be confirmed in either a consent order (option D) or a Tomlin order (option E), the latter is the best way forward as the claimant does not want other customers to be aware that they have supplied the defendant with additional materials at no extra cost. If a Tomlin order is used, this term could be kept confidential by placing it in the schedule to the agreement or in a separate document.

# 5 Statements of Case

## SQE1 syllabus

By the end of this chapter you will be able to apply relevant core legal principles and rules appropriately and effectively, at the level of a competent newly qualified solicitor in practice, to realistic client-based and ethical problems and situations in relation to **statements of case** as follows:

* purpose, structure and content of a claim form, particulars of claim, or defence relating to a claim in contract or tort

* purpose, structure and content of a reply, Part 20 claim and defence to Part 20 claim

* requests for further information about statements of case

* amendments

Note that for SQE1, candidates are not usually required to recall specific case names, or cite statutory or regulatory authorities. These are provided for illustrative purposes only and the sample statements of case are included for the same reason.

## Learning outcomes

The learning outcomes for this chapter are:

* To appreciate how statements of case define the issues in dispute.

* To understand what must be included in different particulars of claim and the principles involved in drafting a defence.

* To understand the role of the reply and defence to counterclaim and when these would apply.

* To know when and how to make a request for further information.

* To understand and apply the procedure for amending a statement of case.

## 5.1 Introduction

### 5.1.1 Overview

Statements of case are the formal documents in which the parties concisely set out their respective cases. They are served between the parties and filed at court. The statements of case are central to the litigation as they ensure that each party knows their opponent's case at an early stage, providing them with the opportunity to assess how strong it is, to determine what evidence is needed to counter it and to consider whether to make an offer to settle and on what terms. At trial, the court will only decide those issues that are raised in the statements of case and so they must be drafted carefully and reviewed continually as the matter develops.

Statements of case are invariably the first documents that are served between the parties and are served in sequence.

- The **claim form** and **particulars of claim** start the process.
- If the case is contested, a **defence** will be filed by the defendant.

Usually, these will be the only statements of case in civil proceedings. However, on occasion, they will not be sufficient and the CPR provide for additional documents that may also prove useful.

- If deemed necessary by the claimant, they will respond with a **reply**.
- The defendant may also file a **counterclaim**; if so, the claimant will need to serve a **defence to the counterclaim**.
- If any party requires additional details of another party's case, they may file a request and a **response to the request for further information** must be served.

### 5.1.2 Some general points

Part 16 of the CPR sets out the requirements and the formalities of statements of case. However, precedents are another useful starting point when drafting these documents, although they must always be tailored to the particular matter that is the subject of the litigation. When drafting, it is important to remember that, although the documents themselves are formal, the style adopted should be clear using plain English where possible. Where a solicitor prepares a party's statements of case, it should be signed in the name of the firm.

### 5.1.3 Ethical considerations

A solicitor must not mislead the court so should only include assertions in the statements of case that are properly arguable. For example, a solicitor should not include a client's allegation that the opponent has acted fraudulently unless there is some evidential basis for this.

What if a client has filed a statement of case and subsequently tells their solicitor before the litigation ends that it contains a material error, the effect of which is to mislead the court? In those circumstances, the solicitor should advise the client to amend the statement of case and, if the client refuses to do so, should cease to act. In order to keep client confidentiality, the solicitor should not inform the court or any other party of the reasons why they are no longer representing their client.

## 5.2 Claim form

In **Chapter 3**, the content and structure of a claim form were discussed in detail and an example provided of a claim form for a specified sum (a debt) incorporating the particulars of claim. However, in most instances where lawyers are involved, the facts are likely to be too complex to fit into the limited space available on a claim form; consequently, a separate particulars of claim will be required.

## 5.3 Particulars of claim

The contents and purpose of the particulars of claim are governed by r 16.4(1) of the CPR. Specifically, the document must include:

(a) A concise statement of the facts on which the claimant relies. This means that it must outline all the facts giving rise to the dispute, to demonstrate the required elements of the cause of action on which the claim is based.

(b) If the claimant is seeking interest, a statement to that effect and the details.

However, the precise contents of the particulars of claim will depend upon the relevant cause of action, for example, whether the claim is for breach of contract or negligence.

### 5.3.1 Claim based on breach of contract

Where the claimant alleges breach of contract, the particulars of claim should deal with the essential material facts that will establish the cause of action.

(a) *The status of the parties*: this is the starting point and, apart from providing background information, these details are required in certain situations. For example, the parties should confirm the defendant's business when relying on sale during the course of that business to establish terms implied by the Sale of Goods Act 1979 or the Supply of Goods and Services Act 1982.

Next, the claimant will set out the chronological events explaining what has occurred. This may include pre-contractual matters if they assist in establishing the claim, such as the request for a sample or relevant pre-contract statements. Thereafter, the particulars of claim will move into the substance of the matter. However, whilst it may appear that the claimant is simply 'telling their story', behind this are the legal elements that underpin their case.

(b) *Existence of contract*: this must be established (although rarely disputed in practice) and will consist of the date, type (written or oral), parties, subject matter and consideration.

Where a claim is based upon a written contract, by paragraph 7.3 of PD 16, a copy of the contractual documents must be attached to or served with the particulars of claim. If the claim is based on an oral agreement, the contractual words used, by whom, to whom, and when and where they were spoken should be specified by virtue of paragraph 7.4 of PD 16.

(c) *Terms*: details of any express terms are included and these will usually be found in the contract itself. Likewise, any implied terms relied upon should be stated specifically.

### ⭐ *Examples*

*In a dispute over a service agreement between a company and an individual, the relevant express term could be referred to in this way:*

- *By clause 5.1 of the Service Agreement, the Defendant agreed not to take up employment with a rival company within 6 months of termination of the Service Agreement.*

*In a dispute over the printing and binding of a biography of a famous entertainer, implied terms are pleaded as follows:*

- *The Contract contained implied terms that the Defendant would carry out the services of printing and binding of the Books with reasonable care and skill and would produce Books of satisfactory quality.*

At this point, the particulars of claim may appear to revert back to a mere description of the facts, perhaps the date that the goods were delivered or the payment of the first instalment. However, in addition to telling the chronological story, this paragraph sets out what parts of the contract have been performed. This is important in limiting the areas of dispute the court will need to consider.

(d) *Breach alleged and particularised*: this section contains details of which terms were breached and specifically how. Examples would be a failure to pay for the goods, late delivery or the poor quality of the items supplied. Initially, the breach is alleged generally.

⭐ **Examples**

- *The Defendant breached clause 5.1 of the Service Agreement.*

- *In breach of the implied terms, the Defendant did not carry out the services of printing and binding the Books with reasonable care and skill and did not produce Books of satisfactory quality.*

Next, under a heading of Particulars of Breach, the details of exactly what the claimant alleges the defendant did wrong must be itemised. This could be quite straightforward such as:

- *The Defendant took up employment with Media Giants Ltd, a rival company of the Claimant, in June 20XX, only 3 weeks after the termination of the Service Agreement.*

Alternatively, a more complex list of how the defendant fell short of the express or implied terms may be required, for example:

- *The binding agent used when printing and binding the Books was only 45% of full strength or was applied at too high a temperature.*

- *The laminate covering the Books was wrinkled and in some places detached from the hard cover.*

(e) *Factual consequences*: this is a continuation of the chronological events where the claimant explains what happened as a result of what the defendant did wrong (the breach). It may be that the poor quality goods supplied to a retailer could not be sold on to consumers or that repair work had to be carried out.

(f) *Damage and loss alleged and particularised*: the loss must be alleged generally, for example:

- *By reason of the Defendant's breaches of the Contract, the Claimant has suffered damage and loss.*

The losses should then be itemised so it is clear to the defendant exactly what is being claimed from them and how this is calculated.

(g) *Interest*: where the remedy sought by the claimant is either damages or the repayment of a debt, the court may award interest on the sum outstanding, but only if claimed. In breach of contract cases, there are three alternative ways of claiming interest as follows:

- The contract itself may specify a rate of interest payable on any outstanding sum.
- If there is no provision in the contract for interest, interest may be claimed under the Late Payment of Commercial Debts (Interest) Act 1998, which gives a statutory

right to interest on commercial debts that are paid late. As the Act is only concerned with commercial debts, it does not apply to unspecified (damages) claims or to a specified amount (a debt) owed by a consumer. The relevant rate of interest is 8% per annum above the Bank of England's base rate on the date the debt became due for payment. The claimant is also entitled to a small, prescribed amount of statutory compensation for the inconvenience of having to recover the debt.

- In all other cases, the court has a discretion to award interest either under s 35A of the Senior Courts Act 1981 (SCA 1981) in respect of High Court cases, or under s 69 of the County Courts Act 1984 (CCA 1984) for County Court cases.

For specified claims, the interest must be precisely calculated as a lump sum for the amount that has accrued from breach of contract up to the date of issue of the proceedings, plus a daily rate so it is easy to provide an updated total. Set out below is a calculation of interest in a specified claim to illustrate this in practice.

### ⭐ Example

*ULaws LLP act for Guy Tibbs, a local builder who is in dispute with one of his customers, Jemma Little. He entered into a written contract to convert her basement into a games room in May [this year]. He finished the work on 12 September but, despite reminders, Jemma has not paid him the contract price of £13,000. The written contract between Guy and Jemma provides that interest is payable on late payment at the rate of 20% per annum from and including the day of completion of the works. Guy issues a claim form on 31 October.*

*He is entitled to interest on £13,000 for 50 days (namely 19 days in September and 31 days in October). For each day, he is entitled to interest of £7.12 (that is £13,000 x 20% ÷ 365 rounded down). Thus, on the claim form, Guy should claim £356.00 by way of interest.*

*Thereafter, £7.12 would be added to the outstanding balance for each day that passes up until judgment is awarded.*

(h) *Summary of relief*: traditionally, although not a requirement of the CPR, the remedies claimed are summarised towards the end of the particulars of claim.

(i) *Statement of truth*: the claim form or particulars of claim must contain a signed statement of truth that its contents are believed to be true (Part 22) as set out in **Chapter 3**.

An example of a particulars of claim for a claim arising out of a dispute over a contract is provided as **Figure 5.1** to give an insight into how the document would look in practice. This relates to a High Court matter.

### 5.3.2 Claim based on negligence

Particulars of claim relating to an action in the tort of negligence will be approached in a similar way, although the content will differ to reflect the legal elements of duty of care, breach of that duty, causation and loss.

The court has a general discretion (which is usually exercised) to award interest on damages in any negligence claim in accordance with s 35A SCA 1981 in respect of High Court claims, and s 69 CCA 1984 for County Court matters. In practice, interest is normally awarded from when the loss was sustained.

**Figure 5.1**  Example of particulars of claim in a High Court case

IN THE HIGH COURT OF JUSTICE

QUEEN'S BENCH DIVISION                                                    20XX No 876

READING DISTRICT REGISTRY

BETWEEN

INDUSTRIAL MANUFACTURING LIMITED                              Claimant

and

HEATECHS LIMITED                              Defendant

PARTICULARS OF CLAIM

1.  At all material times the Claimant was a manufacturer of small industrial machinery parts and the Defendant carried on business as a manufacturer and supplier of central heating boilers and systems.

2.  By a written contract made on 23 April 20XX between the Claimant and Defendant, the Defendant agreed to sell to the Claimant a central heating gas boiler and integrated water pump described in clause 1 as a Heatechs Powerheat Unit Model 312K ('the Unit') for the sum of £70,000. A copy of the contract is attached.

3.  The Claimant bought the Unit from the Defendant who sold it in the course of its business. It was an implied term of the contract that the Unit should be of satisfactory quality.

4.  Further, during a telephone conversation at about 11.30 am on 18 April 20XX, the Claimant by its contracts manager, Ian Jones, expressly or by implication made known to the Defendant (represented by their sales manager, Polly Rees) the particular purpose for which it required the Unit, namely for the purpose of installation in the Claimant's factory at 15 Normandale Lane, Reading 'as part of a heating system required to be in continuous use for 7 days per week'. It was an express and/or implied term of the contract that the Unit to be delivered by the Defendant should be reasonably fit for that particular purpose.

5.  In purported performance of the contract the Defendant delivered the Unit on 25 June 20XX when the Claimant paid the Defendant the agreed sum of £70,000. The Unit was installed by the Claimant into its factory heating system on or about 6 July 20XX.

6.  In breach of the express and/or implied terms the Unit delivered by the Defendant was not of satisfactory quality and was not reasonably fit for its particular purpose.

PARTICULARS OF BREACH

The impeller retaining nut on the integrated water pump was insufficiently secure because the thread was 0.4cm wide whereas the maximum that it should have been was 0.2cm wide.

7.  As a consequence of the breaches of terms the integrated water pump failed to operate and the boiler in the Unit became or had become drained of water on 6 August 20XX and overheated as a result. When the pump effectively re-engaged, cold water flowed into the boiler causing it to explode and rupture on 6 August 20XX and the pipe connections to distort. As a result the boiler house had to be pumped out and repaired and a new boiler installed. During this time the Claimant lost 9 days of production.

8.  By reason of the above the Claimant has suffered loss and damage.

*(continued)*

**Figure 5.1** (*continued*)

<u>PARTICULARS OF LOSS AND DAMAGE</u>

| | | |
|---|---|---|
| 8.1 | Cost of new boiler | £72,500 |
| 8.2 | Cost of installation of new boiler | £4,700 |
| 8.3 | Cost of pumping out boiler house and repairing damaged premises | £17,625 |
| 8.4 | Consequential losses as the result of production losses (estimated) | £25,000 |

9. In respect of damages awarded the Claimant is entitled to interest pursuant to s 35A of the Senior Courts Act 1981 at such rates and for such period as the Court thinks just.

AND THE CLAIMANT CLAIMS:

(1) Damages pursuant to paragraph 8 above;

(2) Interest pursuant to paragraph 9 above.

Dated 10 December 20XX.

*ULaws LLP*

ULAWS LLP

STATEMENT OF TRUTH

I believe that the facts stated in these Particulars of Claim are true. I am duly authorised by the Claimant to sign this statement. I understand that proceedings for contempt of court may be brought against anyone who makes, or causes to be made, a false statement in a document verified by a statement of truth without an honest belief in its truth.

Signed: *D. Smith*

DAVID SMITH

Director of Claimant company

This statement of truth was signed on [date].

The Claimant's Solicitors are ULaws LLP of 133 Great Hampton Street, Birmingham B18 6AQ where they will accept service of proceedings on behalf of the Claimant.

To the Defendant

To the Court Manager.

## 5.4 Defence

The defendant only has a limited amount of time in which to file a defence with the court and, where solicitors are instructed, they will usually draft this as a separate document rather than completing the standard form.

### 5.4.1    Purpose of the defence

The defence sets out the defendant's answer to the claim with the aim being to highlight what issues are in dispute. Rule 16.5 assists in the approach that should be adopted when drafting this document. The defence must state, for each allegation, whether it is:

a)   denied;

b)   not admitted; or

c)   admitted.

Where a defendant denies an allegation, they must state:

*   their reasons for doing so; and

*   their own version of events if different from that given by the claimant.

### ✪ *Example*

*Returning to the case study (above), to satisfy this requirement, the Defence includes a statement as follows:*

*   *Paragraph 3 of the Particulars of Claim is denied. The Defendant has been working with Media Giants Ltd on a consultancy basis only and is not, nor ever has been, employed by them in breach of the Service Agreement or at all.*

A non-admission is made where the defendant has no knowledge of the particular matter alleged.

The effect of the three different responses is summarised in **Table 5.1**.

**Table 5.1**    Defence: effect of defendant's responses to the claimant's allegations

| Response? | Does the claimant need to prove the allegation? |
|---|---|
| Admit | No |
| Non-admission | Yes |
| Denial | Yes |

Considering these issues in the context of a scenario will assist in understanding how this would apply in practice.

### ✪ *Example*

*Hamza is driving to work one day when he is involved in a road traffic accident with Marnie. A few months later, he is served with a claim form and particulars of claim alleging negligence.*

*In his defence, Hamza admits that he has a duty of care to other road users (this is an established duty) and further admits the date of the car accident, that a collision took place and the location where this occurred. As a consequence, the claimant is not required to prove these facts.*

*However, Hamza denies he was at fault, alleging that he had the right of way and that Marnie drove across his path. The effect of this response is that the claimant must provide evidence to prove Hamza was in breach of his duty of care.*

*With regard to the damage or loss alleged to have been sustained by the claimant, Hamza makes a non-admission because he does not know how much Marnie's car cost to repair. This will force the claimant to prove her losses.*

The purpose of the defence is to narrow down the issues between the parties so that only the matters in dispute are tested in court. In the example above, the central issue to determine is who was at fault in causing the collision. If the court rules in the claimant's favour, Hamza is likely to admit the amount of the damages once Marnie produces evidence to prove them, such as a car repair bill.

It is vital not to miss an allegation because the effect is that it is deemed to be accepted. Accordingly, best practice dictates that a systematic approach is adopted to ensure every allegation in the particulars of claim is dealt with and nothing is admitted through omission. This will mirror, as far as possible, the sequence of events in the particulars of claim, with the defence usually answering each paragraph in turn. If more than one allegation is included in the paragraph, these should be dealt with on a point by point basis.

### 5.4.2 Contents of a defence

When drafting the defence, the defendant must comply with the formalities required by the CPR and must include:

- the name of the court;
- the claim number (the unique reference number that is allocated by the court on issue of proceedings);
- the parties;
- the title (DEFENCE);
- the date and signature of solicitors in the name of the firm;
- the statement of truth; and
- details of who is to be served and where.

If the defendant alleges that the relevant limitation period for the claim has expired, the details of this must be given in the defence, for example, when it began and expired, and whether it ran under the terms of a contract or under the Limitation Act 1980. The burden of proof is then normally transferred to the claimant to show the claim is not time-barred.

There are some instances where the burden of proof falls upon the defendant, specifically in relation to:

(a) contributory negligence; and

(b) a failure by the claimant to mitigate its loss.

Where these matters are alleged, they should be made and detailed in the defence.

**Figure 5.2** illustrates how a defence is drafted in the breach of contract claim between Industrial Manufacturing Limited and Heatechs Limited. This defence also illustrates the methodical approach that should be adopted in answering the allegations raised.

**Figure 5.2** Example of a defence in a High Court case

IN THE HIGH COURT OF JUSTICE

QUEEN'S BENCH DIVISION                                                    20XX No 876

READING DISTRICT REGISTRY

BETWEEN

INDUSTRIAL MANUFACTURING LIMITED                           Claimant

and

HEATECHS LIMITED                                        Defendant

DEFENCE

1. The Defendant admits paragraphs 1 to 4 of the Particulars of Claim.

2. The delivery of the Unit referred to in paragraph 5 of the Particulars of Claim was wholly in accordance with the terms of the contract and constituted full and complete performance by the Defendant. Payment of the agreed sum of £70,000 by the Claimant is admitted. No admission is made as to the installation of the Unit by the Claimant as the Defendant has no knowledge of that matter.

3. The Defendant denies it was in breach of contract as alleged in paragraph 6 of the Particulars of Claim, or at all. The Defendant asserts that the Unit supplied was of satisfactory quality and fit for its purpose. In particular, the impeller retaining nut on the water pump was sufficiently secure by means of a 0.4cm thread.

4. The Defendant makes no admission as to the matters stated in paragraph 7 as the Defendant has no knowledge of these matters.

5. As to paragraph 8 it is not admitted that the Claimant has suffered the alleged or any loss and damage as the Defendant has no knowledge of these matters.

6. If, which is not admitted, the Claimant suffered the loss and damage alleged in paragraph 8, it is denied that this occurred as a result of the alleged or any breach of term by the Defendant. Any such loss or damage was caused by the Claimant's installation and/or subsequent use of the Unit.

7. If, which is not admitted, the Claimant suffered the loss and damage alleged in paragraph 8, the Claimant failed to mitigate that loss and damage. In particular, it was unreasonable to stop production for 9 days.

8. In all the circumstances it is denied that the Claimant is entitled to the relief claimed or any relief.

Dated 8 January 20XX.

*Haughton & Co*

HAUGHTON & CO

STATEMENT OF TRUTH

I believe that the facts stated in this Defence are true. I am duly authorised by the Defendant to sign this statement. I understand that proceedings for contempt of court may be brought against anyone who makes, or causes to be made, a false statement in a document verified by a statement of truth without an honest belief in its truth.

Signed: *Darren Bennett*

DARREN BENNETT, Managing Director of the Defendant company

This statement of truth was signed on [date].

The Defendant's Solicitors are Haughton & Co, 19 High Pavement, Reading RD61 4UZ, where they will accept service of proceedings on behalf of the Defendant.

To the Court Manager and the Claimant.

## 5.5    Part 20 claims

In many cases, the only statements of case will be the particulars of claim and the defence. However, a defendant may wish to make their own claim against a claimant, or to bring another party into the proceedings. These additional claims are governed by rules set out in CPR Part 20 and are referred to as Part 20 claims.

### 5.5.1    Counterclaim

A counterclaim arises where the defendant is alleging they have their own cause of action against the claimant. Effectively, they could have taken action against the claimant first and issued proceedings.

⭐ *Example*

*Kendal Plumbers Ltd (KPL) supply and install high quality bathrooms. Edwin Gallagher, who owns a hotel in the Lake District, purchases new bathroom suites for two of the bedrooms. However, on installation, it becomes apparent that there are a number of flaws in the ceramic appearance. Edwin refuses to pay the second instalment as required under the contract and, as a consequence, KPL issues proceedings for the monies due.*

*In response, Edwin files a defence stating that he is not liable to pay for the bathroom suites because they are defective. In the meantime, the toilets have leaked causing extensive flood damage to the floor below. Edwin wants to claim for losses incurred as a result of the damage to his hotel and does so by way of a counterclaim. This will form part of the same document as the defence.*

*This may also be referred to as a 'set off'. Edwin's defence is that he should not have to pay the balance due for the bathroom suites because, if he can establish his counterclaim, it will set off the amount claimed and KPL will have to pay him damages.*

In summary, a counterclaim will be relevant if the defendant has actually suffered loss that is attributable to the claimant. If the defendant simply has a good reason for not paying the monies owed, but has not incurred any loss, they should only file a defence.

### 5.5.2    Structure of a defence and counterclaim

A defence and counterclaim is essentially what the title suggests: a defence and a (new) claim, set out in a single document. The title to the action remains the same but the heading will now be 'DEFENCE AND COUNTERCLAIM'. The document is then sub-divided into two sections, with the defence outlined at the beginning and the counterclaim following on immediately thereafter.

In terms of the content, the best approach to drafting a counterclaim is to treat it as a stand-alone claim, for example, for breach of the Sale of Goods Act 1979 on the basis the goods were not of satisfactory quality. However, rather than repeat aspects that have already been included in the statements of case, such as details of the contract and the incorporation of the implied terms, the counterclaim will refer back to the defence. The first paragraph will simply state that the relevant paragraphs are repeated. The effect of this is that, for example, the existence and terms of the contract are accepted and the defendant's allegation of breach is also confirmed. The rest of the counterclaim will then set out the allegations of loss resulting from the claimants' breach.

In summary:

- A counterclaim is treated as if it were a claim and should be filed with the defence.
- It will form one document, with the counterclaim following on from the defence.
- Permission is not required from the court unless the defence has already been filed.

### 5.5.3    Additional claims

Part 20 also applies to additional claims made by a defendant for a contribution or indemnity or some other remedy against any person whether or not they are already a party. These are referred to as additional claims.

A common scenario is where the defendant wishes to pass the blame, either in whole or in part, onto a third party. The defendant may be seeking a full indemnity from the third party, or a contribution towards any damages they have to pay the claimant.

#### 5.5.3.1    Indemnity

A claim for an indemnity may arise where there is a contractual relationship between the defendant and the third party, in which the latter is obliged by the terms of a contract to indemnify the defendant if they are found liable for the claim. This may also arise by way of statute.

 *Example*

> *Continuing with the scenario above, KPL claim an indemnity against Alpha Bathrooms Ltd (Alpha), the company that manufactured the bathroom suites, alleging that there was an inherent defect in the goods. If KPL lose the claim against Edwin, the liability for any sums the defendant is ordered to pay may be passed on to Alpha.*

#### 5.5.3.2    Contribution

A claim for a contribution can be made where there are joint wrong-doers and the defendant argues that the third party is partly responsible for the harm the claimant has suffered.

 *Example*

> *Toya claims damages from Lisa as a result of a road traffic collision. Lisa alleges that another driver, Jaspar, was partly to blame for the accident. She will claim a contribution from Jaspar towards any damages that she is ordered to pay to the claimant.*

#### 5.5.3.3    Other additional claims

The defendant may also make other additional claims without the court's permission provided this is done either before or at the same time as they file the defence.

 *Example*

> *Farzani is suing Leycester Motors Ltd (LML) because the new car that she purchased from the company has patches of rust underneath the vehicle. LML bring in Fenland Storage Limited as an additional party as they have evidence that the company stored the car outside before delivering it, instead of in a warehouse as they were contracted to do.*

## 5.6    Reply to defence

A claimant may wish to file a reply to the defence but is under no obligation to do so. Replies tend to be used if the claimant wants to respond to matters that have been raised in the defence but which are not covered in the particulars of claim.

## 5.7 Defence to counterclaim

If the claimant decides to dispute the counterclaim, they must file a defence to the counterclaim within 14 days (unless an extension of up to 28 days has been agreed with the defendant). If they fail to do so, the defendant may enter judgment in default on the counterclaim using the procedure outlined in **Chapter 4**.

## 5.8 Amendments to statements of case

In a perfect world, no one would ever have to amend their statements of case. However, sometimes mistakes are made and, on other occasions, fresh information comes to light after the statement of case has been served. CPR Part 17 lists the ways in which these can be amended.

### 5.8.1 Before expiry of the limitation period

The procedure for amending documents prior to the expiry of the limitation period is set out in **Table 5.2**.

**Table 5.2** Amending statements of case (within limitation period)

| After filing but before service | After filing and service |
| --- | --- |
| Amendments may be made any time. | Only with:<br>(a) the written consent of all of the parties; or<br>(b) the permission of the court. |

When applying for permission, the applicant should file a copy of the statement of case with the proposed amendments together with an application notice. The court will then decide whether or not to exercise its discretion to grant the application, taking into account the overriding objective of dealing with the case justly and at proportionate cost. In particular, the court will need to strike a balance between injustice to the applicant if the amendment is refused, and injustice to the opposing party and other litigants in general, if it is permitted.

### 5.8.2 After expiry of the limitation period

Where the limitation period has ended, the court may allow an amendment only in the following three circumstances:

a) to add or substitute a new claim, if this arises out of the same or substantially the same facts as an existing claim;

b) to correct a (genuine) mistake as to the name of a party;

c) to alter the capacity in which a party claims.

## 5.9 Requests for further information

There will be occasions where the statement of case is somewhat confusing or fails to set out the case precisely enough. At this point, CPR Part 18 comes into play. The rule provides that, at any time, either the court or the parties may request further information and, if successful, a party will be ordered to:

(a) clarify any matter that is in dispute; or

(b) give additional information in relation to any such matter.

### 5.9.1 Procedure

The procedure for making or responding to Part 18 requests is as follows:

- If either party requires further information, they must (first) serve a written request on the other party, allowing a reasonable time for the response.

- A request should be concise and strictly confined to matters that are reasonably necessary and proportionate to enable the applicant to prepare their own case or to understand the case they have to answer.

### ✪ *Example*

*KPL receive Edwin Gallagher's defence and counterclaim to their claim. Edwin has not specified what the flaws are that he alleges can be seen in the ceramic bathroom suites. Furthermore, in his counterclaim, he merely states that he is claiming for flood damage to his hotel but without itemising what this entails. As a consequence, KPL contact Edwin asking him to provide sufficient particulars of both the alleged breach and the damages.*

- Requests must be made as far as possible in a single comprehensive document and not piecemeal. If brief, this may be by letter; if not, the request should be made in a separate document, which must be sent to the other party.

- Any request must be headed with the name of the court, the title and number of the claim and identify that it is a Part 18 request. The requests should be set out in separate numbered paragraphs, and state the date for a response.

**Figure 5.3** provides an example of a request for further information under Part 18.

Once the request has been received, the other party must deal with the issues raised.

- The response must be in writing, dated and signed by the party or their solicitor. It should set out the same information as the request and then give details of the response.

- The response must be:
  - served on all the parties;
  - filed with the court; and
  - verified by a statement of truth.

- If a request for further information is not responded to, or cannot be complied with, an application may be made to court under Part 18. The court will grant an order if it is satisfied that the request is confined to matters that are reasonably necessary and proportionate to enable the applicant to prepare their case or to understand the case against them.

**Figure 5.3**   Request for further information

IN THE CARLISLE COUNTY COURT

BETWEEN

KENDAL PLUMBERS LTD                                          Claimant

and

EDWIN GALLAGHER                                          Defendant

CLAIMANT'S PART 18 REQUEST FOR FURTHER INFORMATION

This Request is made on 10 April 20XX and the Claimant expects a response to it no later than 24 April 20XX.

1.   Under paragraph 4 of the Particulars of Claim, please provide a detailed description of the appearance of the ceramic finish on the bathroom suites and an explanation of why this is alleged to be unsatisfactory.

2.   Under the same paragraph, please provide full details of how the flooding occurred and how it is alleged this was due to the quality of the bathroom suites.

3.   Under paragraph 6 of the Particulars of Claim, please provide a detailed description and financial breakdown of all work which it is proposed be undertaken and each and every item of cost it is proposed to incur in respect of:

   (a)  the repairs to the hotel; and

   (b)  the refitting of the rooms affected by the flooding.

*ULaws LLP*

ULAWS LLP

15-16 Park Row, Leeds LS1 5HD

Solicitors for the Claimant

To the Defendant

---

# Summary

- Statements of case are the formal documents that are served by the parties on each other. Their purpose is to define for the court the issues that are in dispute and, as a consequence, to limit the matters that must be proved by the respective parties.

- The term 'statements of case' encompasses claim forms, particulars of claim, defences, counterclaims, replies and responses to requests for further information, but not evidential documents such as witness statements or expert reports.

- The document that begins legal proceedings is the claim form. This may either stand alone or (for more complex matters) be accompanied by separate particulars of claim. The particulars of claim contain a concise statement of the legal and factual basis of the claim, together with details of the alleged breach and the remedies sought, and the interest claimed.

- The defence outlines the defendant's answer to the claim and each allegation in the particulars of claim must be answered, otherwise it is deemed to be admitted. Allegations that are admitted need not be proved by the claimant, but those that are either denied or not admitted must be.

- In most instances, the statements of case will consist of the claim form, particulars of claim and the defence only. However, if the defendant wishes to raise a claim of their own, a counterclaim must be served. The claimant must respond with a defence to the counterclaim if they are to avoid judgment being entered in default. A reply to the defence itself may be filed by the claimant but this is optional.

- If either party requires clarification of or more information on any matter in dispute, a request for further information can be made, to which the other party must respond.

- All statements of case must be verified by a statement of truth.

- Statements of case may be amended but only with the agreement of the other party or the permission of the court after service has been effected.

## Sample questions

### Question 1

A company (the claimant) owns an office building on a business park. When making a delivery of office supplies to the claimant, the defendant loses control of his van and crashes into the reception causing extensive damage. The cost of rebuilding has been assessed as £32,500. The defendant is refusing to accept liability and so the claimant issues proceedings in the County Court.

**Which of the following statements best describes how the claimant should make a claim for interest?**

A The claimant should claim interest pursuant to any relevant term in the contract between it and the defendant.

B The claimant need not claim interest as this will be automatically added to the claim if successful.

C The claimant should set out the basis of its entitlement to interest, but need not calculate the amount owing.

D The claimant must precisely calculate the amount of interest which has accrued up to the date of proceedings.

E The claimant must precisely calculate the amount of interest which has accrued up to the date of proceedings as well as the daily rate of interest which will continue to accrue.

### Answer

Option C is correct. The court may award interest, but only if it is claimed – as a result, option B is wrong.

As the claim is for damages, and is therefore unspecified in nature, all the claimant is required to do is to set out the basis of its entitlement to interest. In this case, that entitlement comes from s 69 of the County Courts Act 1984. Although there may be a contract between the claimant and the defendant, most likely that contract will be limited to the supply of goods by the defendant to the claimant. Any term for interest in that contract will presumably only exist for the benefit of the defendant should the claimant be late in paying any invoices for the supply of those goods. Option A therefore is unlikely to represent the best option on the facts.

It is only when the claim is specified in nature (a claim for monies owing in debt) that the claimant must precisely calculate both the amount of interest which has accrued and the daily rate of interest that will continue to accrue. For this reason, options D and E are both wrong.

## Question 2

The defendant is served with proceedings for damage caused to the claimant's reception building when his van collided into it. He denies liability and files and serves a defence alleging that the reason he lost control of the van was because there were shards of glass on the driveway approaching the reception, which caused a puncture to the front tyre. The defendant alleges that he was a visitor within the meaning of the Occupiers' Liability Act 1957 and that the claimant failed in its statutory duty to safeguard him from danger and a foreseeable risk of damage to his property. He also makes a claim for the cost of repair to his van. This is disputed by the claimant.

**Which of the following statements correctly describes how the defendant should approach drafting his statements of case?**

A   When drafting his defence, the defendant need only admit facts that he accepts and deny those which he disputes.

B   The defendant should adopt a structured approach to drafting his defence, but any facts missed are deemed to have been denied.

C   The defendant should include a counterclaim with his defence if he wishes to claim for the repair of his van.

D   When drafting a counterclaim, the defendant should include all the relevant facts even if these have already been set out in the defence.

E   The counterclaim need not be verified by a statement of truth as it is part of the defence.

## Answer

Option C is correct. Option A is wrong because there is a third option – that of a non-admission and this applies to those facts of which the defendant has no knowledge. Option B is wrong as any facts missed are deemed to be admitted. Option D is also wrong as there is no need to include facts that have already been set out in the defence and the first paragraph will simply state that the relevant paragraphs are repeated. Option E is wrong because all statements of case must be verified by a statement of truth.

## Question 3

The claimant has issued proceedings against the defendant, who files and serves a defence and counterclaim in response. However, the claimant is unable to respond effectively because the contents are lacking in clarity.

**Which of the following statements provides the best advice as to the action the claimant should take first?**

A   The claimant should write to the defendant to request further information on the defence and counterclaim.

B   The claimant should make an application to the court to request further information in relation to the defence and counterclaim.

C    The claimant should apply for permission from the court as they cannot make an application for further information on the defence and counterclaim without this.

D    The claimant does not need to respond to the counterclaim as they are deemed to deny it.

E    The claimant should file a reply to the defence and a defence to the counterclaim based on the information that has been provided by the defendant.

**Answer**

Option A is correct. Under CPR Part 18, the client may request further information from their opponent to clarify any matter that is in dispute or to obtain additional information in relation to any such matter. Before applying to the court, the claimant should write to the defendant to request this – hence, option B is wrong. Option C is wrong as the claimant does not need the permission of the court to request further information on statements of case.

Option D is wrong as the facts state that the claimant disputes the counterclaim and if they do not file and serve a defence, the defendant can enter judgment in default for this aspect. Option E is not the best advice because responding to the defence and counterclaim where the issues are unclear would be contrary to the overriding objective as the statements of case would almost certainly need amending at a later stage.

# 6

# Interim Applications

## SQE1 syllabus

By the end of this chapter you will be able to apply relevant core legal principles and rules appropriately and effectively, at the level of a competent newly qualified solicitor in practice, to realistic client-based and ethical problems and situations in relation to **interim applications** as follows:

- procedure for making an application
- purpose, procedure and evidence required for particular applications:
  - ◦ summary judgment
  - ◦ interim injunctions
  - ◦ interim payments

Note that for SQE1, candidates are not usually required to recall specific case names, or cite statutory or regulatory authorities. These are provided for illustrative purposes only and the sample notice of application is included for the same reason.

## Learning outcomes

The learning outcomes for this chapter are:

- To understand how to make an interim application.
- To understand and apply the procedure for summary judgment.
- To know when and how to apply for an interim payment.
- To appreciate when it is appropriate to apply for an interim injunction.

## 6.1 Introduction

If the parties are unable to resolve their differences by negotiation, they will have little alternative but to issue proceedings. However, cases do not always proceed seamlessly to trial and, in many cases, one or other of the parties will need to bring a particular matter before the court along the way. Applications that are made after litigation starts but before the trial are known as interim applications and they are many and varied. However, in this chapter, only a sample will be covered.

## 6.2 Purpose of interim applications

There are many reasons why a party may consider it necessary to apply to the court but, in most instances, the aim is to ensure that the case proceeds as quickly and efficiently as possible in accordance with the overriding objective. **Table 6.1** contains illustrations of interim applications.

**Table 6.1** Types of interim applications

| Purpose of interim application | Examples |
| --- | --- |
| To ensure compliance with procedural matters | <ul><li>permission to serve a claim form out of the jurisdiction</li><li>challenging the court's jurisdiction</li><li>permission to amend a statement of case or to make an additional claim</li></ul> |
| To request more time | <ul><li>to serve a claim form or a defence</li><li>to serve the list of documents – see **Chapter 8**</li></ul> |
| To assist in preparation for trial | <ul><li>requiring a reply to a Part 18 request for further information</li><li>seeking disclosure of documents</li></ul> |
| To consider penalties | <ul><li>applying for a sanction against the opponent for failing to meet a deadline</li><li>applying for relief from a sanction imposed by the court, such as the imposition of a penalty costs order or the striking out of a claim</li></ul> |

Part 23 of the CPR sets out the general rules governing applications to the court, but these are subject to (additional) express provisions that apply to specific types of applications.

## 6.3 Procedure

Before applying to the court, the parties should seek to resolve matters between themselves so as to comply with the overriding objective and to avoid the imposition of costs penalties. This will usually be achieved by the exchange of correspondence, whether by letter or email, and only if that fails should an application be made.

Under Part 23, the party who is applying (the applicant) must complete an application notice and Form N244 should be used. The party against whom the order is sought is known as the respondent.

**Figure 6.1** sets out an example of a completed notice of application for an interim order (Form N244).

**Figure 6.1**   Completed notice of application for an interim order

| Application notice | Name of court | |
|---|---|---|
| For help in completing this form please read the notes for guidance form N244 Notes. | High Court of Justice Queen's Bench Division | |
| | Fee account number | U38562984 |
| | Claim no. | HQ 001234 |
| | Warrant no. (if applicable) | |
| | Claimant's name (including ref.) | Scandinavian Self-Build Limited (Ref:16845.743/PH/JTL) |
| | Defendant's name (including ref.) | Platinum Developments Limited (Ref: 00945.478/OW/LP) |
| | Date | 31 October 20XX |

1.   What is your name or, if you are a legal representative, the name of your firm?

> ULaws LLP

2.   Are you a   [ ] Claimant          [ ] Defendant          [X] Legal Representative

     [ ] Other (*please specify*)

     If you are a legal representative whom do you represent?          Claimant

3.   What order are you asking the court to make and why?

> An order that summary judgment be granted to the Claimant pursuant to CPR r 24.2(a)(ii) and (b) because the Defendant has no real prospect of successfully defending the claim at trial and there is no other compelling reason why the case should be disposed of at a trial.

4.   Have you attached a draft of the order you are applying for?   [X] Yes   [ ] No

5.   How do you want to have this application dealt with?   [X] at a hearing [ ] without a hearing[ ] at a telephone hearing

6.   How long do you think the hearing will last?   [0] Hours   [30] Minutes

     Is this time estimate agreed by all parties?   [X] Yes   [ ] No

7.   Give details of any fixed trial date or period          Not applicable

8.   What level of Judge does your hearing need?          Master

9.   Who should be served with this application?          Defendant

9a.  Please give the service address, (other than details of the claimant or defendant) of any party named in question 9.

*(continued)*

**Figure 6.1** (*continued*)

10. What information will you be relying on, in support of your application?

    [X] the attached witness statement

    [X ] the statement of case

    [ ] the evidence set out in the box below

---

If necessary, please continue on a separate sheet.

Statement of Truth

(~~I believe~~) (The applicant believes) that the facts stated in this section (and any continuation sheets) are true. I am duly authorised by the Claimant to make this statement. I understand that proceedings for contempt of court may be brought against anyone who makes, or causes to be made, a false statement in a document verified by a statement of truth without an honest belief in its truth.

Signed _T Petersen_____          Dated_31 October 20XX
Applicant('s legal representative) (~~'s litigation friend~~)

Full name _Tobias Petersen

Name of applicant's solicitor's firm _ULaws LLP

Position or office held __Solicitor
(if signing on behalf of firm or company)

---

11. Signature and address details

    Signed     *ULaws LLP*          Dated 31/10/20XX

    Applicant('s legal representative) (~~'s litigation friend~~)

Applicant's address to which documents about this application should be sent

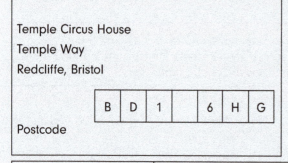

| Temple Circus House | | | | | | | |
|---|---|---|---|---|---|---|---|
| Temple Way | | | | | | | |
| Redcliffe, Bristol | | | | | | | |
| | B | D | 1 | | 6 | H | G |
| Postcode | | | | | | | |

| | If applicable |
|---|---|
| Phone no. | 01823 976235 |
| Fax no. | 01823 976236 |
| DX no. | 103 Bristol |
| Ref no. | 16845.743/PH/JTL |

| E-mail address | tpetersen@ulawsllp.co.uk |
|---|---|

### 6.3.1 Which court?

The application must be made to the court where the claim started or (if relevant) to where it has been transferred.

### 6.3.2 Content

An application notice must state what order is being sought and why. Although there is no specific requirement to provide evidence, as a matter of practical reality, it will be necessary to set out the facts the party is relying on in support of, or for opposing, the application.

If the issues raised are straightforward, the applicant will complete the box to be found on the second page of Form N244. However, if there is insufficient space on the form, a witness statement may be filed at the same time. Furthermore, the party may also rely on the contents of a statement of case, such as the particulars of claim. The application must be verified by a statement of truth.

6.3.2.1 Evidence in support

The witness statement should be made by the person best able to address the relevant points from personal knowledge. If the application is a more technical one, such as for the amendment of a statement of case, this is likely to be the solicitor; whereas in other situations, it may be the client. The statement should:

(a) include the factual information and the evidence in support of the application; and

(b) anticipate the opponent's case, where appropriate.

Sufficient detail must be provided to persuade the court to make the order, as there will be no oral evidence from witnesses at the hearing. Although the solicitor will make submissions, the judge will decide the issue primarily on the basis of the written evidence. Hence, it is important that the witness statement covers all the required points including, if necessary, attaching relevant documents as exhibits.

### 6.3.3 Draft order

Practice Direction 23A states that, except in the most simple of applications, the applicant should attach a draft of the order sought to assist the judge.

### 6.3.4 Service

The application notice must be served on the opponent at least three clear days before the court hearing to allow the other party to respond and to object to the application should they wish to do so. Clear days means that the date of service and of the hearing are excluded, as well as weekends and bank holidays.

### ★ Example

*ULaws LLP are acting on behalf of a company that is engaged in litigation against a defendant. They issue an interim application on behalf of their client. A hearing is listed for Thursday 10 November. Counting back from this date, the three clear days are Wednesday 9, Tuesday 8 and Monday 7 November; so the latest day on which the documents can arrive with the opponent is Friday 4 November (as the weekend is excluded). Given that such documents are deemed served on the second day after being sent by first class post provided this is a business day, ULaws LLP must post the application notice and the witness statement in support no later than Wednesday 2 November.*

### 6.3.5 Consent orders

If the parties have reached agreement on the order they require, they can apply to the court for an order to be made by consent without the need for attendance at the hearing. The parties must ensure they provide the court with any material it needs to be satisfied that it is appropriate to make the order, and usually a letter will suffice. The main advantage of this is the saving of costs for all concerned.

### 6.3.6 Orders made without notice

The general rule is that applications must be made on notice to the other party. This ensures that the opponent is aware of the application so they may file evidence in response and arrange for attendance at the hearing. However, there are exceptions to this rule, usually where:

- there is exceptional urgency; or
- the overriding objective of the CPR would be best achieved by making an order without notice.

The most common examples are where the applicant is applying to freeze their opponent's financial assets or to search their premises. Clearly, in these instances, giving warning of the intended action would defeat the purpose of the application as it would allow time for assets to be moved or destroyed. These type of applications are considered later in this chapter.

Where an application is made without notice to the respondent, the evidence must explain why notice was not given. In addition, the applicant has a duty of full and frank disclosure, which means they cannot take advantage of the respondent's absence at the hearing and must draw the court's attention to evidence and arguments they reasonably anticipate the respondent would wish to make.

If an order is made on an application without notice, the following copy documents must be served on the respondent, as soon as it is practicable to do so:

(a) the court order;

(b) the application notice; and

(c) any supporting evidence.

The respondent may then apply to set aside or vary the order within seven days of service of the order upon them. **Figure 6.2** provides a summary of the procedure under CPR Part 23.

**Figure 6.2**  Overview of interim applications

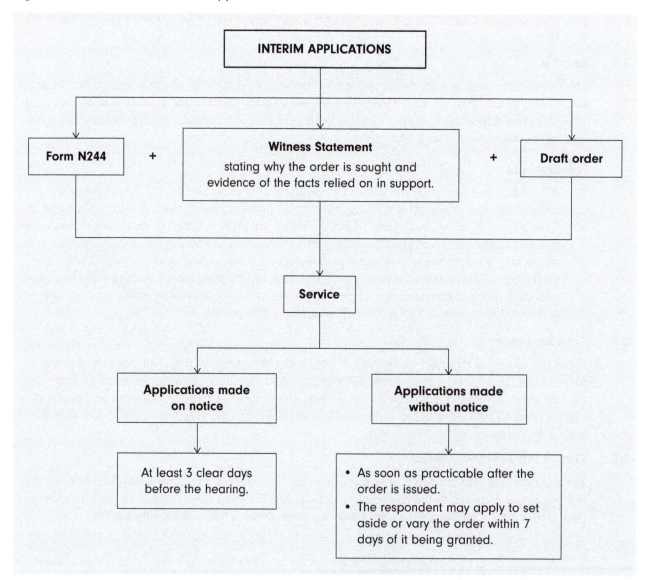

### 6.3.7 Telephone hearings and video conferencing

Many courts now have the facilities to conduct hearings by telephone or video conferencing. This is actively encouraged and, under PD 23A, the general rule is that interim applications with a time estimate of one hour or less will be conducted by telephone if at all possible. However, there are exceptions such as the hearing of an application made without notice to the other party.

## 6.4 Interim costs

Any interim application will involve the parties in expense, for example, in collecting evidence, preparing the notice of application and supporting witness statement, and attending the hearing. A court fee is also payable.

At the end of any interim application, the judge will decide the issue of costs – often referred to as 'pay as you go' litigation. The general costs rule applies with the loser paying the winner's costs. Thus, if the application is granted, it is normal to order the respondent to pay the applicant's costs. However, the type of costs order will depend upon the nature of the application and interim costs orders usually reflect, to a large extent, the conduct of the parties. For example, a party who wants permission to amend their statement of case starts from a weak position as the document should perhaps have been properly drafted in the first place; hence, they may have to pay the costs of the application even if they win.

There are several possible costs orders, but the most common are included in **Table 6.2**.

**Table 6.2**   Interim costs orders

| Term | Effect | When would this apply? |
|------|--------|------------------------|
| [Named party's] costs | The party named in the order is entitled to their costs of the interim application whatever other costs orders are made in the proceedings. These costs are normally summarily (instantly) assessed and ordered to be paid within 14 days. An example would be an order for 'claimant's costs'. This would mean that the defendant must pay the claimant's costs. | When there is a clear 'winner' such as where the claimant succeeds in their application for summary judgment. The unsuccessful party would be ordered to pay the costs. |
| Costs in the case | In an order for costs in the case, no party is named and, at this stage, neither party can recover their costs. It only becomes apparent who is to pay the costs of the interim application at the conclusion of the proceedings. The ultimate loser of the litigation will also be liable for these costs. | This could apply if the court makes a conditional order, for example, that the defendant may continue to defend the proceedings but only if they file a full defence within 14 days. If they fail to do so, only then would the claimant receive the costs of the interim application. |
| No order as to costs | Each party is to bear their own costs of the interim application whatever costs orders are made at the end of the proceedings. | This order is often made when the outcome of the interim application is effectively a draw with neither party being perceived to be at fault. An example may be where evidence later comes to light that requires additional witness statements to be filed. |

Having covered interim applications in general by reference to Part 23, the remainder of this chapter will consider specific examples.

## 6.5 Summary judgment

Once a claim has been served, the defendant may:

(a) do nothing – in which case the claimant will apply for default judgment;

(b) admit the claim, allowing the claim to be enforced; or

(c) file a full defence so the case proceeds to trial.

However, there is a fourth option. Sometimes the defendant will simply file a weak defence, either because their case has no substance or as a delaying tactic to buy more time. This may be because they are looking for additional evidence, or simply that they do not have the available financial assets to pay the claim. If the defence received is poor, the claimant would almost certainly succeed at trial but this would cost them additional time and money. To enable a claimant to bring the matter to an early conclusion, Part 24 of the CPR provides a solution. This is known as summary judgment.

Although such applications are normally brought by the claimant, the defendant may also apply for summary judgment. This may occur if, for example, a litigant in person has filed a weak particulars of claim or one which has no legal basis.

Rule 24.2 states that the court may give summary judgment on the whole of the claim or a particular issue if:

(a) it considers that:

    (i) the claimant has no real prospect of succeeding on the claim; or

    (ii) the defendant has no real prospect of successfully defending the claim; and

(b) there is no other compelling reason why the case should be disposed of at trial.

There are some cases which are clearly not suitable for summary judgment, for example, where there are complex issues that need proper investigation at trial or difficult questions of law. However, Part 24 is a useful mechanism that should be considered by the parties wherever appropriate, particularly as it is consistent with the overriding objective of the CPR to deal with matter justly and at proportionate cost.

⭐ *Example*

*Classic Motoring Ltd (Classic) provide self-build kits for go-karts and other leisure cars including all technical drawings and full build instructions. Joe purchased five kits for his caravan park to provide entertainment for the guests. However, having built the go-karts, they constantly break down so they prove to be entirely unsuitable for their purpose.*

*Joe issues proceedings against Classic for £24,000. Classic files a defence, which simply states: 'The self-build kits supplied were perfectly good and the claimant does not know how to construct them properly'.*

*This is clearly insufficient and, although the claimant would certainly succeed at trial were this to be the only defence submitted, Joe does not want to waste time and money allowing the case to proceed this far. He can apply for summary judgment under Part 24.*

### 6.5.1 No real prospect

In determining whether the claimant has a real prospect of succeeding in their claim or the defendant of defending theirs, the court will consider the evidence and this will vary from case to case. With the increase in litigants in person, there is a risk that claims are pursued or defended with limited understanding of the legal merits of a particular issue or the requirements of evidence. In these situations, the responsibility will fall upon the court to weed out the somewhat hopeless cases.

### 6.5.2 Compelling reason

In addition to the prospect of success being determined, the judge must also be satisfied that there are compelling reasons to allow the matter to proceed to trial. Although this covers a range of situations, the most common reasons would be:

- The need to allow more time for the matter to be investigated, perhaps due to difficulties in contacting an important witness.

- The claim or defence is of a highly complicated and/or technical nature so it can only be properly understood with all the evidence that would be available at a full trial.

- The need to hear from witnesses, particularly if one of the central issues (such as the terms of a contract) is disputed oral evidence.

It is important to bear in mind that the hearing is not the trial. The submissions should be based upon the criteria of Part 24 so the respondent should concentrate on establishing a compelling reason to allow the proceedings to continue and not attempt to argue their case in its entirety. Obtaining an order for summary judgment is not a given and indeed, the easier option may be for the judge to allow the proceedings to continue.

### ⭐ Example

*Continuing with the scenario above, Joe files and serves his application for summary judgment against Classic. The defendant responds with a witness statement from their technical director setting out their submissions as to why they consider their kits to be satisfactory and why Joe is at fault. This is to persuade the court that Classic has a defence with a real prospect of success.*

*However, if summary judgment is to be granted, the judge must also be satisfied that there is no other compelling reason why the matter should be disposed of at trial. Having listened to the evidence, the judge finds against Joe on the basis that Classic's defence does have merit. Furthermore, the matter is too technical to be determined at a summary judgment hearing and would benefit from additional evidence – specifically, from an independent expert.*

In summary:

- a claimant applicant has to prove both that the defendant has no real prospect of successfully defending the claim *and* that there is no other compelling reason why the matter should proceed to trial; but

- a defendant respondent need only succeed in preventing the claimant from proving *one* aspect to ensure the dismissal of the application for summary judgment.

### 6.5.3 Procedure

An application for summary judgment can be made by either party at any time. The only occasion where the court's permission is required is where the claimant wishes to apply before the defendant has filed an acknowledgement of service or a defence. However, given the requirement to convince the judge that the defendant has no real prospect of defending the claim, a claimant will invariably wait until after the defence has been filed.

The procedure is as follows:

- The applicant applies with Form N244 and (usually) a witness statement in support.

- The respondent must:

- ○ be given at least 14 days' notice of the hearing date; and
- ○ file and serve any written evidence at least seven days before the hearing.
- If the applicant wishes to rely on further evidence, this must be filed and served at least three days before the hearing.

**Figure 6.1** referred to earlier in this chapter is an example of a completed notice of application in which the claimant is applying for summary judgment.

### 6.5.4 Possible orders

The judge has a number of possible orders at their disposal.

(a) *Judgment on the claim*: this means that the claimant has succeeded in their application for summary judgment and the matter will proceed to enforcement.

(b) *The striking out or dismissal of the claim*: here, the defendant has succeeded in their application to dispose of the claimant's claim and the case comes to an end.

(c) *The application is dismissed*: the applicant has failed to bring the case to an early conclusion and it will now proceed towards trial.

(d) *A conditional order*: the application has not been granted, but equally the respondent has not succeeded in having it dismissed – neither side has won.

A conditional order will be made where the court concludes it is possible, but not probable, that the claim or defence may succeed. The party will be allowed to continue with the litigation provided they pay a sum of money into court or take a specified step in relation to their claim. This ensures that the party is genuine in their desire and ability to pursue the matter and, in the case of the defendant, they are not merely delaying payment.

### ⭐ Example

*In Joe's claim against Classic, the judge makes a conditional order. She allows Classic to pursue their defence provided they file and serve a full defence within 14 days of the hearing and pay the sum of £24,000 (the value of the claim) into court within 28 days. If Classic fails to do so, their defence will be struck out and Joe will be able to enforce his claim.*

Where the court dismisses the application or makes an order that does not completely dispose of the claim, case management directions are usually given as to the future conduct of the case.

### 6.5.5 Costs

The costs order awarded will depend upon the type of claim and the outcome of the application.

- Where a claimant succeeds in obtaining summary judgment for a specified sum, the court may award fixed costs under Part 45. However, it is open to the claimant to request a higher figure as their costs usually exceed these, and to ask for summary assessment of the costs.

- If a claimant is awarded summary judgment in an unspecified claim, the usual rule applies so that the winner (the claimant) is granted their costs. These will be summarily assessed and a further hearing will be listed to assess the damages payable by the defendant (a disposal hearing).

- If the defendant secures summary judgment so the entire claim is struck out, the court will normally order that the claimant pays the defendant's costs of the whole claim – again, subject to summary assessment.

- If the application is dismissed, the proceedings will continue and the unsuccessful party will pay the successful party's costs of the summary judgment hearing.

- If a conditional order is made, the usual order will be for costs in the case.

Applying for summary judgment is a useful means of bringing the matter to an early conclusion or, at the very least, putting pressure on the opponent to confront the claim.

### 6.5.6 Overview of summary judgment

**Figure 6.3** Summary judgment

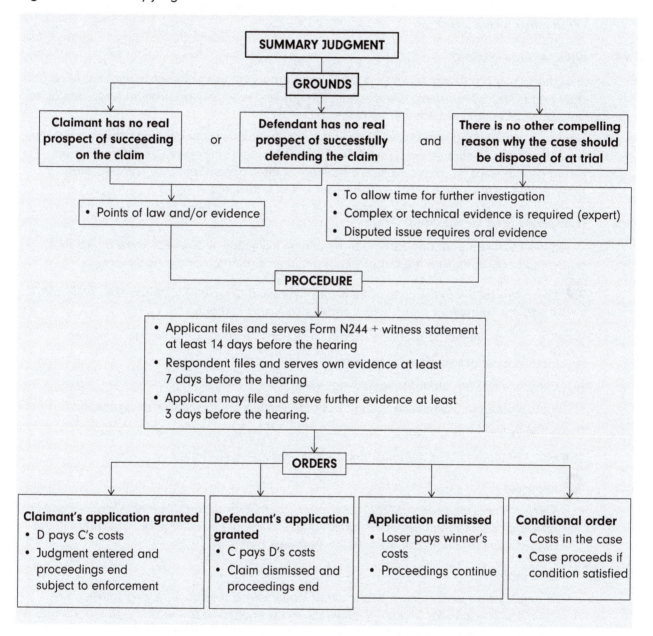

## 6.6 Interim injunctions

Under Part 25 of the CPR, the court has wide powers to grant various interim remedies, including interim injunctions.

### 6.6.1 Who can apply?

Either party may apply for (and be granted) an interim injunction in support of their cause of action.

### 6.6.2    When to apply?

A party may seek an injunction at any time after proceedings have been commenced and, in exceptional cases, even beforehand. However, the court must be satisfied that the matter is urgent or it is otherwise desirable in the interests of justice.

If granted before trial, these orders are known as interim injunctions. They remain in force until the matter comes to trial (or until further order), at which point the court will decide whether or not to make a final injunction.

### 6.6.3    What is an injunction?

Injunctions may be distinguished from other court orders because breach is punishable as a contempt of court. They are a discretionary remedy and may only be granted when damages are not an adequate remedy for the applicant.

There are different types of injunctions but the primary aim is to maintain the status quo – the current position – until the trial. Generally, they will be used to prevent the defendant from taking certain steps, such as soliciting customers of the claimant, but they can also order a party to take action, for example to stop committing a nuisance.

### 6.6.4    Guidelines used by the court

When the court hears an application for an interim injunction, it does not know all the facts and so, to assist in making the correct decision, judges refer to certain guidelines.

 *These are set out in the case of* American Cyanamid Co (No 1) v Ethicon Ltd *[1975] UKHL 1 and are sometimes referred to by reference to this authority.*

When deciding whether to grant an interim injunction, the court will determine whether:

(a)  there is a serious question to be tried;

(b)  damages are an adequate remedy for either side;

(c)  the balance of convenience lies in favour of granting or refusing the injunction; and

(d)  whether there are any special factors.

The effect of these is best demonstrated by considering an illustration.

⭐ *Example*

*Taste of the Caribbean Ltd (TCL) have commenced proceedings against Ocean Foods Ltd (Ocean) alleging that they have infringed their copyright by selling jars of sauce with an almost identical image on the label to their own brand.*

*Outcome 1*

*TCL obtains an interim injunction to stop Ocean selling the sauce having satisfied the court that its claim for breach of copyright is a serious issue to be tried and that damages are not an adequate remedy. The injunction will remain in place until the matter is determined at trial. The aim of the injunction is to prevent TCL suffering further loss of profits in the meantime.*

*Outcome 2*

*At the hearing for the interim injunction, Ocean provides evidence that they will go out of business if the injunction is granted. In contrast, if TCL's application for an injunction is refused, although they will suffer financial losses, both parties will continue to trade. The judge declines to grant an injunction to TCL.*

### 6.6.5 Cross-undertaking

If an interim injunction is granted, the applicant must undertake to the court to pay any damages that the respondent (or any other party affected by the order) sustains by reason of the injunction, if it subsequently transpires that the injunction ought not to have been granted. This is often called the applicant's 'cross-undertaking'.

 *Example*

*Continuing with the scenario (above) as described in Outcome 1, when the action comes to trial, Ocean proves they were not infringing TCL's copyright. As a consequence, Ocean can claim damages for their loss of profits arising from their inability to sell their sauce during the period between the injunction and the trial.*

### 6.6.6 Procedure

As with other types of applications, the party who seeks the order must apply by way of an application notice with evidence in support – usually, a witness statement.

#### 6.6.6.1 Orders obtained with notice

Interim injunctions are usually obtained on notice, so the defendant has prior warning of the hearing. They last until the trial of the claimant's action unless they are set aside earlier by the court, perhaps because of a change of circumstances.

#### 6.6.6.2 Orders obtained without notice

However, under Part 25, the court may grant an interim remedy on an application made without notice if there are good reasons for doing so. This could be due to insufficient time or, more commonly, that giving notice would enable the defendant to harm the claimant in some way, such as destroying evidence that would support the claimant's case. Secrecy is needed because if the defendant learns of the claimant's plans they may try to cause irreparable harm to the claimant before an injunction can be secured.

An injunction without notice takes one of two forms.

(a) The court may fix a date for a further hearing with all parties present, in which case it lasts until the date specified for that hearing. If the defendant successfully argues that the injunction should not be granted, it will be set aside.

(b) Alternatively, rather than fixing a hearing date, an injunction without notice may simply tell the defendant that they may, if they wish, apply on notice for the order to be varied or set aside. In the meantime, the injunction remains in force until trial or further order.

Examples of injunctions that can be made without notice include:

#### Freezing injunctions

These restrain a party from removing their assets from the jurisdiction (England and Wales). If notice was given of such an application, the respondent could simply transfer their assets prior to the hearing. The court must be satisfied that the applicant has a good arguable claim and there is a real risk the respondent will dispose of their assets so as to defeat the enforcement of an eventual judgment.

#### Search orders

A search order compels the respondent to allow their premises to be searched by the applicant, where the applicant believes that the respondent has documents or property belonging to them. Again, if notice was given to the respondent in advance, it would be a simple matter for them to hide the items somewhere else. The court must be satisfied that the applicant appears to have a strong case, they will suffer serious harm if the order is not made and the respondent has incriminating materials in their possession which cannot be obtained by other means.

### ⭐ *Example*

*Junaid Mahmood was employed by Southcity Engineering Ltd (SEL) in a senior management post, but was dismissed. SEL becomes aware that Junaid is about to set up a business in competition. Furthermore, they have discovered that he removed his work laptop containing confidential information in relation to a new, innovatory product belonging to SEL so he could compete with their business. They have obtained evidence suggesting that Junaid will conceal or destroy the laptop if he becomes aware they are taking court proceedings against him. SEL obtains a search order allowing them access to Junaid's premises to enable them to search for the laptop. This could be combined with an interim injunction restraining Junaid from making use of the confidential information.*

Because freezing injunctions and search orders can be quite draconian in their impact upon the respondent, such applications are normally made to a High Court judge and must be supported by evidence in the form of an affidavit. This is a document that is similar in content to a witness statement but it is sworn or affirmed by the person making it.

## 6.7    Interim payments

One particular type of interim remedy also covered by Part 25 is an interim payment. This is an advance payment on account of any damages, debt or other sum (excluding costs) that a defendant may be held liable to pay. The interim payment procedure enables a claimant who has a strong case on liability to avoid the financial hardship and/or inconvenience that might otherwise be suffered because of any delay during the period between the start of the claim and its final determination.

Before making an application to the court, the claimant should try to negotiate with the defendant or the defendant's insurance company to obtain a voluntary interim payment. Only if one is not forthcoming, should an application be made.

### 6.7.1    Timing

A claimant may not seek an interim payment until after the time for acknowledging service has expired, although they can make more than one application during the proceedings.

### 6.7.2    Procedure

An application notice for an interim payment must be served at least 14 days before the hearing date. Evidence must be provided and should set out:

- the amount requested and what it will be used for;
- the amount of the sum of money that is likely to be awarded at final judgment; and
- the reasons for believing that the grounds required by the CPR are satisfied.

Any documents in support of the application should be exhibited to the witness statement. If the respondent wishes to rely on evidence to counter the application, this must be served at least seven days before the hearing. The applicant may then respond with further evidence provided it is served at least three days before the hearing.

### 6.7.3 Grounds

Part 25 of the CPR contains the grounds that must be satisfied before the court will make an interim payment. These are:

(a) the defendant has admitted liability; or

(b) the claimant has obtained a judgment against the defendant for damages to be assessed or for a sum of money; or

(c) the court is satisfied that, if the case went to trial, the claimant would obtain judgment for a substantial amount of money (other than costs).

Usually, an order for an interim payment will only be made if there is likely to be a delay in the assessment of damages, perhaps because the situation is ongoing or particularly complex.

As to ground (c), the burden on the applicant is high. They must prove, on the balance of probabilities, that they *will* succeed and it is not enough that the court considers it likely they will do so. This is a common sense approach because, once the money has been paid out, it may not be possible to obtain its return.

### 6.7.4 Orders

Having established their entitlement to an interim payment, the court has discretion in relation to two questions:

(a) Should an order for an interim payment be made?

If the issues are complicated or difficult questions of law arise, the court may decide not to order an interim payment at all.

(b) If yes, what should the amount be?

If the applicant succeeds, the court cannot order a sum of more than a reasonable proportion of the likely amount of the final judgment and must take into account contributory negligence and any counterclaim. In other words, the court will try and calculate what figure is indisputably due to the claimant and then determine what the defendant is able to pay.

The court may order an interim payment in one sum or in instalments.

### 6.7.5 Effect on trial

The trial judge will not be told about any interim payment order or voluntary payment until after they have determined all issues of liability and quantum, unless the defendant consents. As the purpose of keeping any payment secret is to avoid the trial judge's decision being influenced in any way, it is difficult to see when a defendant would give their consent.

## Summary

- Interim applications are those made between the issue of proceedings and the trial. Their purpose is to obtain directions from the court to push the matter forwards, to obtain clarification of any issues or to seek a particular remedy.

- Part 23 contains the general rules for interim applications, which may be made either with or without notice, and which may be disposed of in the absence of a hearing. However, the parties should attempt to reach agreement before submitting an application.

- Either party may apply using Form N244 – the Notice of Application. This is supported by evidence, usually in the form of a witness statement, and should be accompanied by a draft order.

- Summary judgment may be applied for by either party under Part 24. It is available where the court concludes that there is no real prospect of either the claimant or the defendant succeeding on the claim or in their defence, and there is no other compelling reason why the case should proceed to trial. The advantage of winning an application for summary judgment is that the matter is brought to an early conclusion without the additional cost in time and expense of proceeding further.

- Applications for interim remedies are governed by Part 25, including for interim payments and injunctions.

- Interim injunctions may be granted at any time up to the trial and are reserved for urgent matters or those where the court is satisfied that it would be in the interests of justice. Although such injunctions may be made on notice, doing so would often defeat the purpose as it would allow the defendant to dispose of evidence or to transfer financial assets out of the jurisdiction. Freezing injunctions and search orders may be applied for without notice in these circumstances.

- Interim payments are orders for payments on account of a debt owed or damages sought that the court is expected to order the defendant to pay. Before such an order is made, liability must have been admitted or determined, or the court is satisfied the claimant will win at trial and obtain a substantial amount in damages.

## Sample questions

### Question 1

The defendant has a contract with a hotel to landscape their gardens ready for the official opening on 14 May. They order 2,000 plants and shrubs (the Order) from the claimant for £18,500. However, the Order does not arrive until 20 May (after the event) and so the defendant refuses to pay the invoice. The claimant issues proceedings in the County Court for the monies due and the defendant responds with a defence stating: 'We dispute the payment. The Order arrived too late so we could not fulfil our contract with the hotel. The terms of the contract were agreed orally at a meeting where our sales director made it clear to the claimant's facilities manager that the plants and shrubs had to be delivered by 7 May to allow time for planting and that time was of the essence.' The claimant applies to the court for an order for summary judgment.

**Which of the following answers best describes the likely outcome of the claimant's application for summary judgment?**

A   The claimant will succeed in its application because the defendant's defence does not provide sufficient detail for the court to determine the matter.

B   The claimant may fail in their application because the need to hear oral evidence from witnesses to determine whether time was of the essence is a compelling reason as to why the matter should proceed to trial.

C   The claimant will fail in their application but only because the information provided in the defence is sufficient to demonstrate that the defendant has a real prospect of successfully defending the claim.

D   The claimant may fail in their application because the matter is too complex and technical to be dealt with at a summary judgment hearing and this is a compelling reason why the matter should proceed to trial.

E   The court is likely to make a conditional order as it is possible but not probable that the defence will succeed.

**Answer**

Option B is correct as a central issue is whether the contract contained an express term that time was of the essence and the judge will need to hear oral evidence from the sales director and the facilities manager who were at the meeting where the terms were agreed to determine this issue. This is a compelling reason why the matter should proceed to trial.

Option A is wrong because there is no guarantee the claimant 'will' succeed in their application. Option C is wrong as there are two grounds upon which the court could refuse to grant summary judgment. In addition to deciding that the defendant has a real prospect of defending the claim, the court could also refuse the claimant's application on the basis of compelling reasons (as above).

Option D is wrong because the matter is neither complex nor technical in nature. Option E is not the best answer because of the reasons above, but also the defendant's defence has a greater than 'possible' chance of success on the limited evidence available.

**Question 2**

The company is a pharmaceutical corporation and they have just developed a vaccine for a coronavirus that is sweeping the globe. One of their research scientists is offered significant financial incentives to work for a competitor in producing their own vaccine. The scientist leaves the company and begins work immediately for the competitor. The company is concerned that the scientist will use the confidential information and knowledge they have acquired and this will have a huge impact upon the company's future profits. They have information that the scientist downloaded material onto a mobile device and also that they may be moving to the United States to work in a laboratory there.

**Which of the following best describes the action that the company could take to protect their position?**

A   The company should issue proceedings against the scientist claiming damages for breach of contract and wait for the trial to determine these.

B   The company should apply for an interim injunction to prevent the scientist from using the confidential information that they have obtained.

C   The company should apply for a search order and a freezing injunction against the scientist.

D   The company should apply for an interim injunction to prevent the scientist from using the confidential information that they have obtained together with a search order.

E   The company should apply for an interim injunction to prevent the scientist from using the confidential information that they have obtained, a search order and a freezing injunction.

**Answer**

Option E is correct. The company should apply for an interim injunction to prevent the scientist from using the confidential information they have obtained, a search order to compel the scientist to allow their premises to be searched for the mobile device and a freezing injunction to prevent them from moving their assets to the United States. As all three interim remedies are possible on the facts, options B, C and D are not the best ones.

Whilst option A is a correct course of action, waiting for the trial would mean the damage was done – the competitor would have developed and sold the vaccine and the company would have lost the profits from doing so themselves.

### Question 3

A woman issues proceedings against a company for breach of contract relating to the building of a new house. The company respond with a full defence and a counterclaim for the second instalment, which they allege is owed by the woman for the building works carried out to date. The issues in dispute are complex and highly contested so the litigation is likely to take some considerable time to resolve. The woman has just lost her employment and is in financial difficulties. Her solicitor advises her to apply for an interim payment.

**Is the woman likely to succeed in her application for an interim payment?**

A   Yes, because the woman can apply for an interim payment as soon as she serves the particulars of claim.

B   Yes, because when deciding whether to grant the application for an interim payment, the court may take into account the woman's financial hardship.

C   No, because liability has not been determined and the court must have established liability before an interim payment can be awarded.

D   No, because the litigation is complex and highly contested, so the court cannot be satisfied the woman would obtain judgment at trial.

E   No, because the company have served a counterclaim and this precludes the woman from being granted an interim payment.

### Answer

Option D is the correct answer. The woman would not be granted an interim payment as the court is unlikely to be satisfied that, if the claim went to trial, she would obtain a judgment. Given that the case is complex and highly contested, there is real uncertainty as to which of the parties would succeed in the litigation.

Option A is wrong as the woman cannot apply for an interim payment after serving the particulars of claim; she must wait until after the time for acknowledging service has expired. Option B is wrong because the woman's financial hardship is not a ground on which the court may grant the application.

Option C is wrong because (as stated above) the court may grant an application for an interim payment before liability has been determined provided the court is satisfied that the woman would obtain a judgment for a substantial amount of money against the company should the matter proceed to trial. Option E is wrong because the mere presence of a counterclaim does not preclude the court from granting an interim payment.

# 7 Case Management

## SQE1 syllabus

By the end of this chapter you will be able to apply relevant core legal principles and rules appropriately and effectively, at the level of a competent newly qualified solicitor in practice, to realistic client-based and ethical problems and situations in relation to **case management** as follows:

- the overriding objective
- track allocation
- case management directions for cases proceeding on the fast or multi-tracks
- non-compliance with orders, sanctions and relief
- costs and case management conferences

Note that for SQE1, candidates are not usually required to recall specific case names, or cite statutory or regulatory authorities and these are provided for illustrative purposes only.

## Learning outcomes

The learning outcomes for this chapter are:

- To appreciate the overall approach taken by the courts in resolving disputes.
- To understand what influences the allocation of a case to a particular track.
- To evaluate what directions are appropriate and why, and the different sanctions the court may impose on a party who defaults.
- To recognise the role of a case management conference on the multi-track and how the court deals with the issue of costs.

## 7.1 Introduction

One of the key elements of the CPR is the notion of case management. The aim is to promote justice but in a way that makes the best use of the court's resources, to ensure cases are pushed through efficiently and effectively. Part 3 is a vital tool in achieving this as it provides the court with wide-ranging powers including to make, vary or revoke orders, to strike out a party's statement of case and to impose penalties on a party who falls short in some way. The role of the court is not a passive one and judges are expected to be robust and interventionist in their approach to ensure compliance with rules, practice directions and orders.

## 7.2 The overriding objective

In exercising their powers to manage cases, the courts must comply with the overriding objective of the CPR and this is to be found in Part 1.

(1) The *overriding objective* is set out in r 1.1 of the CPR and the aim is to enable the court to deal with cases justly and at proportionate cost.

(2) The rule then lists the *six objectives* the court should seek to achieve when dealing with cases:

   (a) ensuring that the parties are on an equal footing;

   (b) saving expense;

   (c) dealing with the case in ways that are proportionate to:

   — the amount of money involved

   — the importance of the case

   — the complexity of the issues and

   — the financial position of each party;

   (d) ensuring that the case is dealt with expeditiously and fairly;

   (e) allotting to it an appropriate share of the court's resources, whilst taking into account the need to allot resources to other cases; and

   (f) enforcing compliance with rules, practice directions and orders.

The *importance of these aims* both to the court and to the parties and their legal advisers is emphasised by later provisions:

- CPR, r 1.2 – the court must give effect to the overriding objective when making procedural decisions; and

- CPR, r 1.3 – the parties are required to help the court to further the overriding objective.

It is essential to note that r 1.3 imposes a positive duty upon the parties and the court will expect a high level of co-operation and realism from those involved in the litigation process.

To give practical effect to the overriding objective:

- CPR, r 1.4 – the court must *actively manage* cases.

This means that the courts may tailor their approach to individual cases, adopting a more flexible approach to meet the object of cost-proportionate litigation. The court's active role includes:

(a) encouraging the parties to co-operate with each other in the conduct of the proceedings;

(b) identifying the issues at an early stage;

(c) deciding promptly which issues need to be fully investigated and dealt with at a trial;

(d) deciding the order in which issues are to be resolved;

(e) encouraging the parties to use alternative dispute resolution procedures if appropriate;

(f) helping the parties to settle the case;

(g) fixing timetables or otherwise controlling the progress of the case;

(h) considering whether the likely benefits of taking a particular step justify the cost of taking it;

(i) dealing with as many aspects of the case as it can on the same occasion;

(j) dealing with the case without the parties needing to attend at court;

(k) making use of technology; and

(l) giving directions to ensure that the trial of a case proceeds quickly and efficiently.

The scope of these provisions is extensive. The aim is to ensure tailored directions so that cases progress quickly and efficiently to their conclusion, whilst keeping costs under control.

## 7.3    Allocation to a track

One important way in which cases are dealt with proportionately is by the allocation procedure. Cases are allocated to different tracks or 'routes' to ensure that the most difficult and highest value claims receive greater resources and attention than simpler matters. Different rules apply with the *small claims track* requiring the least formality to recognise the low value of the claims and the fact they are often conducted by litigants in person. The *fast track* is the standard route along which most cases proceed, whereas the *multi-track* incorporates greater flexibility to reflect the variety and complexity of these cases.

### 7.3.1    Provisional allocation

Initially the decision as to track allocation is made by a court officer, but this is only confirmed after the involvement of the parties.

- When a defence is filed, the court will provisionally decide which track appears the most appropriate for the claim.

- The court will then serve on the parties a notice of proposed allocation, requiring them to file and serve a completed directions questionnaire by a specified date.

The directions questionnaire is a key document in the progress of a case and will be used by the court to confirm the track and to determine directions for case management. In claims that have been provisionally allocated to the multi-track, the following documents should also be prepared:

(a) a case summary

(b) a disclosure report

(c) a costs budget and budget discussion report.

These documents will be considered later in the chapter. In addition, a draft order for directions should accompany the return of the questionnaire.

### 7.3.2    Directions questionnaire

Because of the importance of the directions questionnaire, the parties must consult with one another and co-operate in completing it, including attempting to agree case management directions. However, if this proves impossible, perhaps because one of the parties is intransigent, this should not delay the others in filing their completed questionnaires.

The directions questionnaire (Form N181) is divided into 10 parts, lettered A to J as follows:

**Table 7.1**   Contents of the directions questionnaire

| Part | Content |
| --- | --- |
| **A**: Settlement | The solicitor must confirm that they have explained to their client the need to try to settle, the options available and the possible costs sanctions if the client refuses to engage.<br>The parties are asked whether they want a one month stay (suspension of the proceedings) to attempt to settle the matter at this stage.<br><br>• If they all agree, the court will stay (pause) the proceedings for one month.<br>• If not, the party who objects must provide reasons why they consider it inappropriate.<br>• Alternatively, the court may of its own initiative, whether or not any party has requested it, order a stay of any length for this purpose. |
| **B**: Court | Reasons why the case needs to be heard at a particular court should be stated. |
| **C**: Pre-action protocols | The parties must state whether they have complied with any relevant pre-action protocol and, if not, explain their reasons. |
| **D**: Case management information | This includes:<br><br>• whether any applications have been made to the court;<br>• any objections to the provisional allocation of the case and reasons for requesting a different track; and<br>• the scope and extent of disclosure of documents including proposals for how to deal with electronic documents. |
| **E**: Experts | The parties should indicate whether the case is suitable for a single joint expert and, if not, provide details of the expert evidence they wish to rely on at trial including the cost. |
| **F**: Witnesses | The parties must name or provide the number of the witnesses of fact they intend to call at trial and identify the points the witnesses will address. |
| **G**: Trial | A realistic estimate of how long the trial will last must be given. |
| **H**: Costs | If a party is legally represented and the case is likely to be allocated to the multi-track, a costs budget must be filed. |
| **I**: Other information | Any other information that might assist the judge in managing the claim should be stated, including applications that the party intends to make. |
| **J**: Directions | The parties should attempt to agree directions and a draft order must accompany the questionnaire.<br><br>• For the fast track this will usually be standard directions.<br>• For multi-track claims, directions should be based on the specimen directions, which are listed on the Ministry of Justice website. |

7.3.2.1    Failure to file the directions questionnaire

Consequences will follow if a party fails to file the directions questionnaire:

- If the claim is for money in the County Court, the court will serve a notice on the defaulting party requiring compliance within seven days. Failure to do so results in the party's statement of case being automatically struck out.

- In all other cases, the court will make such order as it considers appropriate. This may include an order for directions, to strike out a statement of case or to list the matter for a case management conference.

### 7.3.3    Which track?

In deciding which track to allocate a case, the most important factor will be the financial value of the claim. However, Part 26 sets out other factors to which the court must have regard as summarised below.

**Figure 7.1**    Overview of track allocation

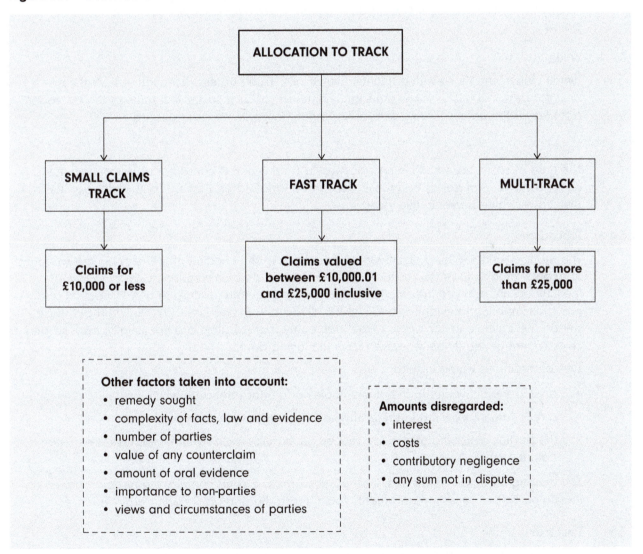

⭐ *Example*

*Alison purchases a kitchen from Bespoke Kitchens Ltd (BKL) – a company that designs and fits high quality kitchens. Alison is dissatisfied with the work and refuses to pay the invoice of £18,000. BKL issue proceedings against Alison, which she defends on the basis that the goods supplied were not of satisfactory quality and the fitting was not carried out with reasonable care and skill. She also counterclaims for the sum of £9,500, this being the cost of repairing the kitchen to an acceptable standard.*

*The case will be allocated to the fast track because the amount of the claim falls between £10,000 and £25,000. The court will not generally aggregate a claim and a counterclaim, and the largest of them will usually determine the financial value, so here this is £18,000.*

*There are no other factors that suggest the case should be allocated to the multi-track as the remedy sought is monetary, the facts and law are not complex (a straightforward breach of contract claim) and there are only two parties involved.*

### 7.3.4 Small claims track   *See update*

This track is intended to provide a proportionate procedure to deal with straightforward claims.

#### 7.3.4.1 Value

'Small claims' are those with a financial value of £10,000 or less, although note that the rules for personal injury claims are slightly different. In such cases, the value of the damages claimed for the pain, suffering and loss of amenity aspect must not exceed £1,000.

#### 7.3.4.2 Type

The type of cases the small claims track would deal with are consumer disputes, disputes about ownership of goods and those between a landlord and tenant (but not for possession). Also, lower value personal injury cases.

#### 7.3.4.3 Procedure

The requirements for the preparation of the case and the conduct of the hearing are designed to enable litigants in person to represent themselves. As a consequence, certain parts of the CPR do not apply to the small claims track, for example, disclosure and inspection and provisions relating to evidence and experts. Directions will be issued by the court but these will be quite simple in content to reflect the reality that solicitors are not usually involved and costs cannot generally be recovered from the losing party.

Typical directions would include:

- each party delivering to the others copies of all documents on which they intend to rely;
- a requirement for them to bring original documents to the hearing; and
- the parties not being allowed to rely on an expert's report without express permission from the court.

The hearing itself is informal and, if all parties agree, a court can make a decision based on the statements of case and documents submitted rather than by hearing oral evidence.

### 7.3.5 Fast track

For the 'middle range' of cases, the fast track is the appropriate way forward.

#### 7.3.5.1 Value

To follow the fast track, the claim must fall on or between the relevant financial value bands of £10,000.01 and £25,000. However, the court will also take into account the likely length of the trial before making a final decision on allocation. Only those cases where the trial is expected to last no longer than one day are generally suitable for the fast track.

7.3.5.2 Procedure

When a case is allocated to the fast track, the court will give directions on how the matter is to proceed to trial and, usually, the court will simply issue standard directions. A typical timetable for preparation of a case allocated to this track is:

| Disclosure | 4 weeks |
| --- | --- |
| Exchange of witness statements | 10 weeks |
| Exchange of experts' reports | 14 weeks |
| Court sends pre-trial checklists | 20 weeks |
| Parties file pre-trial checklists | 22 weeks |
| Hearing (trial) | 30 weeks |

These periods run from the date of allocation. The time between each step is intended to be sufficient to allow the parties to prepare their case, whilst being short enough to discourage tactical litigation such as making technical applications. The court will also fix the date and place of the trial.

Although the parties may agree different directions, these must be approved by the court. They may also agree in writing to vary the timetable but not the trial date nor the date for returning the pre-trial checklists.

7.3.5.3 Differences with the multi-track

There are certain key differences with the approach taken for multi-track cases.

(a) Directions are standard, so not tailored to the individual case.

(b) Expert evidence is more limited. The court will usually order a single joint expert, unless there is a good reason to appoint separate experts, and will rely upon their written report at trial rather than allowing the expert to give oral evidence.

(c) The trial is expected to last no longer than a day.

(d) The power to award costs is more limited and the judge will generally assess these summarily (instantly) at the end of the trial.

### 7.3.6 Multi-track

The third option available for the allocation of a case is the multi-track.

7.3.6.1 Value

Cases that have a value of more than £25,000 will usually be allocated to this track. The multi-track therefore includes an enormously wide range of cases, from the fairly straightforward to the most complex and weighty matters involving claims for millions of pounds and multi-party claims.

7.3.6.2    Procedure

Case management on the multi-track has to reflect this wide diversity of claims. In simpler matters, the standard directions as used on the fast track may be perfectly adequate. Here, the court will usually:

- give directions for the management of the case; and
- set a timetable for the steps to be taken up to trial.

However, in more complex claims, the court will need to adopt a flexible approach. This recognises that the time required for the parties to complete each step may be considerably longer than on the fast track. In such instances, the court will:

- fix a case management conference to ensure that appropriate directions relating to the management of the case are given.

### 7.3.7    The case management conference (CMC)

Because multi-track cases are more complex, a discussion may prove helpful in deciding what actions are necessary to progress the matter to trial and how long these will take. To enable the judge to do this effectively, the 'live' issues between the parties must be evaluated because these will impact upon decisions about what directions are appropriate.

Where this more hands on approach is required, the CMC will:

(a)  review the steps the parties have already taken to prepare the case;

(b)  check their compliance with any directions the court has made (for example, following an application for summary judgment that has been dismissed); and

(c)  consider and give directions about future steps to ensure the claim proceeds in accordance with the overriding objective.

An initial CMC may be listed as soon as a claim is allocated to the multi-track. Often one CMC will prove more than adequate to deal with any issues that arise during the proceedings but, if necessary, the court may order further CMCs to review the progress the parties have made. If the trial is approaching, such a hearing may also be referred to as a pre-trial review but the purpose and substance are similar.

7.3.7.1    Attendance at the case management conference

If a party has a legal representative, an individual who is familiar with the case must attend the CMC. This will usually be someone who is personally involved in the conduct of the case and who has both the authority and information available to deal with any matter that may reasonably be expected to arise. This could include the fixing of the timetable, the identification of issues and matters of evidence.

Where the inadequacy of the person attending leads to the adjournment of the hearing, the court may order that the other party's costs incurred in preparing for and attending the hearing are paid by either the solicitor personally or their firm (known as a wasted costs order).

### 7.3.8    Case summary

Once the parties have served their statements of case, it will become clearer what the issues are. The purpose of the case summary is to describe what matters are still in dispute and which are agreed – effectively, it is an updated case analysis. In most multi-track cases, a case summary will be prepared for the CMC to assist the judge in determining how the case should proceed to trial.

The case summary should set out a brief chronology of the claim, state the factual issues that are agreed and those that are not, and the evidence needed to decide them. The claimant is responsible for preparing the document but, if possible, it should be agreed with the other parties.

⭐ *Example*

*ULaws LLP are advising Bromsgrove Transport Services (BTS) in relation to their claim for negligence against Kwame Nkrumah, trading as Hopwood Vehicles (Kwame). Kwame leased a lorry from BTS for the purposes of transporting gravel to a customer. However, he collided with a tree and caused extensive damage to the vehicle. ULaws LLP draft the case summary. This is set out as a court document with the relevant heading, but then includes the following:*

### Chronology

| | |
|---|---|
| Claim form | 6 May 20XX |
| Particulars of claim | 6 May 20XX |
| Acknowledgment of service | 14 May 20XX |
| Defence | 21 May 20XX |
| Directions questionnaire | 8 June 20XX |

### Agreed Issues of Fact [this is not an entire list]

1.  On 3 January 20XX, the Defendant agreed with the Claimant to hire a DAF c450 lorry ('the Lorry') with Steel Tipper Body for a period of five days commencing on 5 January 20XX.

2.  The Defendant was driving the Lorry on 8 January 20XX when he collided with a tree on the B4294 at Feckenham Cross, Worcestershire.

3.  Substantial damage was caused to the Lorry, which is a write off. The quantum of the damage has been agreed at £58,000 subject to liability.

### Issues in Dispute [this is not an entire list]

1.  Were the brakes of the lorry defective?

2.  Was the Defendant driving negligently by going too fast and/or without due care and attention along the B4294?

3.  Did the Defendant cause the damage to the Claimant's Lorry?

### Evidence Required to Deal with the Disputed Issues [this is not an entire list]

**The Claimant**

Peter Johnson, the managing director of the Claimant will give evidence on all issues relating to liability.

The Claimant wishes to rely upon Alexandra McDowell, an accident reconstruction expert, as to the cause of the collision.

**The Defendant**

The Defendant will give evidence as to his driving and the accident.

The Defendant wishes to rely upon Sundar Pichai, an accident reconstruction expert, as to the cause of the collision.

The case summary would then be signed and dated.

### 7.3.9    Directions on the multi-track

In all cases, an order for directions will be made, with the aim being to provide a 'road map' to take the proceedings all the way to trial in an efficient and cost-effective way. For the more straightforward cases, standard directions may be sufficient. If not, in line with Part 29, the court's general approach will be to list directions covering the following issues:

**Figure 7.2**   Content of directions for the multi-track

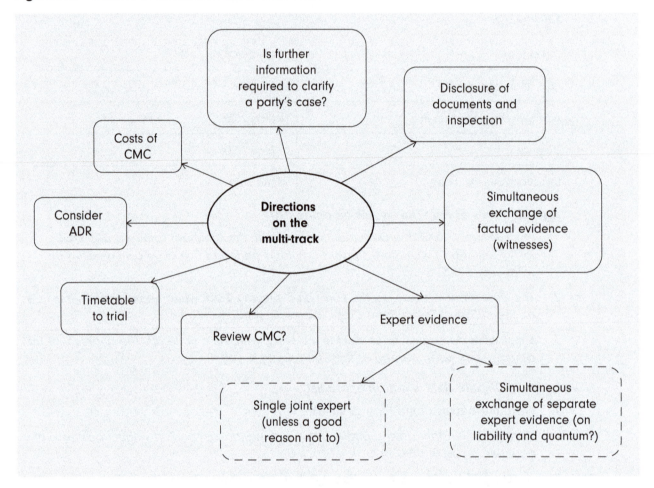

Many of these mirror the standard directions issued on the fast track but usually the provisions are more detailed. To assist in drafting case management directions, the parties can refer to a 'menu' of directions, which may be found online on the Ministry of Justice website. These include the standard directions but also a number of model directions, which may be adapted as appropriate to the circumstances of the particular case.

Unlike the more rigid approach adopted on the fast track, there is some flexibility as to the timing of the steps and the parties may agree in writing to vary the timetable. However, they are precluded from changing any of the following without making an application to the court:

(a)  any case management conference;

(b)  a pre-trial review;

(c)  the return of a pre-trial checklist; or

(d)  the trial or the trial period.

To ensure the flow of communication with the court at all times, it is usual for the parties to be directed to inform the court immediately if the claim is settled and to file a draft consent order giving effect to their agreement. This is in accordance with the overriding objective, and in particular the principles of saving expense and allotting to a case only an appropriate share of the court's resources.

Finally, the issue of costs of the CMC will be determined and, normally, an order will be made for costs in the case (see **Chapter 6**).

### ⭐ *Example*

*Bronwyn Williams has issued proceedings against Grand Finance Plc (GFP) for negligent mis-statement in relation to her pension investments. The case involves the provision of specialist financial advice and a complex analysis of the alleged losses of £2.4 million. The claim is provisionally allocated to the multi-track and the parties file and serve their directions questionnaires.*

*The parties enter into discussions and agree appropriate directions. These are submitted to the court for approval, as required, at least seven days before the CMC. The judge considers the case and agrees with the proposals. As a consequence, the CMC is vacated and the court issues directions for the future conduct of the matter. The order confirms that the case will remain in the multi-track and in addition:*

- *The parties are instructed to consider settling the matter by any means of alternative dispute resolution.*

- *An order is made for standard disclosure and inspection of documents with further specific directions listed in relation to the disclosure and inspection of electronic documents.*

- *Statements of witnesses upon whom the party intends to rely must be served on the other party by a set date and this will include Bronwyn's own statement.*

- *Bronwyn is given permission to rely on evidence from her expert, Sadiq Javid, on whether the investments were appropriate to her needs (liability) and what value the pension should have been if invested correctly (quantum). GFP is given permission to rely on their own named expert in relation to these matters. The court also orders that the experts exchange reports, answer any written questions raised, further discuss any issues that remain in dispute and give oral evidence.*

- *The case is listed for a (review) CMC.*

- *The trial is listed between 25 April and 22 May with a time estimate of six days.*

*Had Bronwen and GFP been unable to reach agreement, to ensure the progression of the case, directions would have been imposed by the judge at the CMC.*

## 7.4 Failure to comply with directions

If a party fails to keep precisely to the directions timetable, this will not generally be an issue provided the parties co-operate and are able to meet certain key dates, such as the CMC and the trial. However, to ensure the case proceeds without delay, if a step is missed:

- any other party may apply for an order enforcing compliance and/or for a sanction to be imposed.

Furthermore, to comply with the overriding objective:

- the trial date is sacrosanct and the court will not allow failure to comply with directions to lead to the postponement of the trial, unless the circumstances are exceptional.

## 7.5 Costs management

Costs management is another way in which the court seeks to control the litigation. It enables the court to manage both the steps to be taken and the costs to be incurred by the parties in multi-track cases, so as to further the overriding objective. Generally, only claims of £10 million or more are excluded from the process. The aim is to ensure that future costs are reasonable and do not become disproportionate by determining what actions should be taken in the proceedings and at what expense.

### 7.5.1 Costs budgets

Costs are managed by the parties being required to provide a costs budget in the prescribed form (Precedent H).

- *What is included?*

  The costs budget consists of:

  ○ a detailed breakdown of the costs and disbursements already incurred (pre-action, issue of proceedings and statements of case) – 'incurred costs'; and
  ○ an estimate of future costs and the assumptions on which those are based for the future phases of the proceedings, namely, case management, disclosure, evidence, pre-trial review, trial preparation and trial stages, along with any ADR or settlement discussions and contingencies. These are known as 'budgeted costs'.

  A budget must be dated and verified by a statement of truth signed by a senior legal representative of the party.

- *What must the parties do next?*

  Costs budgets must be filed:

  ○ with the directions questionnaire for claims of less than £50,000; and
  ○ no later than 21 days before the first CMC for all other claims.

  Having done so, the parties must complete a budget discussion report (Precedent R) no later than seven days before the first CMC. This itemises the figures for phases that are agreed and those that are not, with a brief summary of the grounds of dispute.

- *What is the judge's role?*

  The judge will review those costs which are disputed by systematically cross-referring between the parties' proposed directions and their budgets to ensure the suggested costs are reasonable and proportionate to the case in hand. The budget will then be revised as necessary. The court normally conducts a costs and case management conference at the same time but they may be held separately in complex cases.

- *What if a party wants to change a costs budget?*

  Once a costs budget has been agreed or approved by the court, it is extremely difficult to amend or update it. Consequently, it should be drafted with great care as inadequacies and mistakes will not be rectified. Only if the other party agrees – which is unlikely – or the court can be persuaded that there have been significant developments, for example the need for an additional expert's report that could not have been anticipated, may it be revised. However, this is a rare event. In such circumstances, the parties must file a budget variation summary sheet (Precedent T). The rigidity of the process is one reason why litigation has become so front-loaded. It is much easier to draft a costs budget that accurately reflects the likely costs if much of the work has already been completed.

- *What if a party acts oppressively?*

  If one party considers that another is acting oppressively in seeking to cause the applicant to spend money disproportionately on costs, an application can be made to the court, which will grant such relief as may be appropriate. This is to ensure that parties with 'deep pockets' do not take advantage of their financial position to discourage their opponent from continuing with the litigation.

⭐ *Example*

*Mason Care Homes Plc (Mason) are suing Health Procurement Ltd (HPL) for breach of contract. They are claiming £3.2 million for the defendant's failure to source appropriate medical supplies and equipment. After the costs budgets have been filed and agreed, Mason become aware of a further 1,000 documents, which had been incorrectly stored for reasons unconnected to them. The disclosure of these documents has a knock-on effect on the experts' reports, which will need to be updated.*

*Mason ask HPL to agree to an upward revision of their agreed costs for the disclosure and evidence phases but this is refused; so Mason apply to the court for an order to vary their budget setting out the changes made, the reasons for these and the defendant's objections. The application is granted as the court is satisfied that the assumptions upon which the disclosure and evidence phases of Mason's costs budget were agreed have been significantly departed from through no fault of the claimant.*

### 7.5.2 Failure to file a costs budget on time

If a party files their costs budget late or not at all, there are significant consequences for that party and (potentially) their lawyers. Rule 3.14 provides that, unless the court orders otherwise, the party will be treated as having filed a costs budget consisting only of the court fees. Thus, unless the court gives relief from this automatic sanction, that party will not be able to recover any of its future legal costs, apart from court fees, from another party.

⬤ *In the case of* Andrew Mitchell MP v News Group Newspapers Ltd *[2013] EWCA Civ 1537, the claimant sued The Sun newspaper in relation to their coverage of an incident that took place outside Downing Street. Although of interest to the wider public because it involved a government minister, the case was significant to the legal profession as it was the first time r 3.14 was used in such a high profile case. Mr Mitchell's lawyers were six days late in filing their costs budget without any adequate excuse and so were treated as having filed a budget consisting of court fees only. Although the solicitors agreed to continue to act, the effect was that they conducted expensive and strongly contested litigation with no prospect of being paid for their work after the date of the sanction.*

The subsequent rejection of the solicitors' appeal against the sanction led to a shift in the way dispute resolution matters were conducted as meeting deadlines became of paramount importance.

### 7.5.3 Costs management order

As a further means of ensuring costs are kept in check, the court is now highly likely to make a costs management order. Such an order is imposed unless the judge is satisfied that the litigation can be conducted justly and at proportionate cost.

In the order the court will:

a) record the extent to which any incurred or budgeted costs are agreed between the parties; and

b) in respect of the budgeted costs that are not agreed, record the court's approval after making appropriate revisions.

#### 7.5.3.1 Effect of a costs management order

The court will thereafter control the parties' budgets in respect of recoverable costs. If at trial one party is ordered to pay another party's costs to be assessed by the court on the standard (usual) basis, the court will not depart from the receiving party's last approved or agreed budget unless satisfied there is a good reason for doing so. The consequence is that the parties are tied to their costs budget figures even if the litigation proves far more expensive than anticipated.

### 7.5.3.2 Effect if no costs management order

If there is no costs management order, there is more flexibility when dealing with costs. Where there is a difference of 20% or more between the costs claimed by the receiving party and the costs as set out in the budget, the receiving party must provide a statement of the reasons for the difference. It is then a matter for the court to decide whether the additional amounts can be recovered.

### 7.5.4 Summary of case and costs management

Set out below is an overview of the provisions relating to costs management.

**Table 7.2** Costs management

| Costs management | |
|---|---|
| (a) What is a costs budget? | A statement of costs already incurred and those anticipated for the future conduct of the litigation. |
| (b) When must a costs budget be filed? | Either:<br><br>• with the directions questionnaire (claims under £50,000); or<br>• no later than 21 days before the CMC. |
| (c) What if a party files a costs budget late or not at all? | They will be treated as having filed a budget consisting of court fees only. |
| (d) What can be done? | A party may apply for relief from this sanction under r 3.9 (see later in this chapter). |
| (e) How are the costs decided? | • A budget discussion report must be filed by both parties highlighting costs agreed and disagreed no later than seven days before the CMC.<br>• The parties should then seek to agree those costs.<br>• If not, the court will review costs. |
| (f) What if the party's budgeted costs are considered to be too high? | If the judge is not satisfied that the litigation can be conducted justly and at proportionate cost, a costs management order will be made. |
| (g) What if the party wants to revise their costs budget? | The party will have to persuade the court there have been significant unanticipated developments since the budget was filed. |
| (h) What happens at the end of the case? | • A party awarded its costs on the standard basis will recover its last approved or agreed budgeted costs unless the court is satisfied there is a good reason for departing from them.<br>• Costs awarded on the indemnity basis and incurred costs are assessed by the court in the usual way. |

Finally, **Figure 7.3** provides an overview of both case and costs management in the multi-track, including the key role played by the CMC.

**Figure 7.3** Case and costs management

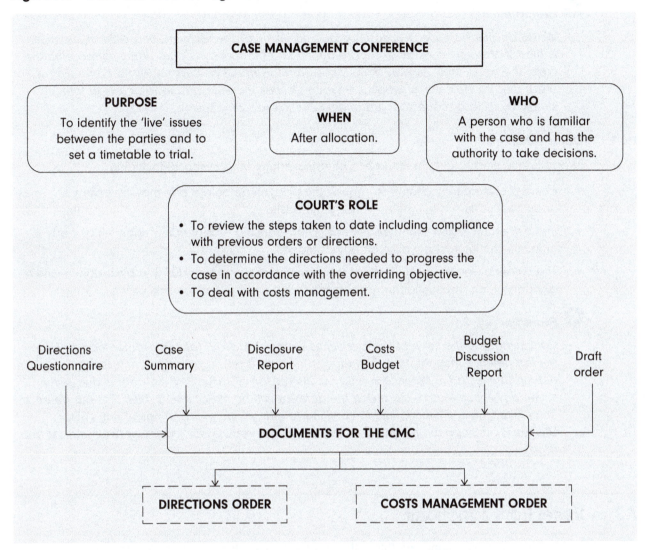

## 7.6 Court sanctions

There is little point in having directions if a party can simply ignore them and so, to ensure compliance with the overriding objective, the CPR provide the court with a range of sanctions.

### 7.6.1 Striking out a statement of case

CPR, r 3.4 gives the court the ultimate sanction of striking out a party's case so their claim or defence comes to an immediate halt. The two most common scenarios where the court may exercise this power are:

- the statement of case discloses no reasonable grounds for bringing or defending the claim; and

- there has been a failure to comply with a rule, practice direction or court order.

These would include a particulars of claim that does not set out any facts indicating what the claim or the defence is about – for example, 'money owed £5,000'. Also, those statements of case that contain a coherent set of facts but where those facts, even if true, do not disclose any legally recognisable claim or defence so they are 'doomed to failure'.

 *Example*

*Water Utilities Plc issue proceedings against Akhil for the recovery of a debt. A defence is filed that simply consists of a bare denial that the money is due. When considering the case, the judge may, as part of their case management powers under Part 3, make an order that the defence is struck out. Water Utilities Plc will be able to obtain judgment simply by filing a request for judgment (with interest and costs).*

### 7.6.2 Other sanctions

In addition to striking out, the court has other sanctions at its disposal including:

- *Costs*: a common sanction is to require the party in default to pay the other party's additional costs on an indemnity (penalty) basis.

- *Interest*: orders could be made increasing or reducing – depending upon which party is at fault – the interest payable on any damages.

- *The unless order*: if a party has not taken a step in the proceedings in accordance with a court order, an application may be made to the court for an 'unless' order.

 *Example*

*Continuing with the case of Water Utilities Plc against Akhil (above), rather than striking out the defence immediately, the judge is far more likely to order that unless the defendant files a full defence setting out his reasons for denying the debt is due, within seven days of service of the order, the defence will be struck out. If Akhil files the defence as ordered, he will be allowed to continue to defend the proceedings; if not, Water Utilities Plc may obtain judgment simply by filing a request for judgment (with interest and costs).*

## 7.7 Relief from sanctions

If the court imposes a sanction, this will take effect unless the party applies to obtain relief, in other words, to overturn the penalty. Unless the sanction is the payment of costs, in which case the party in default will have to appeal against the order, r 3.9(1) will apply. In deciding whether to grant relief, the court will consider all the circumstances of the case, so as to enable it to deal justly with the application, including the need:

(a) for litigation to be conducted efficiently and at proportionate cost; and

(b) to enforce compliance with rules, practice directions and orders.

To seek a reprieve from a penalty imposed, the party must apply promptly and support their application with evidence addressing the factors outlined below.

*In Denton v TH White Ltd [2014] EWCA Civ 906, the appeal court ruled that, when considering a party's failure to comply with any rule, practice direction or court order, the court should adopt a structured approach as follows:*

*(a) The first stage is to identify and assess the seriousness or significance of the relevant failure. If a breach was not serious or significant, relief is usually granted.*

*(b) The second stage is to consider why the failure or default occurred.*

(c) *The third stage is to evaluate all the circumstances of the case so as to enable the court to deal justly with the application. Factors would include whether the trial date could still be met and the effect the failure to comply and the granting of relief would have on each party.*

In recent times, judges have taken a robust approach to such applications and the party will face an uphill task to convince the court to grant relief. However, the judges have also warned that a party could be penalised if they seek, unreasonably, to take advantage of a mistake by an opponent where the failure concerned a minor or technical breach that had no effect on the litigation.

## Summary

- The court is required to further the overriding objective by actively managing cases.

- To assist with this process, defended cases are provisionally allocated to one of three tracks. The small claims track is the most informal and is designed for claims with a value of up to £10,000, the fast track is the standard route for cases of over £10,000 and up to £25,000, whilst the multi-track is reserved for the higher value and more complex cases over £25,000.

- Thereafter, all the parties must complete a directions questionnaire so the judge has the relevant information to confirm or change the track, as appropriate.

- The court will give directions at the track allocation stage. These vary depending upon the track but will cover issues such as disclosure, witnesses of fact, expert evidence and the steps required to take the matter to trial.

- In the multi-track, a case management conference will usually be held at which the court will also consider the question of costs. The parties are required to file costs budgets and a budget discussion report. The court may take control of costs by imposing a costs management order.

- The court has a number of sanctions at its disposal to enforce compliance with the overriding objective. These include the power to strike out statements of case, to impose penalty costs orders and to make unless orders.

- A party may apply for relief from a sanction imposed but this may not be granted.

## Sample questions

### Question 1

The claimant issues proceedings against the defendant for breach of contract arising from the installation of a heating system in their plant nursery. The claimant claims that, due to inherent defects within the system, the heating failed to come on at the appropriate temperature on the night of 23 November. As a consequence, the claimant's entire stock of valuable roses died causing losses of £43,000 and damage to their reputation in the industry. This is disputed by the defendant who submits that the fault lay with the claimant in its operation of the system. Both parties have instructed experts. The claimant is a multi-national company whereas the defendant is an individual.

**Which of the following best describes the approach the court would take when seeking to comply with the overriding objective?**

A   The aim of the court is to deal with the case justly and at reasonable cost. As a consequence, the court directs that a single joint expert be appointed to deal with liability.

B   The court must manage cases as best as possible and the parties are required to assist the court in furthering the overriding objective.

C   The court will concentrate entirely on the merits of the case and will have no regard for the difference in status and financial position of the claimant and the defendant.

D   The court will take account of the fact this is a complex breach of contract claim requiring expert evidence and the level of damages sought is £43,000.

E   The court will allocate all the resources the claimant requires to resolve the matter because of the importance of the matter to the claimant.

**Answer**

Option D is correct because when deciding the appropriate approach to the matter, the court will consider the amount of money involved and should also take account of the complexity of the issues.

Option A is wrong because the overriding objective requires the court to deal with cases justly and at 'proportionate' cost – not 'reasonable' cost. Also, it would be more usual for the parties to instruct separate experts in a case of this value. Option B is wrong because the court must manage cases 'actively' rather than 'as best as possible' although the second part of the statement is correct.

Option C is wrong as one of the objectives that the court should seek to achieve when dealing with cases is to ensure the parties are on an equal footing with the financial position of each party being a factor. Option E is wrong as the court will allocate 'an appropriate share of the court's resources' to the case and not all the resources the claimant requires. It is, however, correct that the court will take account of the importance of the case to the parties.

**Question 2**

The claimant has issued proceedings in the County Court for £24,500 against the defendant. The particulars of claim state that: 'The claim is for building work provided by the defendant which was sub-standard'. The court provisionally allocates the claim to a track. The defendant completes the directions questionnaire as required and files it at court, but the claimant fails to file their questionnaire.

**Which of the following statements best describes how the matter will proceed?**

A   The court will provisionally allocate the claim to the multi-track.

B   The defendant could apply to strike out the claim on the basis that it discloses no realistic grounds for bringing the claim.

C   The court could grant an order that unless the claimant files full particulars of claim setting out their reasons for claiming the damages within seven days of service of the order, the claim will be struck out.

D    The court will serve a notice on the claimant requiring them to file the directions questionnaire within seven days failing which the claimant's statement of case may be struck out.

E    If either party fails to comply with any future directions issued by the court, the court will automatically impose a sanction to ensure the trial is not postponed.

## Answer

Between the options provided, Option C provides the best answer as to how the case should proceed. Option A is wrong as the amount in dispute is less than £25,000 and so the case will be allocated to the fast track. Option B is wrong because a claim will be struck out if it has no reasonable (not realistic) prospect of success. Option D is wrong because, in the circumstances described – a claim for money in the County Court – the claimant's statement of case will be automatically struck out if the claimant does not file its directions questionnaire within seven days.

Option E is not an appropriate way forward (and therefore a wrong answer) because the court will not automatically impose a sanction. If a party fails to keep to the directions timetable, the parties should co-operate to ensure they meet certain key dates, such as the case management conference and the trial. However, if a step is missed, the other party may apply for an order enforcing compliance and/or for a sanction to be imposed.

## Question 3

A claimant issues proceedings against the defendant, a structural engineering company, for the sum of £340,000 in relation to the negligent construction of a road bridge. The case is allocated to the multi-track and a case management conference is listed. The client telephones for an update and asks for an email to be sent advising them on the litigation process at this stage of the proceedings.

**Which one of the following statements correctly describes what might happen at a case management conference?**

A    The purpose of the case management conference is to review the steps the parties have taken to prepare the case, check their compliance with any directions the court has made and give directions for the future conduct of the case.

B    At the case management conference, if agreement cannot be reached between the parties, a costs management order will be imposed in every case to ensure that future costs are kept under control.

C    In the multi-track, directions will be tailored to the circumstances of the particular case and will often include a direction that a single joint expert be appointed.

D    The parties must file a costs budget and failure to do so on time will result in the automatic sanction that the defaulting party's future recoverable costs are limited to 50% of their actual costs (unless relief is obtained from the sanction).

E    If either party has already been sanctioned in their conduct of the litigation, they must apply for relief from that sanction, but that application can only be heard after the case management conference, as the conference can only address directions for the future conduct of the case.

**Answer**

Option A correctly summarises what might happen at a case management conference.

Option B is wrong, as a costs management order will not be imposed in every case. However, such an order will usually be made unless the judge is satisfied that the litigation can be conducted justly and at proportionate cost.

Option C is wrong in that, on the multi-track, it is more common for a judge to grant permission that each party can instruct their own expert. Option D is also wrong. If either party fails to file its costs budget on time, the automatic sanction applied is that the defaulting party's future recoverable costs will be limited to any court fees that have been paid (unless relief is obtained from that sanction).

Option E is wrong. If either party has already been sanctioned, an application for relief from that sanction will usually be heard at the case management conference, provided the application has been made properly and in good time, and there is time to deal with the application during the conference hearing itself.

# 8 Disclosure and Inspection

## SQE1 syllabus

By the end of this chapter you will be able to apply relevant core legal principles and rules appropriately and effectively, at the level of a competent newly qualified solicitor in practice, to realistic client-based and ethical problems and situations in relation to **disclosure and inspection** as follows:

- standard disclosure
- orders for disclosure
- specific disclosure
- pre-action and non-party disclosure
- electronic disclosure
- privilege and without prejudice communications
- waiver of privilege

In this chapter, disclosure is often referenced by r 31.6 and may be referred to as such in the SQE assessment. Otherwise, references to cases, statutory and regulatory authorities are provided for illustrative purposes only, and the sample list of documents is included for the same reason.

## Learning outcomes

The learning outcomes for this chapter are:

- To understand the role and scope of disclosure and inspection.
- To be able to apply the definition of legal professional privilege.
- To understand what applications can be made for disclosure.
- To appreciate the effect of marking correspondence 'without prejudice'.

## 8.1　Introduction

Once the parties have filed and served their statements of case, the court will issue directions for the future conduct of the proceedings. The first of these is usually a requirement for the disclosure and inspection of documents.

The main purpose of this step is to enable the parties to evaluate the strengths and weaknesses of their case in advance of the trial. This will assist them in making an informed decision about whether to pursue the matter or whether to seek an early settlement. The parties are required to reveal to each other any documents that have a bearing on the case, even if they are unhelpful to the party giving disclosure and which they would rather keep hidden.

Disclosure is usually achieved by completing a list of documents. The parties may then inspect, that is read, some of the other party's documents. This is to ensure they are not taken by surprise at the trial and that the court has all the relevant information to ensure justice is done.

Disclosure is governed by Part 31 of the CPR, which applies to all claims except those allocated to the small claims track.

## 8.2　Disclosure of documents

Disclosure is defined in Part 31 as follows:

- a party discloses a document by stating that it exists or has existed.

This is done by preparing and serving a list of documents on all the other parties, the format of which is considered later in the chapter.

### 8.2.1　Definition

Documents are defined as anything in which information of any description is recorded. Consequently, it includes written documents, audiotapes, videotapes and photographs although this is not an exhaustive list. Electronic documents, such as emails, word-processed documents and databases are also subject to disclosure.

The definition under the CPR is extensive, but the crucial words are 'information ... is recorded'. This is what determines whether or not the document forms part of disclosure. It is irrelevant whether it is admissible or whether a party wishes to rely upon the actual document itself at trial.

## 8.3　Disclosure on each track

Different provisions apply to disclosure depending upon the track to which the claim has been allocated.

### 8.3.1　Small claims track

The usual direction is that each party shall, at least 14 days before the date of the final hearing, file and serve on every other party copies of all documents (including any expert's report) on which they intend to rely at that hearing.

### 8.3.2　Fast track

On the fast track, an order for standard disclosure will invariably be made.

### 8.3.3    Multi-track

Although standard disclosure is usually ordered, the court may tailor the order to the requirements of the particular case, taking account of the importance of the issues and the complexity of the matter. This necessitates a more involved procedure as set out in **Table 8.1**.

**Table 8.1**    Overview of disclosure on the multi-track

| Disclosure on the multi-track | |
| --- | --- |
| How do the parties notify the court of their requirements for disclosure? | By compiling a disclosure report. |
| When must this be filed and served? | Not less than 14 days before the first case management conference (CMC). |
| What happens next? | Not less than 7 days before the first CMC the parties must discuss and seek to agree a proposal for disclosure that meets the overriding objective. Any agreed proposal must be filed at court. |
| What orders for disclosure can the court make? | An order for standard disclosure or any other order that the court considers appropriate. |
| Examples? | An order:<br>• dispensing with disclosure;<br>• for specific disclosure;<br>• disclosure on an issue by issue basis. |

In recognition of the variety of cases that are dealt with on the multi-track, the parties have the benefit of a menu of options for disclosure from which they can select the most appropriate for their particular matter. These may be accessed on the Ministry of Justice website. Judges can make orders that cover the entire spectrum from dispensing with disclosure entirely to what Lord Jackson referred to as the 'keys to the warehouse approach' – although both of these will be very rare in practice. More commonly, the court will order something in between such as the provision of disclosure in stages or on an issue by issue basis – perhaps that disclosure is only required on the issue of liability but not causation. A more complex example is an order that a party should disclose any documents it is reasonable to suppose may contain information which enables that party to advance its own case or to damage that of another party's case, or which leads to an enquiry that has either of these consequences.

However, it should be borne in mind that, to deal with concerns about the potentially huge task of disclosure a party may face, the court is required actively to consider limiting disclosure to deal with the case justly.

## 8.4    Standard disclosure

Standard disclosure is defined in CPR, r 31.6 and requires a party to disclose:

(a)  the documents on which they rely; and

(b) the documents which:

(i) adversely affect their own case;

(ii) adversely affect another party's case; or

(iii) support another party's case.

In practice, documents falling within this definition are often called 'Rule 31.6 documents'.

Although there appear to be four possibilities, they mirror each other so that effectively the requirement is to disclose any documents that help or hinder the party. Most clients will be happy to provide their solicitors with favourable documents, namely those containing information on which they intend to rely. However, they may be less forthcoming with documents that adversely affect their own case or support their opponent's. Litigants often find it difficult to accept that they are required to provide their opponent with the means to defeat them. However, not only is this a requirement of the CPR, but it is a mutual obligation so they should receive similar disclosure from the other party.

The references to 'the case' are those issues that are in dispute and the parties should concentrate their efforts in searching for documents that impact on these. There is no need to search for and disclose documents that record only information relating to agreed matters.

## ⭐ Example

*ULaws LLP act for Country Fare Limited (Country Fare), which runs a large farm shop in Worcestershire. On 16 June 20XX, Country Fare entered into a contract with Rural Dairies Ltd (RDL) for the provision of fresh milk to their business. However, a dispute has arisen between the parties and Country Fare is refusing to pay the outstanding invoice. RDL has now issued proceedings against Country Fare for the monies due.*

*There is no dispute that a contract existed between the parties and that delivery was made, so they do not need to search for documents relating to these aspects. However, the issues of liability and quantum are contested as Country Fare are alleging that the milk had gone sour and they had to source alternative supplies at short notice to sell in their shop. Country Fare defend the claim and make a counterclaim on this basis.*

*There must be full disclosure of any documents that record information relevant to the alleged breach of contract and the loss. This would include documents on which Country Fare would rely, for example, any written contract providing for the quality of the milk, an email from the store manager (Jagdev Singh) to the owner of the business (Elisabeth Jenkins) explaining the milk was sour and the invoice for the alternative supplies obtained from Green Farms Ltd.*

*However, Country Fare would also be required to disclose an email from the store manager to a junior employee (Naomi McMahon) in which he asks why the milk was left outside for two hours on one of the hottest days of the summer. This records information relevant to the issue of liability and must be disclosed, despite it adversely affecting Country Fare's own case and supporting RDL.*

### 8.4.1 Control of documents

The duty to disclose is limited to documents in the party's control (CPR, r 31.8). This means documents that:

(a) either are or were in their physical possession;

(b) they have a right to possess; or

(c) they have a right to inspect.

⭐ *Example*

*Continuing with the case study, Country Fare's disclosure obligations would include any documents they possess such as the contract and any correspondence received from RDL. It would also include the originals of any letters sent to the opponent (used to possess).*

*Documents covered by a party's right to possess would include those held by third parties. Examples would be the statements of case that are retained on Country Fare's solicitors' file (information is recorded on these – it is irrelevant what use of the document will be made at trial) and documents relating to the claim for loss of profits that their accountants may have.*

*With regard to the right to inspect, although not relevant in this case study, a person has the right to inspect their medical records, for example.*

## 8.5 The duty to search

All parties to the proceedings are subject to a duty to search for documents.

### 8.5.1 Scope of search

A party is required to make a reasonable and proportionate search for all documents that:

(a) adversely affect their own case;

(b) adversely affect another party's case; or

(c) support another party's case.

Documents on which the party intends to rely are not listed but, presumably, the party would look for these anyway as it is in their interests to do so.

What is reasonable depends upon:

- the number of documents involved;
- the nature and complexity of the proceedings;
- the ease and expense of retrieval of any particular document; and
- the significance of the document.

Thus, if a document is peripheral to the main issues and would be expensive to locate, it would not be reasonable for the party to be ordered to search for it. In contrast, if the claim is of a high value, the search required is likely to be more extensive than for a low value one.

### 8.5.2 Limitations

The duty to search is not exhaustive and a party may limit the extent of their search in several ways:

- by not searching for documents that came into existence before a particular date; or
- by specifying a particular place or places they search; or
- by limiting the categories of documents.

Any such limitation would need to be justified.

⭐ *Example*

*Gillian has issued proceedings against her former solicitors, Throp & Co, for negligence. Throp & Co limit their search in the following ways:*

- *By time: they do not search for documents that pre-date 10 May [two years previously] as this was the date when they were first instructed by Gillian.*

- *By location: they limit their search to the main office and the branch office that dealt with Gillian's case.*

- *By category: Throp & Co only search for documents that relate to the subject matter of the client's current negligence claim.*

- *By type of electronic storage devices: they search for documents on their office computers but not mobile devices.*

- *By keywords: the solicitors search the electronic devices using Gillian's full name.*

These limitations will be acceptable if the court is satisfied they would not affect a proper investigation into the merits of the case. Arguments concerning the extent of the disclosure provided may arise after lists of documents have been sent, in the context of an application by the dissatisfied party for further disclosure. However, it is sensible and more cost effective to avoid them by proposing (and hopefully agreeing) any limitations earlier in the proceedings, either when drafting the disclosure report or attending a directions hearing. This would also be in accordance with the overriding objective.

 **Example**

*Continuing with Gillian's claim against Throp & Co, she is unhappy with the limits on disclosure her opponent has imposed. In particular, she is aware that it is common practice for solicitors at the firm to work from home and so the location may need to be widened to take account of this. In addition, more information would be required as to what mobile devices are used in the firm and why these are excluded.*

Note that if the search is limited in any way, this must be specifically stated in the list of documents (see below).

### 8.5.3 Electronic documents

Electronic documents include those which are readily accessible from computer systems and other electronic devices and media, but also those stored on servers and back-up systems even if they have been deleted. There are special rules that apply because the sheer volume of such documents is such that disclosure could become a mammoth task.

The CPR require the parties to manage electronic documents to minimise the cost incurred in disclosure and to use technology to ensure that the search is undertaken efficiently and effectively. To keep the work involved to a sensible level, the parties must discuss and (if possible) agree such matters as the categories of electronic documents to be disclosed, how data will be exchanged, the format for inspection and any limitations, for example, what keywords will be used. This must be done before directions are given for the conduct of the case and the parties may, if they wish, use an electronic disclosure questionnaire for this purpose.

At the case management conference, the parties will discuss disclosure and the court will then either give written directions on how electronic disclosure will proceed or order a separate hearing to deal with this aspect.

## 8.6 How disclosure is made

Once the party has gathered together the documents, they are disclosed by way of a list and this is achieved by the completion of Form N265. The contents of the list of documents are as follows.

(a) *Formalities*: the court, the claim number and the parties are set out in the top right hand corner.

(b) *Disclosure statement*: the party must sign to confirm the extent of the search made to locate any documents. They must also certify that they understand their duty of disclosure and that, to the best of their knowledge, the duty has been carried out.

A legal representative cannot sign the disclosure statement on behalf of their client. Where the party is a partnership, LLP, company or corporation, an individual in that organisation who was responsible for overseeing the disclosure process should sign. The name, address and the office or position that the signatory holds in the disclosing party or the basis upon which they have made the statement on behalf of the party must be included.

A party may decide not to permit inspection of a category or class of documents because they consider it would be disproportionate to the issues in the case. If so, they must explain their reasons on the disclosure statement, for example, the difficulty or expense such a search would have entailed or the documents' marginal relevance.

The duty of disclosure is regarded so seriously that proceedings for contempt of court may be brought against anyone who makes a false disclosure statement without an honest belief in its truth. It is also a continuing duty so that if, after signing the statement and at any time before the proceedings are concluded, the party becomes aware of additional documents, they must prepare and serve a supplemental list of documents. Having done so, if they wish to rely upon the 'new' document at trial and the opponent does not agree, they will have to obtain the court's permission.

(c) *The list*: this is on the final page and consists of three parts.

'Part 1' – In the first part of the list are documents that are within the party's control and which they do not object to the other party inspecting. These are usually numbered and listed in date order with a concise description, for example, email from A to B dated 10 May 20XX or contract dated 15 October 20XX between X and Y.

'Part 2' – In the second section are those documents which are in the party's control but where there is an objection to inspection, usually because they are privileged (discussed later in this chapter).

'Part 3' – The final, third part sets out the documents that are not privileged from inspection but are no longer in the party's control. The list must state what happened to the documents, for example, that they were lost or destroyed in a fire. The most common scenario where this arises is in relation to correspondence – a copy of a letter retained by solicitors on their file would be disclosed in Part 1, and Part 3 might state: 'The original of the letter from the claimant's solicitors to the defendant dated 12 October 20XX which was last in the claimant's control on the day it was posted.'

The importance of disclosure is underlined by the fact that a party who fails to disclose a document may not rely on it at trial unless the court permits and, if such a document is harmful to their claim or defence, their case could even be struck out.

Set out below is the defendant's completed list of documents for the claim by Rural Dairies Ltd against Country Fare Limited. This is provided to illustrate how the list would be drafted in practice, although the actual wording may vary.

**Figure 8.1** Example of a completed list of documents

# List of documents: standard disclosure

**Notes**

- The rules relating to standard disclosure are contained in Part 31 of the Civil Procedure Rules.

- Documents to be included under standard disclosure are contained in Rule 31.6

- A document has or will have been in your control if you have or have had possession, or a right of possession, of it **or** a right to inspect or take copies of it.

| In the | |
| --- | --- |
| Worcester County Court | |

| Claim No. | WR 20 2869 |
| --- | --- |
| Claimant (including ref) | Rural Dairies Ltd (ref 485001/AP/C) |
| Defendant (including ref) | Country Fare Limited (ref UL/CF/47) |
| Date | 15 November 20XX |

Click here to clear all fields

Click here to print form

## Disclosure Statement

I, the above named

☐ Claimant      ☑ Defendant

☐ Party (if party making disclosure is a company, firm or other organisation identify here who the person making the disclosure statement is and why he is the appropriate person to make it)

state that I have carried out a reasonable and proportionate search to locate all the documents which I am required to disclose under the order made by the court on (date of order)   18 October 20XX

☑ I did not search for documents:-

☑ pre-dating   1 June 20XX

☑ located elsewhere than

The Defendant's offices at Country Fare Farm Shop, Manor Road, Worcester WR11 5TB

☐ in categories other than

☐ for electronic documents

☑ I carried out a search for electronic documents contained on or created by the following: (list what was searched and extent of search)

On the Defendant's databases and email accounts.

**N265** Standard disclosure (10.05)                                                      HMCS

(*continued*)

**Figure 8.1** (*continued*)

☑ I did not search for the following:-

☑ documents created before | 1 June 20XX |

documents contained on or created by the ☐ Claimant ☑ Defendant

☐ PCs      ☑ portable data storage media

☐ databases      ☑ servers

☑ back-up tapes      ☑ off-site storage

☐ mobile phones      ☐ laptops

☑ notebooks      ☑ handheld devices

☑ PDA devices

documents contained on or created by the ☐ Claimant ☐ Defendant

☐ mail files      ☐ document files

☐ calendar files      ☐ web-based applications

☐ spreadsheet files      ☐ graphic and presentation files

documents other than by reference to the following keyword(s)/concepts
(delete if your search was not confined to specific keywords or concepts)

| Rural Dairies Ltd |

I certify that I understand the duty of disclosure and to the best of my knowledge I have carried out that duty. I further certify that the list of documents set out in or attached to this form, is a complete list of all documents which are or have been in my control and which I am obliged under the order to disclose.

I understand that I must inform the court and the other parties immediately if any further document required to be disclosed by Rule 31.6 comes into my control at any time before the conclusion of the case.

☐ I have not permitted inspection of documents within the category or class of documents (as set out below) required to be disclosed under Rule 31(6)(b)or (c) on the grounds that to do so would be disproportionate to the issues in the case.

**Signed** | |      **Date** | |

(Defendant)

(*continued*)

**Figure 8.1** (*continued*)

List and number here, in a convenient order, the documents (or bundles of documents if of the same nature, e.g. invoices) in your control, which you do not object to being inspected. Give a short description of each document or bundle so that it can be identified, and say if it is kept elsewhere i.e. with a bank or solicitor

I have control of the documents numbered and listed here. I do not object to you inspecting them/producing copies.

1. Statements of case and other court documents - various dates
2. Correspondence between the Claimant's solicitors and the Defendant's solicitors - various dates
3. Contract between Rural Dairies Ltd and Country Fare Limited dated 16 June 20XX
4. Email from Jagdev Singh to Elisabeth Jenkins dated 27 June 20XX
5. Email from Jagdev Singh to Naomi McMahon dated 27 June 20XX
6. Invoice from Green Farms Ltd dated 28 June 20XX
7. Copy letter from Elisabeth Jenkins to the Claimant dated 29 June 20XX

List and number here, as above, the documents in your control which you object to being inspected. (Rule 31.19)

I have control of the documents numbered and listed here, but I object to you inspecting them:

(1) Correspondence, attendance notes and similar documentation, instructions to counsel and counsel's advice recording communications between the Defendant's solicitors and the Defendant, and the Defendant's solicitors and Counsel.

(2) Correspondence between the Defendant's solicitors and witnesses, both expert and factual, including proofs, statements, reports, drafts and similar documentation.

Say what your objections are

I object to you inspecting these documents because:

As to the documents referred to at (1) above, these were created for the sole or dominant purpose of giving or receiving legal advice and so are covered by legal professional advice privilege.

As to the documents referred to at (2) above, these were created when this litigation was reasonably contemplated or after this litigation was commenced for the sole or dominant purpose of obtaining or collecting evidence to be used in this litigation and so are covered by legal professional litigation privilege.

List and number here, the documents you once had in your control, but which you no longer have. For each document listed, say when it was last in your control and where it is now.

I have had the documents numbered and listed below, but they are no longer in my control.

The original of the copy letter referred to in Part 1. This was last in the Defendant's control on the day the original was posted or otherwise sent.

## 8.7 Withholding inspection of documents

There are some instances where a party can legitimately withhold documents and this is usually because they come within the definition of legal professional privilege. Such documents must still be disclosed in the list but there are two key differences:

(a) the other parties cannot inspect them; and

(b) they are described generically.

This is in direct contrast with Part 1 documents, which must be described precisely so the other party can identify what they are.

⭐ *Example*

*Continuing with the case study of the sour milk, each non-privileged document would be described clearly in Part 1 of the list, for example:*

- *Contract between Rural Dairies Ltd and Country Fare Limited dated 16 June 20XX.*

*However, privileged documents would be combined together in Part 2 in a broad description such as:*

- *Correspondence, attendance notes, instructions to counsel and counsel's advice created for the sole or dominant purpose of giving or receiving legal professional advice and so covered by legal advice privilege.*

- *Correspondence between the claimant's solicitors and witnesses, both expert and factual, including proofs, statements, reports, drafts and similar documentation created when this litigation was reasonably contemplated or commenced for the sole or dominant purpose of obtaining evidence and so covered by legal professional litigation privilege.*

The effect is that particular documents are disclosed but otherwise concealed under an umbrella description, thus preventing identification of their maker, any recipient and the contents. However, only those documents that satisfy the legal tests for legal professional privilege qualify for this special treatment.

### 8.7.1 Legal professional privilege

The advantage to a party of a document being privileged is that, whilst it is disclosable, it cannot be inspected. The most common type of privilege used is legal professional privilege, consisting of advice privilege and litigation privilege. To qualify, the document must satisfy the legal requirements and a party cannot claim privilege simply because the document is adverse to their case or is confidential.

#### 8.7.1.1 Legal advice privilege

Legal advice privilege is essential as it would be difficult for lawyers to advise their clients effectively and honestly without it. Because the purpose is to allow free access to the legal profession, solicitors, licensed conveyancers, legal executives, in-house lawyers, barristers and foreign lawyers are all protected; but the privilege does not extend to legal advice given by a non-lawyer such as an accountant. Furthermore, advice privilege only applies where the sole or dominant purpose of the communication is to seek or to give legal advice. If the document has a dual purpose, the dominant one must be established. If the court finds this was, for example, to obtain commercial advice from the lawyer, the document is not privileged. Thus, clients need to be careful when communicating with their solicitors.

It is important not to confuse documents that are to be used at a trial with the disclosure process. For example, an attendance note that records advice given at a meeting between the client and their lawyer would not be referred to at trial, but is disclosable. This is because the note contains information on which the client would rely or which might adversely affect their case, perhaps concerning a discussion about the strengths and weaknesses of the evidence.

### 8.7.1.2 Litigation privilege

Litigation privilege is more complex as there are three distinct aspects that must be satisfied. The document must be a communication:

(a) passing between the client or lawyer and a third party;

(b) which came into existence when litigation was contemplated or ongoing; and

(c) which was produced with a view to the litigation, either for the sole or dominant purpose of giving or receiving legal advice in regard to it, or for obtaining evidence to be used in the litigation.

Examples would include a report from an expert obtained by a solicitor in order to advise their client on existing or contemplated proceedings, or witness statements obtained by a legal executive for the purpose of using as evidence.

### 8.7.1.3 Overview of legal professional privilege

**Table 8.2** Legal professional privilege

| Type of privilege | Definition | Examples |
|---|---|---|
| Advice | Communications between a client and their lawyer prepared for the sole or dominant purpose of giving or receiving legal advice. | • Letters or emails seeking or giving advice between solicitor and client.<br>• Attendance notes of a meeting between solicitor and client.<br>• Instructions to counsel and counsel's advice. |
| Litigation | **Who?**<br>Communications passing between the client or the lawyer and a third party...<br><br>**Timing?**<br>• ...provided they came into existence after litigation was contemplated or commenced...<br><br>**Purpose?**<br>• ...and were made for the sole or dominant purpose of obtaining advice or for using as evidence in the litigation. | • Letter to a witness, proofs of evidence and witness statements.<br>• Instructions to an expert and their report.<br><br>• After the client makes an appointment with their lawyer to discuss proceedings.<br>• After proceedings are issued.<br><br>• An expert's report to advise on whether a contract was breached.<br>• An accountant's report on the losses suffered.<br>• The statement of a witness who saw the accident. |

In most instances, it will be clear that a document is privileged but issues may arise.

 *Example*

*Eastleigh Forge Ltd (EFL) is a company that manufactures steel components for the motor industry. One of their employees, Marek, suffers extensive burns in an accident that occurs when he is working at a machine on the factory floor. He brings proceedings against EFL*

*for his injuries and loss of earnings claiming that the machine had a fault. This is denied by EFL who claim that Marek failed to use the guard provided for the machine.*

*Zhen works next to Marek and he now provides a written statement to EFL's solicitors stating that the guard on the machine they were both working at was in place but that the machine had a fault with its temperature controls. This is disclosable because it falls within standard disclosure – it is a document that records information which supports another party's case (Marek's) and also adversely affects EFL's case. EFL would want to 'hide' the statement but they can only do so if it is privileged from inspection. The statement is a communication passing between their solicitors and a third party (Zhen) which came into existence after litigation had commenced. Furthermore, it was obtained for the sole or dominant purpose of obtaining evidence on who was to blame for the accident and thus is covered by litigation privilege. As a consequence, the statement will go into Part 2 of the list of documents.*

*EFL carry out a search of their files for any relevant documents and forward a copy of a report, which they obtained immediately after the incident, to their solicitors. EFL commissioned the report from a health and safety expert to establish the cause of the accident. If the only purpose was to ensure that appropriate safety measures were taken to prevent a repetition of the accident, the report is not privileged from inspection and must go in Part 1 of the list. But what if it was obtained for the additional purpose of asking EFL's solicitors to advise on litigation that EFL thought Marek might bring?*

*Where more than one purpose applies, the document is only privileged from inspection where the dominant (or main) purpose for which the document was brought into existence was for use in pending or contemplated litigation. Thus, if EFL obtained the report mainly to prevent a repetition of the accident, it will not be privileged from inspection. However, if the reason for the report was primarily to enable its solicitors to advise on the litigation they believed Marek would bring, it will be.*

### 8.7.2 Waiving privilege

Privilege is the right of the client and not their lawyer. The client may give up, or waive, that privilege. Waiver will often occur during litigation because it is the only way to advance the proceedings. For example, while a party's solicitors are drafting statements of case and witness statements, they are privileged from inspection; but once these are served on the other side, the privilege is waived. Here it is intentional but sometimes waiver of privilege occurs by mistake.

 *Example*

*A barrister is instructed to advise a claimant on the evidence in a claim. In error, the barrister's chambers send the letter with the enclosed advice to the solicitors acting for the defendant. The solicitor reads the letter and immediately appreciates that, although it concerns their client's case, it was meant for the claimant's solicitors. What should they do?*

*Option 1 – read the advice*

*Applying the SRA Code, principle 7 would suggest continuing to read the letter and the enclosure as it is in the defendant's best interests to know what advice the claimant is receiving about the evidence in the case.*

*Option 2 – do not read the advice*

*Principles 1, 2 and 5 suggest otherwise as reading the advice would not uphold the proper administration of justice, nor uphold public trust and confidence in the solicitors' profession and would lack integrity.*

### *Action required*

*The solicitor should return the advice to the barristers' chambers pointing out the error and confirming they have not read it. However, they should not inform their client – the defendant. SRA Code 6.4(d) provides that the general duty to make a client aware of all relevant information does not apply if that information is contained in a privileged document that has been mistakenly disclosed.*

### 8.7.3 Without prejudice correspondence

Without prejudice correspondence will record information as part of a party's genuine attempt to settle a case. The correspondence will probably therefore satisfy the definition of standard disclosure as it is likely to set out the strengths of a party's case and may also contain concessions that are adverse to their case and support the opponent. Remember that it is irrelevant to standard disclosure that the recipient of a document has already seen it. The point of marking correspondence without prejudice is so the *trial judge* is unaware of the content whereas, in contrast, the disclosure process is just between the parties.

Accordingly, like any other correspondence between the parties that meets the test for standard disclosure, those documents marked without prejudice should be disclosed and no privilege from inspection claimed.

## 8.8 The right of inspection

Having received the opponent's list, the party is entitled to inspect documents contained in Part 1. They cannot inspect documents in Part 2 because they are covered by legal professional privilege and those in Part 3 are no longer in the party's control. The request to inspect must be made in writing and granted within seven days, although a longer period is often agreed between the parties. Rather than going to inspect the documents personally, a party may ask for copies of the documents if they agree to pay reasonable copying costs. Large numbers of copies of electronic documents are often provided on an external hard drive, otherwise USB memory keys or DVDs are commonly used.

## 8.9 Summary of disclosure

To assist in understanding disclosure, **Figure 8.2** sets out an overview.

**Figure 8.2**  Overview of the disclosure process

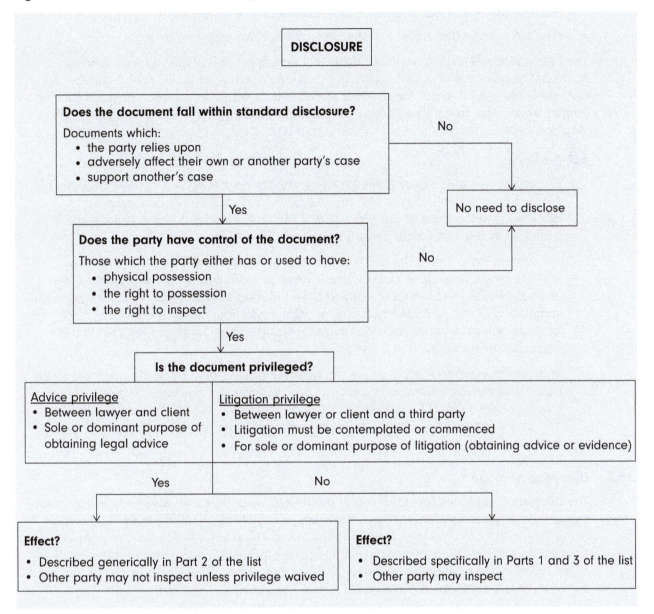

## 8.10  Orders for disclosure

To ensure that disclosure is complied with properly, the CPR provide mechanisms to assist a party who is dissatisfied with their opponent's efforts. However, before applying to the court, the party should write to the other side first as this may lead to a quicker and cheaper resolution of the issue. If this fails, an application notice (Form N244) must be filed at court accompanied by a witness statement, and served on the opponent.

### 8.10.1  Specific disclosure

Once the list of documents has been served, the contents should be scrutinised carefully. If the disclosure appears inadequate, an application may be made for specific disclosure under CPR, r 31.12. This could request an order that the party:

- carry out a more extensive search; and

- disclose any further documents located as a result of that search; or

- disclose specific documents that the party would have expected to see.

The application will require a witness statement in support. This should explain why the applicant believes the document exists, perhaps because the party has seen it previously, and justify the application. It may be that the document is vital to establish an issue such as liability or the information contained will enable the party to pursue a line of enquiry into the disputed facts.

### ✪ Example

*Continuing with the case of Eastleigh Forge Ltd, the parties serve their list of documents. Marek's lawyers are unhappy with the disclosure provided by EFL and issue an application to the court on the grounds that EFL have failed to conduct a reasonable search or to disclose key documents adverse to their case.*

*The witness statement in support is completed by Marek's solicitor, Kieron. He submits that EFL should have gone back further in time, as there was a similar accident five years previously, and the search should have included the managing director's personal computer and mobile phone because he often works from home. The solicitor also requests a number of specific documents including copies of records relating to the inspection of the machine in question.*

*In deciding whether or not to make the order for specific disclosure, the court takes into account all the circumstances of the case and, in particular, the overriding objective. The court concludes that EFL has failed adequately to comply with its disclosure obligations and so the application is granted. EFL are required to provide the specific disclosure requested.*

### 8.10.2 Disputing privilege

The disclosure provisions could (in theory) be abused by parties who wish to hide documents that are unhelpful to their case. To overcome this, an application can be made to the court under CPR, r 31.19 to challenge a claim for privilege. The court may require the party claiming privilege to produce the document, invite any person (whether or not a party) to make representations and will determine whether it has been correctly categorised. If not, the court will order that the document be revealed to the opponent.

However, the effectiveness of this option is limited by the broad nature of the claim for privilege and the general description in Part 2 of the list of documents, which makes it difficult for a party to evaluate whether privilege is being correctly claimed or not.

## 8.11 Pre-action disclosure

The pre-action protocols require the parties to prospective litigation to share information. However, there is no general obligation on a party to show their opponent the contents of documents or to disclose those which are adverse to their own position. Although a request can be made to the other party in this regard, the only way to compel such disclosure is by way of court order. Therefore, prior to a claim form being issued, the parties may to a large extent select those documents they wish to show and keep all the others hidden.

To overcome this, a party may issue an application for pre-action disclosure under CPR, r 31.16. This procedure is normally used where a party is unsure as to the strength of their case, so they can then make an informed decision as to whether to issue proceedings against the intended defendant.

The application must be supported by a witness statement and the court must be satisfied that:

- both the applicant and the respondent are likely to be a party to subsequent proceedings;

- the documents sought would come within standard disclosure; and

- disclosure is desirable to dispose fairly of the anticipated proceedings, assist the dispute being resolved without proceedings or save costs.

## 8.12 Non-party disclosure

Where proceedings have commenced, a party can apply for disclosure against a non-party (r 31.17) if this would help to resolve an issue in the case. The most common use of this procedure is where a party indicates in their list of documents that they no longer have a document in their possession, but that X does. The other party may then write to X asking for a copy of the document. If X refuses to supply that copy voluntarily, an application may be made for non-party disclosure against X.

The application must be supported by evidence and disclosure will only be ordered if:

(a) the documents in question are likely to support the applicant's case or adversely affect the case of another party; and

(b) disclosure is necessary to dispose fairly of the case or to save costs.

The order must specify the documents to be disclosed; and require the non-party to identify which documents are no longer in their control and which are privileged.

 *Example*

*Returning to the case of Eastleigh Forge Ltd, Marek's solicitor requests copies of documents concerning any maintenance carried out on the machine that is the subject of the litigation. EFL respond by stating that the machine is serviced each year by a specialist company, Jenner Engineering Ltd (JEL) but they only have the last three reports. Marek wants the service report covering the previous accident, which occurred five years ago, and so his solicitor writes to JEL requesting this. When no response is received, an application is made for non-party disclosure. The court grants the application as it is satisfied that the service report from JEL is likely to support Marek's case and is necessary to dispose of the case fairly. This is because the information would demonstrate whether there was a history of poor health and safety at EFL's factory.*

## Summary

- Disclosure is an important step in the litigation process and full disclosure is required to ensure justice.

- Standard disclosure is the usual order on the fast track. This requires the parties to disclose all documents that record information upon which they intend to rely, which are adverse to either party's case or which support the opponent's case. A more tailored approach may be taken to disclosure on the multi-track.

- Disclosure is usually effected by serving a list of documents (Form N265). This contains a disclosure statement setting out the extent of the search carried out and confirmation that the party understands and has complied with their duty of disclosure.

- The duty of disclosure is ongoing and continues throughout the proceedings. Proceedings for contempt of court may be brought against anyone who makes a false disclosure statement without an honest belief in its truth.

- Some documents may be withheld from inspection although they must still be disclosed. This is usually because the document satisfies the requirements for legal professional advice or litigation privilege. If a party suspects that privilege has been claimed inappropriately, an application may be made to the court to challenge this.

- Documents may be inspected within seven days of disclosure, either personally or by requesting copies.

- A party who is dissatisfied with the disclosure provided by the opponent may apply to the court for an order for specific disclosure.

- Disclosure may be ordered prior to proceedings being issued or against a non-party, if appropriate.

## Sample questions

### Question 1

A solicitor is conducting proceedings on behalf of a client. The court makes an order for directions and the solicitor writes to the client outlining their standard disclosure obligations.

**Which of the following statements should the solicitor make to the client?**

A   The court order requires you to carry out an exhaustive search for documents sparing no expense.

B   Once you have listed all of the documents that is the end of your disclosure obligations.

C   If you have lost any documents then that is unfortunate, but there is no need to give me details of these.

D   In due course, I will produce a draft list of documents for your approval. You will need to consider this carefully because you will sign the disclosure statement confirming that you understand your duty to give disclosure and have complied with it. If that statement is wrong, you could be imprisoned for contempt of court.

E   Once the list has been served, that is it and your opponent cannot obtain disclosure of any documents that have been missed.

### Answer

Option D is correct. Option A is wrong because the CPR require a reasonable and proportionate search (not an exhaustive one). Option B is wrong as disclosure is a continuing obligation throughout the proceedings. Documents that have been lost or destroyed must still be disclosed (in Part 3 of the list) so option C is wrong. Option E is wrong because a party who is dissatisfied with their opponent's disclosure does have options available to them, for example, applying for an order for specific disclosure or to dispute privilege claimed.

### Question 2

A couple issue proceedings for £15,000 against a company for breach of a written contract in relation to the provision of a buffet at their wedding. The couple allege that several of the guests were unhappy that no vegetarian options were provided and additional food had to be purchased for them on the day. The couple send an email to the company making these complaints about the buffet. The company respond by pointing to a checklist that the couple were asked to complete in which the vegetarian option was not ticked. The company deny the food supplied was not in accordance with the terms of the contract. There is no dispute that full payment was made by the couple to the company. During the course of the negotiations, a 'without prejudice' letter is sent from the couple's solicitors to the company offering to accept £10,000 in settlement.

**Which of the following best describes the documents that the couple would need to disclose if the court orders standard disclosure?**

A    The contract, the proof of payment, the email of complaint, the checklist and the without prejudice letter.

B    The contract, the email of complaint, the checklist and the without prejudice letter.

C    The contract, the email of complaint and the checklist.

D    The contract, the email of complaint and the without prejudice letter.

E    The checklist and the without prejudice letter.

### Answer

Option B is correct as the only document that does not need to be disclosed is the proof of payment (and A is wrong for this reason). This is because there is no dispute that full payment was made and so the document does not record any information relevant to the disputed issues between the parties.

Option C is not the best answer – the without prejudice letter should also be disclosed as it falls within standard disclosure. The letter most probably records information upon which the couple will rely as part of their claim, and the fact that the couple will now accept £10,000 is adverse to their claim for £15,000. The effect of a document being marked in this way is that it cannot be shown to the judge at trial but disclosure takes effect between the parties and, in any event, both have seen the letter.

Option D is wrong because the checklist must also be disclosed as it adversely affects the couple's case and so comes within the definition of standard disclosure. Option E is not the best answer as the couple will want to rely upon the contract as to the disputed issue of the provision of the food as well as the email recording the detail of their complaint that is disputed by the company.

### Question 3

A company manufactures scooters. On testing the finished product, it becomes apparent there is a problem with the brakes. The manufacturing company obtains a report from their quality control department to check the reason, which concludes that the cause may either have been a temporary glitch in the software or a fault with the brakes themselves. The manufacturing company instructs solicitors and issues proceedings against one of its parts suppliers (which supplied the brakes) for breach of contract and to claim damages including loss of profits. The proceedings are defended and the court directs that standard disclosure is given.

**Which of the following approaches should the manufacturing company's solicitors take when completing the list of documents?**

A    Any confidential document must be disclosed but may be included in Part 2 of the list.

B    Attendance notes of meetings between the manufacturing company and their solicitors need not be disclosed as they will not be relied on at trial.

C    Instructions to counsel and counsel's opinion may be disclosed in Part 2 of the list as they fall within the definition of advice privilege.

D    All witness statements obtained must be disclosed in Part 1 of the list of documents.

E    The report from the quality control department is subject to litigation privilege and should be disclosed in Part 2 of the list.

**Answer**

Option C is correct. Option A is wrong because documents may only be disclosed in Part 2 if they satisfy the test of legal professional privilege – confidentiality is irrelevant to answering this particular question. Option B is also wrong as attendance notes of meetings between the client and their solicitor would fall within the definition of standard disclosure and so must be disclosed. However, they are protected by legal advice privilege and would be described generically in Part 2.

Witness statements, whether helpful or not to the manufacturing company, would be subject to litigation privilege and disclosed in Part 2 of the list – hence, option D is wrong. If the party decides to rely upon any of the witnesses, privilege is waived at the next stage in the proceedings when the parties exchange the witness statements of those witnesses that they intend to rely on at trial.

Option E is wrong because the report does not satisfy the requirements of litigation privilege. It was commissioned before litigation was contemplated and the purpose was to establish the cause of the fault with the brakes, and not with a view to litigation for the sole or dominant purpose of obtaining advice or evidence.

# 9 Evidence

## SQE1 syllabus

By the end of this chapter you will be able to apply relevant core legal principles and rules appropriately and effectively, at the level of a competent newly qualified solicitor in practice, to realistic client-based and ethical problems and situations in relation to **evidence** as follows:

- relevance, hearsay and admissibility
- the burden and standard of proof
- expert evidence
  - opinion evidence
  - duties of experts
  - single joint experts
  - discussion between experts
- witness evidence
  - witness statements
  - affidavits

Note that for SQE1, candidates are not usually required to recall specific case names, or cite statutory or regulatory authorities. These are provided for illustrative purposes only and the sample documents are included for the same reason.

## Learning outcomes

The learning outcomes for this chapter are:

- To understand how the courts control evidence.
- To appreciate the role and content of witness statements and affidavits.
- To recognise what evidence is admissible, how hearsay evidence is defined and the approach the courts take to this.
- To understand how opinion evidence is dealt with and the role of expert evidence.

## 9.1 Introduction

Having outlined their respective cases in the statements of case, the parties will concentrate on proving or disproving the issues raised by putting forward their evidence in support. The rules governing how this is achieved and specifically what evidence may be used in civil proceedings are to be found in Parts 32, 33 and 35 of the CPR.

In particular, the court may control the evidence by giving directions as to:

- the issues on which it requires evidence, whether liability, causation or quantum;
- the nature of the evidence it requires to decide those issues, for example, an expert's report;
- the number of witnesses of fact a party may call at trial; and
- the way in which the evidence is to be placed before the court, whether orally or by relying upon written statements.

When exercising its powers, the court will bear in mind the overriding objective in CPR, r 1.1 to decide matters justly and at proportionate expense. This will involve the court being actively involved throughout the proceedings, up to and including the trial. Even at this late stage, the judge could, for example, decide that an issue which had been raised is no longer important and order that any evidence relating to it should be excluded.

## 9.2 Burden and standard of proof

A trial judge is likely to have to evaluate many different types of evidence, such as oral evidence from witnesses of fact (sometimes referred to as lay witnesses), experts' written reports and the parties' own documents. In determining the outcome of a case, judges must bear in mind the burden and standard of proof, both of which must be considered.

### 9.2.1 Legal burden of proof

The burden of proof refers to the party's duty to produce sufficient evidence to establish their allegation or argument.

#### 9.2.1.1 General rule

The legal burden of proof lies with the claimant and each fact must be proved unless it is admitted by the opponent. For example, a claimant alleging breach of contract must prove that a contract existed between the parties, the defendant broke the relevant express and/or implied terms of the contract, and the claimant suffered loss as a result.

#### 9.2.1.2 Exception

The exception to this is where the defendant in civil proceedings has been convicted of a relevant criminal offence. Under s 11 of the Civil Evidence Act 1968, the burden of proof is reversed – unsurprising given the higher standard of proof required to obtain a conviction in the criminal courts. Thus, if a defendant wishes to argue they should not have been convicted they must prove this, meaning that the legal burden has shifted on this point.

⭐ *Example*

*Jakob and Barney are the claimant and defendant (respectively) in civil proceedings having been involved in a road traffic collision. Barney's vehicle hit the back of Jakob's car while it was stationary, waiting to enter a busy roundabout. Before the proceedings started, Barney was convicted of careless driving in the local magistrates' court in relation to the accident. Jakob gives details of the conviction in the particulars of claim, stating that it relates to the issue of the defendant's negligent driving. Barney argues that he was wrongly convicted but, if he is to succeed in his defence, he will have to prove this to the satisfaction of the court.*

9.2.1.3  The defendant

There are a few occasions where the burden of proof falls on the defendant, for example, contributory negligence, where the defendant must prove that the claimant's failure to take care contributed to the damage suffered.

 *Example*

*Continuing with the scenario (above), Barney alleges that Jakob was not wearing a seat belt at the time of the accident and this was partly responsible for his injuries. Barney must prove this fact if he is to succeed in reducing the damages payable.*

### 9.2.2  Standard of proof

In civil cases, the claimant is required to prove a fact on the balance of probabilities. This requires the judge to be persuaded that the claimant's version of events is more likely to be true than the defendant's. In simple terms, there must be a certainty of greater than 50 per cent.

## 9.3  Witness statements

The general rule is that any fact upon which a party intends to rely must be proved at trial by oral evidence. However, this rule is modified in practice as much of the evidence in a civil litigation case is actually dealt with in writing.

Under Part 32, if a party wishes to call a witness, they must serve a witness statement on the other parties setting out all the facts which that witness would be allowed to give orally at trial. Inadmissible or irrelevant material should not, therefore, be included. If the statement is not served for any reason, the witness will only be allowed to speak at trial with the court's permission and this would be a rare occurrence.

### Witness summaries

Sometimes it will be very difficult to obtain a witness statement, perhaps because the person is uncontactable abroad, or to persuade a witness to give a statement (for example, it will be against their current employer and they fear being dismissed). In these circumstances, the party can apply to the court without notice for an order to serve a written witness summary. This will contain:

- the witness's name and address;
- the evidence the witness can provide, if it is known; or if not
- the matters on which the witness would be questioned at trial, namely, the relevant disputed issues.

Witness summaries are less satisfactory to the party than a statement but they may be useful where the alternative is no evidence at all.

### 9.3.1  Form and content

Rules relating to the form of witness statements are set out in the Practice Direction attached to CPR 32, and they list the formalities required for the statement to be valid. It is important that these are complied with as a failure to do so may result in the court refusing to admit the witness statement as evidence.

(a) The statement should be headed with the title of the proceedings and details such as the name of the witness, the number of the statement and the date in the top right hand corner.

(b) In the opening paragraph should be the witness's address, their occupation or description, whether the statement is made as part of their employment or business and, if so, the name of the business and whether they are a party to the proceedings.

(c) The paragraphs must be numbered with all numbers, including dates, being expressed as figures and not words, thus, 'five people' should read '5 people'. The format for dates would be, for example, 16 January 2021 and not 16.01.2021.

(d) The statement should normally follow the chronological sequence of the events.

(e) The function of the witness statement is to set out in writing the evidence that the individual wants to provide on behalf of the party that called them. Historically, such evidence was given orally at the trial but now, to save time, the witness statement usually replaces this.

(f) Consequently, it should be written in the first person and expressed in the witness's own words as far as possible.

(g) The witness must also indicate which of the statements are made from their own knowledge and which are based on information and belief, naming the source if appropriate. Also, the process by which the witness statement was prepared must be included, for example, face to face or over the telephone with a party's solicitor.

(h) Any documents that are attached are formally exhibited, for example, 'AP1'.

(i) Under PD 32 para 20.2, it must be verified by a statement of truth in the format:

'I believe that the facts stated in this witness statement are true. I understand that proceedings for contempt of court may be brought against anyone who makes, or causes to be made, a false statement in a document verified by a statement of truth without an honest belief in its truth'.

Unlike statements of case, a witness statement cannot be signed by a legal representative.

There are special provisions that apply where the statement cannot be given in English. In such cases, the statement should be drafted in the witness's own language with the date and the details of the translation being included in the statement.

Although the content of witness statements will vary significantly, the style and layout will not and **Figure 9.1** provides an illustration.

⭐ *Example*

*In this matter, the claimant (Scandinavian Self-Build Limited) issued proceedings against the defendant, Platinum Developments Limited, for payment due under a contract to supply three self-build 'Lillehammer' house kits. The defendant's defence is that the kits were defective because the claimant's specification for construction of the house foundations did not comply with Building Regulations requirements.*

*The statement on the opposite page details the evidence that the managing director of the claimant company intends to give on behalf of Scandinavian Self-Build Limited.*

### 9.3.2 Directions for exchange

Once the case has been allocated to a track, the court will give directions as to when and how witness statements are to be exchanged and this is usually completed simultaneously. The reason is to prevent one party having an advantage over the other by seeing their opponent's witness statement first. In most cases, the statements will be exchanged a few weeks after disclosure and inspection of the documents, although the interval will vary depending upon

**Figure 9.1** Example of a witness statement

On behalf of the Claimant

J Waggett

1st

Exhibit: JW1

Dated: 31/10/20XX

IN THE HIGH COURT OF JUSTICE

QUEEN'S BENCH DIVISION

BETWEEN

CLAIM NUMBER HQ 001234

SCANDINAVIAN SELF-BUILD LIMITED — Claimant

and

PLATINUM DEVELOPMENTS LIMITED — Defendant

**WITNESS STATEMENT OF JAMES WAGGETT**

I, James Waggett, company director of 2 The Firs, Christlethorpe, Guildshire GU17 6WL will say as follows:

1. I am the Managing Director of the Claimant and I am authorised by the Claimant to make this witness statement.

2. The facts and matters set out in this statement are within my own knowledge unless otherwise stated, and I believe them to be true. Where I refer to information supplied by others, the source of the information is identified; facts and matters derived from other sources are true to the best of my knowledge and belief. I have made this witness statement following a face to face meeting with the Claimant's in-house solicitor, Yasmin Ansari.

3. On 23 April 20XX, the Claimant received a telephone call from Mr Bold on behalf of the Defendant about the Lillehammer kit. The Claimant's sales manager, Mrs Halls, took the call.

4. I have spoken to Mrs Halls, who is a very senior sales operative who has worked for the Claimant for almost 10 years. Mrs Halls informs me that Mr Bold explained that the Defendant was a developer, and that, if it made a good profit on these 3 kits when they were built, it would be looking to acquire more. She quoted him a price of £180,000 for the 3 kits which he accepted. She then explained in accordance with company policy that this was an all-inclusive price to include the kit, technical drawings, specifications for Building Regulations approval and full build instructions.

5. I refer to Mrs Halls' note of the conversation marked **JW1**. It can be seen that at no point did Mrs Halls say that the Lillehammer houses when built would comply with Building Regulations. This is in line with company policy, as, although we are confident that if our kits are built precisely to our specifications the finished houses will comply with Building Regulations, we clearly have no control over whether a customer is able to follow the specification or not...

[The witness continues with the narrative].

...

16. The Claimant's specification for the foundations are considerably more stringent than the Building Regulations requirements. I understand from the District Surveyor's Department that the Defendant's foundations complied with neither this specification nor Building Regulations.

I believe that the facts stated in this witness statement are true. I understand that proceedings for contempt of court may be brought against anyone who makes, or causes to be made, a false statement in a document verified by a statement of truth without an honest belief in its truth.

Signed: *J Waggett*

Dated: 31/10/XX

*(continued)*

**Figure 9.1** (*continued*)

---

**Exhibit JW1** [Separate document]

*23/4/XX- 10.18 am*

*Adrian Bold, MD Platinum Developments Ltd*

*Wants 3 Lillehammer kits for small development behind Waitway.*

*Quoted him £180,000 10% deposit. Balance due 2 months (to allow for building of houses and building regs approval)*

*Confirmed price includes plans and Building Regs Approval.*

*He is happy to deal on these terms.*

I verify that this is the document marked JW1 exhibited to my witness statement dated 31 October 20XX.

Signed: *J Waggett*

---

the complexity of the matter. This allows the witness an opportunity to review their evidence after having taken into account any documents that have been inspected.

### 9.3.3 Use at trial

Having served a witness statement on the other side, the witness will usually be called to give oral evidence at trial. Before the hearing, the judge will have read all the witness statements that were exchanged. These form part of the trial bundle (see **Chapter 10**). The witness will go into the witness box, take the oath or affirm, be shown a copy of their statement and confirm the contents are true. It is then assumed that the witness has said, from the witness box, everything in their statement and so this stands as their evidence- (or examination-)in-chief. Unless the court gives permission for additional examination-in-chief (see below), they will then be subject to questioning by the other side's advocate – known as cross-examination.

It is essential that the statement is comprehensive because a witness cannot add to it at the trial unless the court gives permission, and this will be the exception rather than the rule. Such an event will only occur if the judge is satisfied there is a good reason why the evidence was not dealt with in the statement itself – perhaps because it needs to be amplified or a new relevant matter arose after the statement was served.

---

## 9.4 Affidavits

Affidavits are sworn statements of evidence and they differ from witness statements as the maker has to swear or affirm before a solicitor (not their own), or other authorised person, that the contents of the affidavit are true. Prior to the CPR, affidavits were the usual means of submitting evidence but they have been replaced in this role by witness statements. There are now only a few occasions where it is necessary to use an affidavit, including applications for a freezing injunction or a search order.

---

## 9.5 Witness evidence

When drafting witness statements, or indeed affidavits, it is important to be aware of the rules of evidence and how these apply to civil proceedings.

### 9.5.1 Relevance

The starting point is that any evidence included must be relevant. On a practical level, there is little point in the witness setting out vast amounts of irrelevant material as this will not assist in deciding the case and will simply prolong the trial unnecessarily. Furthermore, its inclusion would fall foul of the rules of evidence, which state that:

- *irrelevant* material is not admissible.

Relevance is judged by reference to the issues the court is called upon to decide.

#### 9.5.1.1 When is evidence relevant?

Evidence from a witness of fact is admissible when it addresses relevant facts, namely those which are in dispute and which have to be proved by the party calling the witness. These should be apparent from comparing the particulars of claim with the defence – the facts not admitted and denied are in dispute.

 *Example*

*Dawn issues proceedings for negligence against her solicitor, Razwana, arguing that Razwana did not represent her properly in her employment claim against a former employer. In her defence, Razwana admits that, as a lawyer, she owes a duty of care to Dawn as her client and so no evidence is required on this issue. However, she denies being in breach of the duty. She submits that Dawn did not provide her with full instructions of what happened during the incident leading up to her dismissal from her employment. Razwana calls Erin, a paralegal who sat in on the meeting, as a witness on her behalf. Erin may give evidence on what was said at the discussion as this is relevant to the disputed question of liability (namely who is at fault).*

### 9.5.2 Opinion

#### 9.5.2.1 General rule

The general rule is that opinion evidence is not admissible because the function of a witness is to give evidence of relevant facts from which the court can draw its own conclusions.

However, there are some situations where it is difficult for a witness to separate fact and opinion.

#### 9.5.2.2 Facts personally perceived

Under s 3(2) of the Civil Evidence Act 1972, a witness may give a statement of opinion if made as a way of conveying relevant facts personally perceived by them. If this test is satisfied, the evidence is admissible.

Strictly speaking, rather than stating their opinion, the witness should list the facts that they saw which led them to reach their conclusion. However, if they fail to do so, even though the accuracy of the witness's assessment of the speed or the level of intoxication might be challenged, the evidence would usually be admissible.

What the witness cannot do is to draw any conclusion from their evidence as this is the role of the court. So, for example, the witness to the road traffic collision cannot say in evidence that (in their opinion) the defendant's speed was 'excessive in the circumstances' or 'too fast' because it is for the trial judge alone to determine if the defendant was driving negligently.

#### 9.5.2.3 Expert evidence

In contrast to witnesses of fact, experts are permitted to express their opinions in court and this is considered later in the chapter.

Set out below are two examples of when a witness of fact can give an opinion.

**Table 9.1**   Opinion evidence: witnesses of fact

| Opinion | Based on facts personally perceived |
|---|---|
| A witness to a road traffic collision gives evidence that she saw the vehicle being driven 'at about 60 miles per hour' before it rounded a corner and ran into the back of the defendant's vehicle. | Although this is clearly an opinion, there are few alternatives other than simply describing the speed as 'fast', which is of limited value. Many people would be able to estimate the speed of a vehicle to some extent. |
| A witness to an assault expresses the view that the assailant was 'drunk'. | The witness is reaching a conclusion based on the physical characteristics she observed about the assailant such as slurred speech, glazed eyes, an unsteadiness of gait, breath smelling of alcohol and so on. |

### 9.5.3   Hearsay evidence

Special considerations apply where hearsay evidence is to be used.

#### 9.5.3.1   Definition

The definition of hearsay is set out in s 1(2) of the Civil Evidence Act 1995. In summary, it is:

- a statement made outside court;

- which is repeated in court;

- to prove the truth of the matter stated.

The statement must be a relevant fact or an admissible opinion. It can be oral or written and may be repeated in court in a document or by the witness whether in their witness statement or in oral evidence. The crucial aspect that determines whether such statements are hearsay is the purpose – the reason is to prove the truth of the words said. In other words, the trial judge is being asked to rely on the repetition of the words (the evidence) to reach a decision in the case. The easiest way to understand hearsay is to work through some examples.

### ⭐ Examples

(a) *Richard was involved in a road traffic collision with Samira. He is disputing liability. Richard gives evidence that the other driver (Samira) got out of her car and said: 'I'm so sorry – I just didn't see you!' This is an oral statement made by Samira outside court – at the scene of the accident. Richard is repeating it in court to prove the truth of the matter stated, namely that Samira did not see his vehicle and was, therefore, to blame for the accident.*

(b) *When Deiza booked a holiday with Fancy Tours Ltd, the agent assured her that the hotel would be quiet and peaceful and close to the beach. However, the hotel was next to a noisy building site and some distance away from the beach. Deiza is now suing for misrepresentation and wishes to repeat in evidence the oral statements made to her by the agent. This will be relevant evidence on the issue of liability but it will not be hearsay because Deiza is not repeating them to show the truth of the statements – in fact, the opposite, that she was lied to. This will assist her in proving that she relied on false representations.*

Hearsay evidence may either be first hand or multiple as demonstrated by the examples in **Table 9.2**.

**Table 9.2**   Hearsay evidence

| First hand hearsay | Multiple hearsay |
| --- | --- |
| Shona gives evidence of something she was told by Padraig (in order to prove the truth of Padraig's statement). | Shona also gives evidence of something Padraig was told by Himesh (in order to prove the truth of what Himesh said). |
| Mary keeps a diary and records what she sees one day. Her diary is used at the trial to prove the truth of its contents. | Mary records what she was told by Lucy. Mary's diary is used at the trial to prove the truth of what Lucy said. |

The common thread to all of these is that the witness is not giving evidence of what they personally know. In Shona's case, she is repeating what Padraig said; whereas with Mary, it is the diary itself that contains the statement being relied upon. This becomes multiple hearsay where the information is relayed through more than one person before it is recorded. In the first example, Himesh tells Padraig who tells Shona so the details are passed down a chain before being repeated in court. In Mary's case, the diary is recording what someone else (Lucy) told Mary – she did not actually see the event herself.

### 9.5.3.2   Using hearsay evidence

Section 1(1) of the Civil Evidence Act 1995 provides that hearsay evidence is admissible in civil proceedings. However, there are notice requirements under s 2 and further details are contained in CPR Part 33.

- If the party intends to call the witness whose statement contains hearsay evidence, they simply need to serve the other party with the statement.

- The opponent must then decide whether to ask the court to order that the maker of the original statement attends for cross-examination or serve notice of intention to attack the credibility of the hearsay evidence.

⭐ *Example*

*In the scenario above, the claimant wants to rely upon Shona's evidence and so her witness statement is served on the defendant. Shona's statement contains hearsay as she is repeating what Padraig said to her to prove the truth of the matter stated and the court will be asked to take this into account when determining the relevant issue. The defendant reads Shona's statement and, as Padraig's (hearsay) statement is crucial to the issue of liability, decides to request the court to order him to attend court to be cross-examined. The defendant also serves notice that, in the event Padraig cannot attend, they will attack the credibility of the statement he made to Shona.*

- If the party does not propose to call the witness to give oral evidence but instead intends to rely upon the witness statement itself, the whole statement becomes hearsay. This obviously limits the opponent's options as they cannot cross-examine the witness and so they must be given advance warning of the situation.

How is this achieved? When serving the witness statement, it is essential that the party intending to rely on the hearsay evidence informs the other parties that the witness is not being called to give oral evidence and explains the reason why. This is done by way of a hearsay notice, which should be served at the same time as the witness statement.

*Example*

*Continuing with the scenario above, Shona cannot attend court to give evidence because she is ill in hospital. The claimant exchanges her witness statement with the defendant and serves a hearsay notice in the format below. This will ensure that the hearsay evidence is admissible at the trial. However, as before, the defendant can make an application to the court to order that the maker of the hearsay statement (Padraig) attends for cross-examination or serve notice of intention to attack the credibility of the hearsay evidence.*

## Heading/title of proceedings

## Hearsay Notice

This notice is given pursuant to the Civil Procedure Rules 1998, Rule 33.2(1)(b) and (2) and s 2(1)(a) of the Civil Evidence Act 1995.

TAKE NOTICE that the Claimant intends to rely on the following hearsay evidence at trial:

The witness statement of Shona McCafferty. A copy is served herewith pursuant to the court order of 3rd April 20XX. It is not proposed to call Shona McCafferty as a witness at trial as she is in hospital and is too ill to attend.

[Date]

[Signed]

[Address for service]

If a party does not comply with the notice requirements, the hearsay is still admissible but the failure may be taken into account when assessing the weight to be given to it, or when making a costs order at the end of the trial.

9.5.3.3 Weight to be attached

Although hearsay evidence is admissible, it is important to remember that it is 'second best' evidence of a fact. Out-of-court statements are not made on oath or with any form of affirmation. It is not uncommon for a person to lie, or to make ill-considered statements that are inaccurate. Furthermore, the greater the number of times a statement is repeated, the more likely there is to be an error.

Because the maker of the hearsay statement is not present at the hearing, they cannot be cross-examined. As a consequence, their memory or powers of observation cannot be challenged and the trial judge is unable to assess the reliability of the statement by observing the witness's demeanour.

So how does the court approach the issue of hearsay? The judge will begin by considering these questions:

(a) What issue, if any, does the hearsay evidence address?

(b) How important is that issue in the case?

(c) What other evidence is available on the same issue?

(d) Is the hearsay evidence more probative than any other evidence the party could obtain through reasonable efforts?

There are also statutory safeguards, which may be found in s 4 of the Civil Evidence Act 1995. These provide guidelines to assist the judge in assessing the weight that should be attached to hearsay evidence. It provides that the court must have regard to all the circumstances and, in particular, to the following:

(a) Whether it would have been reasonable and practicable for the party adducing the evidence to have called the person who made the original statement as a witness. Only if the reason is a credible one, such as the person being dead or abroad and not contactable, is the statement likely be given some weight; otherwise, why not call the person to give oral evidence?

(b) Whether the original statement was made contemporaneously with the events in question, so that the facts referred to in it are fresh in the memory of the person making it. A note made of a car registration number immediately after the car drives off will generally be more reliable than one made the next day, week or month.

(c) Whether the evidence involves multiple hearsay as there is always the danger of mishearing, exaggeration and general inaccuracy through repetition.

(d) Whether any person involved had any motive to conceal or misrepresent matters, for example an employee who makes the statement with a view to pleasing their employer.

(e) Whether the original statement was edited, or was made in collaboration with someone else, as this may suggest collusion, for instance.

(f) Whether the circumstances suggest an attempt to prevent proper evaluation of the weight of the evidence, perhaps because notice was given so late that the other party did not have a fair opportunity to respond to it.

Hearsay may appear quite confusing but below is a clear structure to assist in determining whether a statement is hearsay or not.

**Figure 9.2** Hearsay evidence

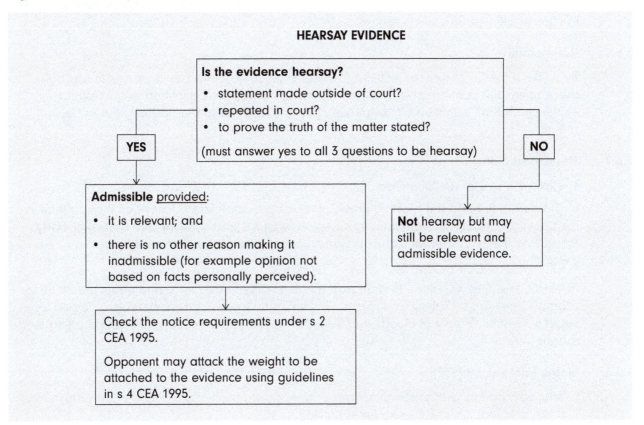

## 9.6 Expert evidence

Expert evidence is often crucial to the outcome of civil proceedings and its use is governed by Part 35. Such evidence may be required to establish the breach of contract, perhaps a surveyor in a case involving defective building work; or damages, for example an accountant to prove loss of profits.

However, the parties do not have an unlimited right to use expert evidence and, as part of its case management powers, the court will restrict such evidence to that which is reasonably required to resolve the issues. This may include:

- refusing to allow any expert evidence at all;
- limiting the number of experts either generally or in relation to specific issues;
- directing that the parties must agree experts; or
- limiting expert evidence to written reports.

No party may call an expert without obtaining permission. This will usually be considered at the directions stage, either when the case is allocated to the fast track or at a case management conference on the multi-track.

The court will need to be satisfied that expert evidence is necessary to decide an issue in dispute or to assist the judge in doing so. Factors taken into account will include the value of the claim and proportionality, and the likely costs.

The judge will also require information on:

- the name of the expert where practicable;
- the field the person is an expert in;
- their knowledge and experience to ensure they are suitable to give their evidence; and
- the issues the expert will address.

Expert evidence is often crucial to the outcome of the case and so it is in the parties' interests to comply with the CPR in this regard.

### 9.6.1 Admissibility

By s 3(1) of the Civil Evidence Act 1972, 'where a person is called as a witness in any civil proceedings, his opinion on any relevant matter on which he is qualified to give expert evidence shall be admissible in evidence'. This is in contrast to the position with witnesses of fact.

### 9.6.2 The expert's duty

The expert's duty is set out in Part 35.

✓ The duty *is* to assist the court by providing objective, unbiased opinions on matters within their own expertise. Although in many cases an expert is instructed by one particular party, the duty to the court overrides any obligation to the person who instructed them.

X The duty is *not* to assume the role of an advocate.

However, this does not mean that an expert has no duty to the party who instructed them; for example, they will be subject to the usual implied term to exercise reasonable care and skill under s 13 of the Supply of Goods and Services Act 1982 when considering and drafting their report.

### 9.6.3 Single joint expert (SJE)

Where both parties wish to submit expert evidence on a particular issue, the court may direct that the evidence is given by one expert only.

- When is an SJE appropriate?

  The court will decide if an SJE is appropriate by considering a number of factors including whether:

  (a) it is proportionate to have separate experts for each party on a particular issue;

  (b) the instruction of an SJE is likely to assist in resolving the issue more speedily and in a more cost-effective way; and

  (c) there is likely to be a range of expert opinion.

- Who chooses the expert?

  If agreement cannot be reached on who this will be, the court will select the expert from a list prepared by the parties.

On the fast track, the usual order is for an SJE to be appointed unless there is a good reason not to do so, rather than allowing each party to instruct their own. Where an expert is jointly instructed, they will send their report simultaneously to both parties with the costs being shared. Furthermore, in fast track cases, such evidence will normally be given by means of written reports and the experts will not be permitted to give oral evidence at the trial.

### 9.6.4 Separate instruction of experts

In contrast, for multi-track cases, it is more common for the parties to instruct their own experts. Factors taken into account are the amount in dispute, the importance to the parties and the complexity of the issue.

 *Example*

*Anya has a large amount of money to invest, which she received from an inheritance. She instructs Clevedon Finance Ltd (Clevedon) to advise her on what investments to make but, over time, it becomes apparent that the shares are under-performing. After following the relevant pre-action protocol, Anya issues proceedings for professional negligence for the sum of £450,000, which Clevedon defends. Because of the complexity of the issues and the amount in dispute, the court grants permission for the parties to instruct separate experts.*

*Anya and Clevedon will each instruct an expert to cover the issue of liability, namely whether Clevedon breached their duty of care to invest the funds with reasonable care and skill; and to deal with quantum, specifically what would the value of Anya's share portfolio have been if they had done so. This will provide the court with information on what investments Clevedon should have made on behalf of Anya and (consequently) her losses.*

### 9.6.5 Procedure

If separate experts are ordered, the court will also make further directions in an effort to streamline the trial as much as possible by narrowing down the issues the experts need to comment upon. These include the following:

- *Exchange*: a deadline will be imposed for exchange of the experts' reports.

- *Questions*: each party may, within 28 days, put written questions to the expert for clarification of their report. The expert's answers are treated as part of the report.

- *Discussion*: the court may order a without prejudice discussion between the experts, usually in the absence of the parties or their legal representatives, and the contents will not be referred to at trial unless the parties agree. The purpose of the discussion is not to settle the case but to narrow down the issues and to identify:

  ○ the extent of any agreement between them;

  ○ the points of and short reasons for any disagreement;

- ◦ what action, if any, may be taken to resolve these; and
- ◦ any further material issues not yet raised and the extent to which these are agreed.

- *Written joint statement*: following the discussion, a written joint statement must be prepared for the court and signed by the experts stating the issues on which they agree and those on which they disagree with a summary of the reasons. Copies should be provided to the parties.

- *Oral evidence*: the judge will decide whether the expert may give oral evidence at trial. Although there is a presumption that the court will rely upon written reports, it is common on the multi-track for experts to be called to give evidence.

### 9.6.6 Form of expert evidence

Detailed instructions for the form and content of an expert's report are to be found in Part 35. As far as the content is concerned, this will vary from a few pages to a lengthy document depending upon the complexity of the case. Regardless of this, the formalities must be complied with and an expert's report must:

(a) be addressed to the court;

(b) give details of the expert's qualifications;

(c) give details of any literature or other material that the expert has relied on;

(d) contain a statement setting out the substance of all facts and instructions;

(e) say who carried out any examinations, measurements, tests or experiments, their qualifications and whether the expert supervised;

(f) where there is a range of opinion, summarise this and give reasons for the expert's own opinion;

(g) include a summary of the conclusions reached; and

(h) contain a statement that the expert understands their duty to the court and has complied with this, and is aware of the requirements of Part 35 and related guidance.

The report must also be verified by a statement of truth as follows:

> I confirm that I have made clear which facts and matters referred to in this report are within my own knowledge and which are not. Those that are within my own knowledge I confirm to be true. The opinions I have expressed represent my true and complete professional opinions on the matters to which they refer.

#### 9.6.6.1 Effect of the expert failing to comply with Part 35

If the breach is serious, the party may not be allowed to rely on that expert's evidence, but in most cases, the judge will simply take account of the breach when deciding what weight should be given to the expert evidence.

#### 9.6.6.2 Professional conduct issues

When drafting the report, the expert must set out all the instructions, whether written or oral, which are material to the opinions expressed or upon which their opinions are based. This is to ensure that the report is not influenced in any way. For example, a surveyor who is instructed to value a property on the basis of a quick sale may well arrive at a different figure than if asked to provide an optimal valuation.

Legal representatives should, therefore, be aware that their instructions are not privileged from inspection and could be scrutinised by the court should the court find reasonable grounds to consider the statement of instructions to be inaccurate or incomplete.

### 9.6.7 Overview of expert evidence

**Figure 9.3** Expert evidence

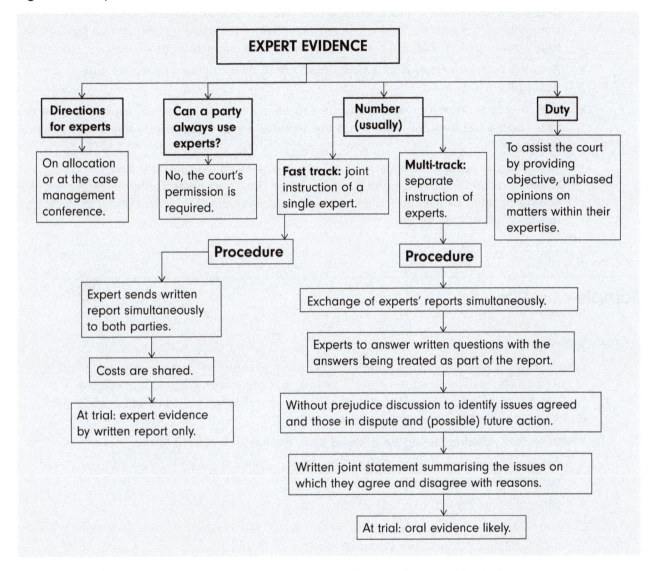

## Summary

- A witness statement is a written statement containing the evidence the witness would be allowed to give orally at trial. It must comply with the formalities required by CPR Part 32 and be verified by a statement of truth.

- The function of a witness statement is to set out in writing the person's evidence-in-chief so it must be expressed, so far as possible, in the witness's own words. The statement should address the disputed issues in an orderly manner and this will usually be chronological.

- Only admissible evidence may be included. Facts that are irrelevant to the issues in dispute are inadmissible, as is opinion evidence unless this is based on facts personally perceived by the witness.

- The starting point for hearsay evidence is that it is admissible. It only becomes inadmissible if it contains irrelevant material or opinion evidence that a witness of fact cannot give. In this way, it is no different from 'ordinary' evidence. However, it is second best evidence and its weight will be carefully assessed by the court. What makes it distinct is the notice requirements and the party intending to rely on the hearsay must comply with these.

- In contrast to witnesses of fact, experts can give an opinion. Their evidence will be admissible if it is relevant and within the expertise of the expert, in the correct format (as provided for by CPR Part 35) and the court has given permission for its use.

- An expert's primary duty is to the court and not to the party that instructed or is paying them.

- The court may order that such evidence is to be given by a single joint expert, which is the norm on the fast track, or that each party instruct their own expert and this is usual on the multi-track.

- The court can require the experts to answer questions on their reports, take part in a without prejudice discussion and submit a written joint statement. Furthermore, the experts can be directed by the court to give evidence orally at the trial or the court may decide to rely upon the written reports.

## Sample questions

### Question 1

A lawyer issues proceedings on behalf of their client (a man) against a company for breach of contract. The lawyer drafts the client's witness statement and writes to him enclosing it. The client asks for information about the process – specifically what formalities are required and what may be included in the content.

**Which of the following should be omitted from the letter of advice to the client?**

A The witness statement must comply with the formalities required by the CPR and should include a statement of truth.

B The statement should, so far as possible, be expressed in the man's own words.

C The man can only include evidence that he would be allowed to give orally so irrelevant and inadmissible evidence must be excluded.

D The man may use his witness statement to argue his case and to make observations about the evidence of other witnesses.

E The man must indicate which statements are made from his own knowledge and provide the source of any information which is not.

### Answer

Option D should be omitted. The man should only give factual evidence and it is not the function of the witness statement to argue his case or to make observations about the evidence of other witnesses. Option A correctly identifies that the witness statement must comply with CPR Part 32. Option B correctly provides that the statement will stand as the man's evidence-in-chief; and option C correctly states that the witness statement is subject to the usual rules of evidence. Option E is another requirement of the CPR.

## Question 2

A woman purchases a car from a local garage after the salesman assures her that the vehicle has never been involved in an accident (statement 1). When she drives the car, it bursts into flames and, on inspection by an expert, it becomes apparent that the vehicle had been completely rebuilt after a collision two years previously. The woman sues the company that sold her the car and includes in her witness statement evidence of the comment that was made to her by the salesman (statement 1) and also what her friend told her afterwards, namely that the company was 'dodgy' (untrustworthy) – statement 2.

**Which of the following correctly describes the evidence the woman may give in her witness statement?**

A    Both statements are admissible hearsay.

B    Statement 1 is not hearsay but is admissible as it is relevant to an issue in dispute. Statement 2 is hearsay but it is inadmissible because it is opinion evidence.

C    Both statements are inadmissible opinion evidence.

D    Statement 1 is not hearsay but is admissible as it is relevant to an issue in dispute. Statement 2 is admissible hearsay.

E    Statement 1 is admissible hearsay and statement 2 is inadmissible opinion evidence.

### Answer

Option B is correct.

Statement 1 is admissible evidence: it is relevant to the issue of misrepresentation as the woman is alleging that the statement was false and that she relied upon it to purchase the car. However, it is not hearsay. Although it is an oral statement made by the salesman outside court (at the garage), which the woman repeats in court, she is repeating it to prove it was said and not that it is true.

Statement 2 is hearsay: it is an oral statement made by her friend outside court that the woman is repeating to prove its truth – that the company is untrustworthy. However, the evidence is inadmissible because it is opinion and not based on facts personally perceived by the woman's friend (just as the friend could not give this evidence herself to the court, so the woman cannot repeat it to the court).

## Question 3

A company wishes to call evidence from experts in support of their claim for breach of contract. The case involves a dispute about the installation of an online booking system for the company's national and international hotel chain. There have been numerous problems with the system including rooms being double booked and customers' details being lost. The defendant argues that this is due to the claimant's employees' failure to operate the system properly rather than the highly technical defects alleged by the company. The company is claiming £125,000 being the cost of a replacement system and £1,395,250 as damages for loss of profits.

**Which of the following best describes the approach that the court will take to expert evidence?**

A   Each party will be granted permission to instruct experts on the issues of liability and quantum.

B   The experts will be ordered to meet to identify the areas of agreement and disagreement and the judge will be made aware of these discussions.

C   Although it is preferable for the expert's evidence to be included in the form of a report, a written statement is also acceptable.

D   The duty of the expert is primarily to the party instructing them but they must bear in mind their additional duty to the court.

E   The court will order that the issues are to be decided on the basis of the written reports alone.

**Answer**

Option A is correct. Because of the complexity of the issues and the amounts in dispute, this case is not suitable for a single joint expert and each party would be granted permission to instruct separate experts on both liability and quantum.

Option B is wrong in that, whilst there would be a discussion between the experts (whether face to face or by telephone or video conference), this is without prejudice and so the judge would not be made aware of what was discussed. Option C is wrong as, to be admissible, the expert's evidence must be in the form of a report that complies with Part 35. The overriding duty of the expert is to the court – hence, option D is wrong – although the expert also owes a duty to the party instructing them to exercise reasonable care and skill. Option E is wrong because, although a court could order that the issues be decided on the basis of written reports only, this is unlikely in a dispute over technical matters involving the suitability and operation of an online booking system and the claim for damages of over £1 million is likely to be hotly contested.

# 10

# Trials and Appeals

## SQE1 syllabus

By the end of this chapter you will be able to apply relevant core legal principles and rules appropriately and effectively, at the level of a competent newly qualified solicitor in practice, to realistic client-based and ethical problems and situations in relation to:

**The trial:**

- summoning witnesses
- preparations for trial
    - purpose of pre-trial checklists and hearings
    - purpose of trial bundles
- trial procedure
- the nature and effect of judgment

**Appeals:**

- permission
- destination of appeals
- grounds for appeals

Note that for SQE1, candidates are not usually required to recall specific case names, or cite statutory or regulatory authorities and these are provided for illustrative purposes only.

## Learning outcomes

The learning outcomes for this chapter are:

- To appreciate how to prepare for trial and what goes into a trial bundle.
- To understand the use of a witness summons.
- To understand the trial procedure and the appeals process.

## 10.1    Introduction

Only a small number of cases reach trial as the vast majority settle. However, if this proves impossible, the parties must prepare for the final hearing although much of the work should have been completed beforehand. Indeed success depends, to a significant extent, on the quality of the parties' preparation, as a judge cannot help but be influenced if the paperwork is inadequate or the witnesses fail to attend when required.

Once the trial commences, the responsibility for the case will pass to the advocate and more complex matters will usually be conducted by a barrister or a solicitor advocate. Depending upon the outcome, the parties may consider appealing the judge's decision and this raises an entirely different set of factors, which will also be covered in this chapter.

## 10.2    Attendance of witnesses    *See update*

Most witnesses will attend the trial voluntarily – after all, they have already co-operated by providing a witness statement. To ensure there are no issues on the day, witnesses should:

- be asked, at an early stage, if there are any dates when they cannot attend; and
- be notified of the trial date without delay.

Details of a witness's availability must be given to the court on the directions questionnaire (thus, early in the proceedings) and also in the pre-trial checklists as the case approaches the final hearing. The aim is to ensure that the trial, should it prove necessary, is not delayed for any reason.

### 10.2.1    Witness summons

Even where witnesses have been kept fully informed and involved, if there is any doubt about whether a witness will attend voluntarily, the matter should not be left to chance and a witness summons should be sought. This is a document issued by the court requiring a witness to:

- attend court to give evidence; and/or
- produce documents to the court.

The court's permission is required and a witness summons should be served at least seven days before the date on which the witness is required to attend court. It is binding and if they fail to appear, the witness may be fined or even, in High Court proceedings, imprisoned for contempt. The summons will normally be served by the court and, to be effective, the witness must be offered or paid:

(a)  a sum reasonably sufficient to cover their expenses in travelling to and from the court; and

(b)  compensation for loss of time as specified in Part 34.

The advantage of serving a summons is that the judge is more likely to be sympathetic to an adjournment of the trial should the witness fail to attend. However, it would be unusual to witness summons an expert as they are required to keep those instructing them informed of their availability.

### ⭐ *Example*

*The case between Eastleigh Forge Ltd (EFL) and their employee, Marek, is listed for trial on 15 November. Bettina is another employee who worked with Marek. She is an important witness as she states that Marek did not wear the safety equipment provided in clear breach of EFL's policies and procedures. However, Bettina has now left the employ of EFL and says that she 'no longer wants to be involved'. She has failed to respond to*

*EFL's solicitors' letter notifying her of the trial date and asking her to confirm that she will give evidence. To ensure her attendance, the solicitors apply for a witness summons and this is served on Bettina with an offer to pay her travel expenses to court and a sum of money to cover the loss of one day's wages. Bettina attends the trial as she does not want to face proceedings for contempt of court.*

## 10.3 Preparations for trial

If counsel is representing the client, it is important that they are briefed in plenty of time for the hearing to ensure they are fully prepared. In more complex cases, a conference may be held so that any potential problems can be discussed and removed. In addition, before the trial, all the steps required by the CPR must be completed and any court orders or directions complied with.

### 10.3.1 Pre-trial checklists and reviews

As the parties approach the trial, there will be a flurry of activity to make sure the hearing can proceed smoothly to avoid a costly adjournment. On the fast and multi-tracks, pre-trial checklists (also known as listing questionnaires) play a vital role in this and must be completed fully by the parties.

- *Purpose*: to ensure the parties have complied with all the directions and the trial is ready to proceed.

- *Timing*: the completed pre-trial checklist must be filed at court no later than eight weeks before the trial date.

- *Role*: the judge will review the checklists to decide whether further directions are needed and whether a review hearing is necessary before the trial. This is referred to as a listing hearing on the fast track and a pre-trial review on the multi-track.

- *Failure to comply*: if neither party comply, the court will order that unless a completed checklist is filed within seven days, the claim, defence and counterclaim will be struck out; if only one party does, the court will fix a hearing to ensure the case is ready for the trial.

In heavy cases, generally those where the trial is likely to last longer than 10 days, the trial judge may order a pre-trial review to personally check the progress of the matter. The parties' representatives are expected to attend to assist in ironing out any last minute glitches before the case is listed, so the court's resources are not wasted. To ensure that decisions can be made, the representative must be familiar with the case and have the authority to deal with any issues that may arise.

After these steps have occurred, the court will:

(a) give a time estimate and set a timetable for the trial if deemed necessary;

(b) fix the place of trial; and

(c) confirm the actual date of the trial or state the week within which it will begin.

Thereafter, the court will order that a trial bundle of documents be prepared.

### 10.3.2 Trial bundles

A trial bundle is a file of all the documents the judge may need to decide the case. It is indexed and paginated for ease of reference so that the documents can be accessed quickly by all those involved, thus promoting the efficient use of the court's resources. To ensure the bundle is not too unwieldly, case law suggests that, generally, it should be no longer than 250 pages in length. So how are trial bundles dealt with in practice?

- *Who*: the claimant or (if they are legally represented) the lawyer who has the conduct of the claim on their behalf will usually prepare the bundle but the contents should be agreed wherever possible.

- *When*: the bundle must be filed between seven and three days before the start of the trial.

- *What*: the trial bundle should include the key documents, for example:

  ○ the claim form and all statements of case;
  ○ a case summary and/or chronology where appropriate;
  ○ requests for further information and responses;
  ○ witness statements;
  ○ notices of intention to rely on hearsay evidence;
  ○ experts' reports and responses;
  ○ directions orders; and
  ○ any other necessary documents containing evidence that a party intends to rely on.

The party filing the trial bundle should supply identical copies to all other parties to the proceedings and for use by the witnesses.

### 10.3.3  Case summary

In multi-track cases, each party should prepare a case summary – often called a 'skeleton argument' – for use at trial. This is designed to assist both the court and the parties by indicating what points are still in issue, and the nature of the argument about the disputed matters. The case summary will (concisely):

(a) review the party's submissions of fact in relation to each of the issues with reference to the evidence;

(b) set out any propositions of law to be relied upon; and

(c) identify any key documents that the trial judge should, if possible, read before the trial starts.

## 10.4  The trial    *See update*

If the matter cannot be resolved, the parties will have no option but to proceed to a trial so that the judge can break the deadlock.

### 10.4.1  Venue

The County Court has hearing centres throughout England and Wales and both fast and multi-track cases will take place at these. In contrast, the High Court is based at the Royal Courts of Justice in London, but there are District Registries in many cities, which act as trial centres.

### 10.4.2  Trial timetable

For more complex cases, a specific timetable may be determined in advance as the trial will be listed for several days. However, fast track trials should only last one day and the usual order of events is as follows: *→amend statement of case →adduce more evidence*

10.4.2.1  Preliminary issues

Any outstanding issues will be addressed before the trial starts. Although this could include substantive law, more frequently it will involve points of procedure such as requesting permission to amend a statement of case or to adduce additional evidence. However, generally, these matters will have been dealt with earlier in the proceedings.

*Procedural matters.*

### 10.4.2.2 Opening speeches

If permitted by the judge, the claimant may make an opening speech setting out (briefly) the background to the case and the facts that remain in issue.

### 10.4.2.3 Examination-in-chief  → witnesses

Normally, the claimant and their witnesses of fact will be called first. Because their statement stands as their evidence-in-chief, the witness will usually just be asked to take the oath or affirm, identify their witness statement in the trial bundle and confirm it is true. Every word in the statement is then treated as having been said by the witness in evidence.

Only if they need to amplify their statement (perhaps to clarify a point) or to give evidence in relation to new matters that have arisen since, will the witness say any more. Even then, the permission of the judge must be obtained. In the event that additional evidence is allowed, the advocate cannot lead on matters in dispute between the parties and should only ask open questions, such as: 'What did you see?' 'What happened next?'

Expert evidence will be given as previously directed by the court – either written reports or by way of oral evidence. Traditionally, the claimant's expert will go first, but the court has the power to make alternative orders such as that the parties' experts give evidence simultaneously on an issue by issue basis.

### 10.4.2.4 Cross-examination  → leading questions allowed.

Next, the witness will be cross-examined by the opponent's advocate. The purpose is to put their own client's case and whilst, rather optimistically, this may extract favourable evidence, this is not the main reason. In most instances, the witness will not change their story but cross-examining them ensures there is no implied acceptance of that evidence. The advocate will also seek to discredit the witness by highlighting inconsistencies or gaps in their evidence, so they appear less believable.

At this stage, there are fewer constraints on the advocate, who may ask leading or closed questions to keep control of the witness. Such a question is one which suggests the answer, for example: 'When the defendant supplied the goods, they did not match the sample, did they?' Often the response is limited to either yes or no, thus discouraging the witness from expanding their answer to re-emphasise their own case. Witness answers judge not opponent advocate. Hostile witness = cross examination by their sides advocate.

### 10.4.2.5 Re-examination

If necessary, the witness may be re-examined by their own advocate. However, this can only relate to matters that have been raised by the cross-examination and the lawyer should consider carefully whether doing so would actually improve the situation. As with examination-in-chief, only open questions may be put to the witness.

### 10.4.2.6 Closing speeches

After the evidence has been given, the defence advocate will usually make a closing speech followed by the claimant's advocate. The aim is to summarise the law and the facts in the most favourable light to convince the judge of the validity of their case.

### 10.4.2.7 Judgment

The judge will either deliver their judgment immediately or (if the case is complex) reserve judgment to a later date. The judgment will take effect on the day it is made unless the order specifies a different date.

The effect of the judgment is to bring the main proceedings to a conclusion. The judge will begin by determining liability, specifically whether the claimant has established their cause of action, for example breach of contract or negligence, before going on to review the evidence and to provide reasons for their decision.

If the defendant has won, this will be the end of the substantive proceedings. However, if the claimant has been successful, the court will need to consider what remedies to grant and this will usually be the payment of a sum of money (quantum). In a specified claim, the total will be calculated, whereas in an unspecified claim the judge will consider each category of damage that the party is claiming in turn. The judge will also rule on whether interest will be paid, the rate and for what period.

Finally, there is the question of costs. The general rule is that the unsuccessful party will be ordered to pay the costs of the successful party, although the court may make a different order. At the end of a fast track trial, the judge will also summarily assess the amount payable. In contrast, at the conclusion of a multi-track trial, the judge will only determine who should pay costs and the amount will be determined at a later hearing (known as a detailed assessment), unless agreement can be reached between the parties.

**Figure 10.1** The nature and effect of a judgment

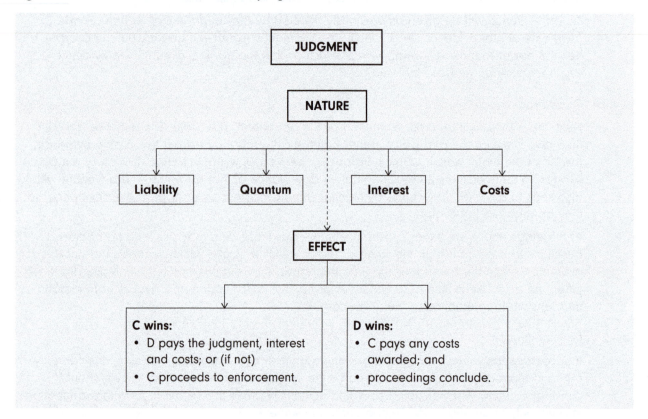

Once the judgment has been made, what happens next? If the claimant has succeeded at trial, they have the right to recover the monies awarded including costs and interest and, if not paid, enforcement action may be taken. In contrast, if the defendant has won, the only outstanding issue will be the payment of any costs awarded. Where the court orders the payment of an amount of money (including costs), this must be paid within 14 days unless the order specifies otherwise.

### 10.4.3 Hostile and unfavourable witnesses

Sometimes, witnesses may not 'perform' as hoped or anticipated and this may be for a variety of reasons.

- An unfavourable witness does so for entirely proper reasons – perhaps they have genuinely forgotten a fact or now interpret the situation in a different way. This is always a risk given the inherent unpredictability of trials and has to be accepted by the party calling them.

- In contrast, a hostile witness fails to come up to proof because they are unwilling to support the party who called them. They may refuse to answer or tell lies so their evidence now differs from what is in their statement. In this instance, the party calling the person may ask the judge to declare them a hostile witness. The effect is that the advocate may now attack the witness's credibility or cross-examine them as if they were a witness for the other side. Clearly, this is not ideal but is a useful way of limiting the damage the witness is inflicting on the party's case.

## 10.5   Appeals

Despite the best endeavours of the lawyers and the judge, there will be occasions when mistakes are made or one party may simply be dissatisfied with the outcome and feel that justice has not been done. If this occurs, the remedy available is the appeals process. Appeals serve two purposes: the private purpose, which is to do justice in particular cases by correcting wrong decisions, and the public one of maintaining public confidence in the administration of justice by making such corrections and clarifying and developing the law.

### 10.5.1   Permission to appeal: grounds

For first appeals, permission will be given only where the court considers that the appeal has a real prospect of success or there is some other compelling reason why it should be heard. There has to be a realistic, as opposed to a fanciful, prospect of success. A compelling reason why the appeal should be heard could be, for example, if there is an important question of law or general policy at stake that requires consideration by the higher courts. If the appeal is to the Court of Appeal or the Supreme Court, the case must also raise an important point of principle or practice.

Second appeals are much rarer and permission is required from the Court of Appeal itself before the judges will hear the case. The grounds are as above.

 *Example*

*Leonard issues professional negligence proceedings against his accountants. He attempted to serve the claim via email without obtaining the defendant's solicitors' confirmation that they would accept service in this way as required by the CPR. Unfortunately for Leonard, his failure to properly serve the document meant the deadline had expired and the claim was struck out. He appealed the decision to the High Court, which agreed with the lower court that there was no good reason to validate the service.*

*Leonard decides to continue to the Court of Appeal, arguing that the appeal has a real prospect of success or there is some other compelling reason why it should be heard. Because this is his second appeal and, in any event, is being made to the Court of Appeal, Leonard must also establish there is an important matter of principle or practice. He succeeds in this aspect by arguing that his case raises the issue of what (if any) special consideration and leniency should be given to litigants in person in navigating the CPR. The Court of Appeal grants permission as the judges agree this is of general public importance given the increasing presence of litigants in person in the civil justice system.*

*However, Leonard is disappointed when the judges find against him on the basis that, although a lack of representation may justify making allowances in case management decisions and in conducting hearings, it will not usually justify applying a lower standard of compliance to litigants in person with rules or orders of the court.*

### 10.5.2 Permission to appeal: procedure

There is no right to appeal and the procedure for obtaining permission is governed by CPR Part 52.

- In most cases, the request will be made at the end of the trial and the judge will decide whether to grant permission.

- If the request is unsuccessful, or none is made, then the party can apply for permission from the appeal court itself. The appeal court will usually deal with such a request on paper, without a hearing. However, in the Court of Appeal, the judge must list the matter for an oral hearing no later than 14 days after the relevant direction if they decide that the application cannot be fairly determined without the presence of the parties.

The requirement to obtain permission acts as a deterrent to those litigants who refuse to accept a court's decision.

### 10.5.3 Timing

The aggrieved party has 21 days to appeal against a County Court or High Court decision; and 28 days to apply for leave to appeal from the Court of Appeal to the Supreme Court.

### 10.5.4 Destination of appeals

The appeal will normally lie to the next court up. However, the route of appeal depends on:

- the court from whose decision the appeal is brought ('the lower court'); and
- who made the decision.

In the civil courts, matters are decided by different levels of judge and this impacts upon the appeals process. In the *High Court*, the case may be heard either by a High Court judge, a master or a district judge. If the decision is made by a High Court judge, the route is straightforward as the matter must be appealed to the Court of Appeal. However, if the judge is of lesser seniority, the appeal goes up the next rung of the ladder to a High Court judge.

In the *County Court*, cases may be decided by circuit judges or district judges. If the former, the appeal is to a High Court judge; if the latter, to a circuit judge.

The common thread is that the appeal is to a judge who is next in the hierarchy, as summarised below:

**Table 10.1** Destination of appeals

| Decision of: | Appeal made to: |
|---|---|
| District judge of the County Court | Circuit judge of the County Court |
| Master or district judge of the High Court | High Court judge |
| Circuit judge | High Court judge |
| High Court judge | Court of Appeal |

From the Court of Appeal, a further appeal would lie to the Supreme Court but, generally, the decision of the appellate court will be the final decision and very few cases will reach the highest courts. This is because judges of the quality of Lords Justices of Appeal are a scarce and valuable resource, and it is important that they are used effectively and only on work that is appropriate to them.

 *Example*

*In Leonard's case (above), the initial decision to strike out his claim was made by a district judge of the High Court. He appealed to a High Court judge and, thereafter, to the Court of Appeal (his second appeal). Only in rare cases will judges allow further appeals but, given the importance of the issue and its implications for others, Leonard applies for and is granted permission to pursue his case all the way to the Supreme Court. Unfortunately, he is unsuccessful and the judges confirm the decision of the Court of Appeal. However, they also take the opportunity to give guidance on the practicalities of dealing with litigants in person, in particular stating that a solicitor has no obligation to point out the mistakes of an opposing litigant in person and indeed cannot do so without their own client's authority, which is unlikely to be given.*

10.5.4.1 Leapfrog appeals

A leapfrog appeal is one that is heard by a higher appellate court than usual. Appeals that would normally take place in the County or High Court will jump over these to the Court of Appeal; whereas for appeals that would ordinarily be dealt with in the Court of Appeal, the destination of the appeal would be the Supreme Court.

It is only on rare occasions that the court has the power to order that the appeal be transferred straight to the Court of Appeal. Permission may be granted where the matter raises an important point of principle or practice, or there is some other compelling reason why the Court of Appeal should hear it.

It is also possible (although very unusual) for cases to proceed straight from the High Court to the Supreme Court should the issue be deemed of sufficient importance. Leapfrog appeals only occur in exceptional circumstances, usually related to the urgency of the matter. There are two stages in the process:

(a) the grant of a leapfrog certificate by the trial judge; and

(b) the grant of permission to appeal by the Supreme Court.

Such appeals arise where the case involves a point of law of general public importance concerning, for example, the construction of a statute or statutory instrument; or a matter of national importance.

**10.5.5 Grounds of appeal**

On what basis may an appeal court grant an appeal? The appellant will have to persuade the appeal court that the decision of the lower court was either:

(a) wrong (as to law, interpretation of facts or exercise of discretion); or

(b) unjust because of a serious procedural irregularity in the proceedings of the lower court.

 *Example*

*In Leonard's case, it was agreed by all parties that service by email was not effected in accordance with the CPR. However, the issue for the court was whether service should be validated given that Leonard had been communicating with the solicitors by email for some time and they were aware from the email attaching the claim form that proceedings had been issued. Leonard sought to argue (ultimately unsuccessfully) that the court's decision to refuse this was wrong in relation to the exercise of the judge's discretion in this regard.*

### 10.5.6 Overview of appeals

**Figure 10.2** The appeals process

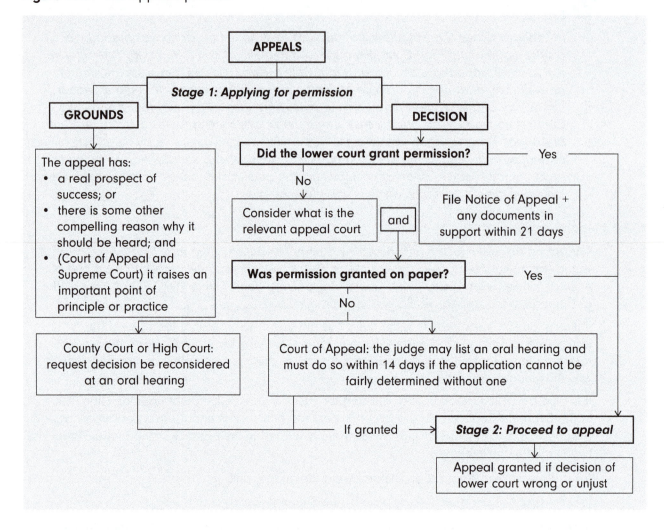

---

## Summary

- Preparation for trial includes ensuring the attendance of witnesses, drafting a case summary and preparing trial bundles.

- The court ensures that the case is ready to be listed for trial with the assistance of pre-trial checklists and (if necessary) a pre-trial review.

- The order of events at trial will usually be: opening speech by the claimant's advocate, the presentation of the claimant's case followed by the defendant's case (including witnesses and expert evidence) and closing speeches by both.

- At the conclusion of the trial, the judgment will determine the contested issues including liability, quantum, interest and costs.

- There is no automatic right of appeal in civil cases – permission is always required. Permission can be obtained either from the court that made the decision, or from the court that will hear the appeal.

- The grounds for permission require the appeal to have a real prospect of success or for there to be some other compelling reason why it should be heard.

- An appeal may be granted if the decision of the lower court was wrong or unjust because of a serious irregularity.

# Sample questions

### Question 1

The claimant has issued proceedings against the defendant. Negotiations break down and the matter is proceeding towards trial on the multi-track.

**Which of the following statements is correct?**

A   A witness summons should be issued for all witnesses to ensure their attendance at trial.

B   The parties must complete a pre-trial checklist.

C   The court will list the case for a pre-trial review in every case.

D   Each party must prepare their own trial bundle.

E   A case summary is not required as it only applies to the fast track.

### Answer

Option B is correct as the parties must complete a pre-trial checklist to assist the court in establishing that all directions have been complied with and that the claim is ready to proceed to trial. Option A is wrong because a witness summons will not be required in 'all' cases. It will only usually be applied for where there is some doubt about a witness of fact attending voluntarily, although a witness may require a summons to show their employer. Option C is wrong because the court will not always list the case for a pre-trial review.

Option D is wrong as the claimant (or their lawyer if they are legally represented) is responsible for preparing the trial bundle unless the court orders the defendant to do so but, in any event, it will be a joint bundle. A case summary may be ordered for the multi-track but not generally for cases allocated to the fast track – hence, option E is wrong.

### Question 2

A claim for breach of contract proceeds to trial and a timetable is set by the court.

**Which of the following statements best describes what will happen at trial?**

A   The order of events is likely to be preliminary issues (if any), examination of the claimant's witnesses, examination of the defendant's witnesses, closing speeches by both advocates.

B   A witness's statement stands as their evidence so examination-in-chief will usually be limited to requiring the witness to take the oath, identify their personal details and confirm that the contents of their witness statement are true.

C   A witness may always add to or expand their witness statement to clarify a point or to clear up any ambiguities.

D   Witnesses may be asked open, leading or closed questions by the advocates for both parties.

E   The judgment will address all disputed issues of liability and (where relevant) quantum, but the issue of costs is always reserved for a subsequent hearing.

**Answer**

Option B is correct. The witness statement stands as that witness's evidence-in-chief.

Option A is wrong because, ordinarily, the claimant will be given permission to make an opening speech, once preliminary issues have been addressed and before witnesses are examined. Option C is also wrong. Although a witness may amplify their statement to clarify a point or give evidence in relation to new matters which have arisen since they signed their statement, they will not 'always' be able to do so, as permission of the judge must be obtained first.

Option D is wrong because, when examining their own witness, an advocate can usually only ask open and non-leading questions. Closed and leading questions can generally only be used during cross-examination.

Option E is not the best answer. If the case is proceeding on the fast track, the judge will summarily assess costs when giving judgment. If the case is proceeding on the multi-track, the judge will, when handing down judgment, usually order who shall pay whose costs, but will leave the quantification of those costs to a subsequent detailed assessment (if the parties cannot agree the matter).

**Question 3**

A claim between the claimant and the defendant is heard by a district judge in the County Court. At the end of the trial, the judge gives judgment. The claimant is unhappy with the outcome and wishes to appeal.

**Which of the following statements best describes the approach that would apply to the claimant's appeal?**

A   The claimant's appeal will be heard by a circuit judge.

B   The claimant has 14 days in which to appeal the decision.

C   The claimant must apply for permission to appeal to the trial judge.

D   Permission will be granted but only if the court considers that the appeal would have a real prospect of success.

E   If dissatisfied with the decision of the appellate court, the claimant will usually be allowed to appeal further to a court higher up in the hierarchy.

**Answer**

Option A is correct. Because the matter was decided by a district judge in the County Court, the appeal will be heard by the next level of judge – a circuit judge. Option B is wrong because the claimant has 21 days to appeal against a County Court decision (as here). Option C is wrong because the claimant may also apply for permission to appeal to the appeal court itself. Option D is wrong as there are two grounds on which permission to appeal may be granted, the other being that there is some other compelling reason why it should be heard. Option E is also wrong as in most cases, the decision of the appellate court will be the final decision as the grounds on which a second appeal may be permitted are very onerous.

# 11 Costs

## SQE1 syllabus

By the end of this chapter you will be able to apply relevant core legal principles and rules appropriately and effectively, at the level of a competent newly qualified solicitor in practice, to realistic client-based and ethical problems and situations in relation to **costs** as follows:

- costs management and budgeting
- inter-partes costs orders (interim and final)
- non-party costs
- qualified one-way costs shifting
- Part 36 and other offers
- security for costs
- fixed and assessed costs

In this chapter, offers to settle are known as Part 36 offers and may be referred to as such in the SQE1 assessment. Otherwise, references to cases, statutory and regulatory authorities are provided for illustrative purposes only.

## Learning outcomes

The learning outcomes for this chapter are:

- To understand how costs are decided between the parties including how to conduct a detailed assessment of costs on the multi-track.
- To appreciate the difference between fixed costs and summary assessment of costs.

- To understand how to safeguard the claimant's position on costs; when a claimant is not liable for the defendant's costs even if they lose; and when a non-party may be responsible for costs.
- To evaluate the role and consequences of Part 36.

## 11.1 Introduction

Costs are an important aspect of litigation and should be considered throughout. The amount the case is likely to cost and the probability of recovering costs from the opponent will be crucial factors in a client's decision as to whether to issue proceedings at all. As the matter progresses, there may be interim hearings at the end of which costs orders will be made. Then, at the conclusion of the trial, the judge will determine which party is to be responsible for paying the outstanding costs.

Because either the claimant or the defendant may be ordered to pay costs, the successful party is referred to as 'the receiving party' and they are entitled to payment of their costs from the unsuccessful one – 'the paying party'. These terms will be used throughout this chapter.

## 11.2 The general rule

The term 'costs' includes solicitor's charges, disbursements such as court fees, expert's fees and even pre-action costs. Provisions relating to costs may be found in CPR Part 44 and the general rule is that the unsuccessful party pays the successful party's costs. However, this is only the starting point and the judge has discretion to make different costs orders if deemed appropriate.

## 11.3 Costs management and budgeting

Costs will be an issue throughout the case from the moment when the solicitor is first instructed until its conclusion whether by settlement or at trial. The court becomes involved at an early stage, particularly in multi-track cases. Before the case management conference is heard, the parties must file a costs budget setting out the costs incurred to date and those anticipated for the future. The court may also impose a costs management order giving greater control over costs, the effect of which is summarised in **Table 11.1**.

**Table 11.1**   Effect of costs management order

| Effect of **Costs Management Order** on the **Multi-track** | • A party awarded its costs on the **standard basis** at trial will normally recover the amount of its last approved or agreed budgeted costs.<br>• On the standard basis, the court may depart from the budgeted costs only if persuaded there is a good reason to do so, for example where the costs of a phase were:<br> ◦ not incurred at all; or<br> ◦ much less than budgeted.<br>• Costs awarded on the **indemnity basis** and incurred costs will be assessed by the court in the usual way, unless agreed. |
|---|---|

Even if such an order is not made, the court will have regard to any costs budgets when assessing costs. Costs budgets and costs management are covered in further detail in **Chapter 7**.

## 11.4 Procedure for determining costs

How costs are dealt with varies depending upon the track to which the claim has been allocated.

- *Small claims track*: legal costs are not recoverable and so the costs payable will only relate to disbursements.
- *Fast track*: the costs will usually be summarily assessed.
- *Multi-track*: a detailed assessment of the costs will be carried out.

However, although these are the general rules, the situation with regard to costs is often more complex.

### 11.4.1 Fixed costs

In certain situations, the CPR fix the amount of costs the party may recover from their opponent. This is entirely separate from the arrangement between the party and their own lawyers, which is governed by contract.

The advantage to a litigant of fixed recoverable costs is that they know in advance how much will have to be paid to the other party should they lose the case. However, fixed costs are less attractive to the successful party as they are extremely unlikely to recover all their costs and will often have to pay the shortfall to their own solicitor.

Fixed costs cover various steps in the proceedings. For example, a claimant who applies for default judgment will usually only be able to claim the costs that are fixed by Part 45 of the CPR, whatever sums they have actually spent so far. Most of the costs incurred in enforcing a judgment are also fixed. However, in some instances such as an application for summary judgment, it may be possible for the parties to agree a higher sum to offset the harshness of this rule and, in these circumstances, the judge will usually concur.

On the fast track, although fixed costs do not generally apply to the costs of bringing the claim and pursuing it to a final outcome, they are imposed on the advocate who prepares and appears at trial.

 *Example*

> Kathryn is the advocate representing two clients, both of whom win their cases at trial. The first is a breach of contract dispute of £7,000; here, the fixed costs for preparing the case and appearing at trial are £690. The second is a negligence claim for more than £15,000 with fixed costs of £1,650. Because these costs are fixed under Part 45, the court can only award the exact amount, with these sums being recoverable from the opponent.

### 11.4.2 Summary assessment

If costs are not fixed, a different process applies. Summary assessment involves the court determining the amount that is payable immediately, at the end of the hearing. The general rule is the court should, unless there is a good reason not to do so, make a summary assessment of the costs:

(a) at the conclusion of a fast track trial; and

(b) at any other hearing that has not lasted more than one day.

To assist the court, the parties must file and serve a statement of costs – a detailed breakdown of their costs – no less than two days before a fast track trial and at least 24 hours before an interim hearing. As with any aspect of litigation, there are risks inherent in allowing a judge to determine the issue and so the parties should seek to agree costs if at all possible.

### 11.4.3 Detailed assessment

If the court cannot make a summary assessment of costs – usually because there is insufficient time – an order will be made for the detailed assessment of those costs. In the multi-track, costs will generally be dealt with in this way.

Within three months of the date of the judgment or order, the receiving party must serve on the paying party a Notice of Commencement of detailed assessment proceedings together with their bill of costs and evidence in support, such as receipts. If the paying party wishes to challenge the bill, the following steps occur:

(a) The paying party has 21 days to serve points of dispute.

(b) The receiving party has 21 days to file a reply.

 *3 months from the date of the order/judgement.*

(c) The receiving party must then file a request for an assessment hearing within three months of the expiry of the period for commencing detailed assessment proceedings.

(d) If the costs claimed are less than £75,000, the court undertakes a provisional assessment where the judge decides what costs are allowable in the absence of the parties.

(e) If either party is unhappy with the provisional assessment, they may request an oral hearing within 21 days; but if the party fails to achieve an adjustment in their favour by at least 20% they will be ordered to pay the costs of the hearing. This is to discourage parties from trying their luck at reducing the costs without being confident of success.

Given the robust attitude taken by judges in determining what costs are appropriate, it is preferable to avoid this procedure by agreeing costs.

## 11.5 Inter-partes costs: interim

Inter-partes is a term that means 'between the parties'. As the claim progresses towards trial, there may be hearings along the way to determine interim matters. These could include applications for summary judgment, to set aside a default judgment or to strike out a party's statement of case. At the end of each of these interim hearings, the question of costs must be considered. The judge will determine who is to pay the costs of the particular application and will usually summarily (instantly) assess the amount.

The types of costs orders that apply and their effect are detailed in **Chapter 6**.

## 11.6 Inter-partes costs: final

Once settlement has been reached or the court has given its judgment at trial, the question of costs will arise. There are two issues to consider, namely who pays and how much.

As to the first question, the usual rule is that the loser pays the winner's costs. However, establishing the amount of costs that should be paid tends to lead to more discussion or even dispute.

### 11.6.1 Factors in assessing the amount of costs

To assist the judge, CPR, r 44.4 sets out factors that the court should take into account in deciding the amount of costs the receiving party is entitled to. These are:

(a) the conduct of the parties and the efforts made to try and resolve the dispute;

(b) the value of any money or property involved;

(c) the importance of the matter to the parties;

(d) the complexity of the matter;

(e) the skill, effort, specialised knowledge and responsibility involved;

(f) the time spent on the case;

(g) the place and circumstances in which the work was done; and

(h) the receiving party's last approved or agreed budget.

Looking at these will ensure that each case receives a full consideration of the issues. However, before going into the detail of the costs, the judge must first check on what basis they were ordered – either on the standard or the indemnity basis.

### 11.6.2 The standard basis

The standard basis will apply in most cases and costs awarded on this basis must be proportionate to the matters in issue. The CPR provide that total costs will be proportionate if they bear a reasonable relationship to the sums in issue, the value of any non-monetary relief in issue, the complexity of the litigation, any additional work generated by the conduct of the paying party and any wider factors.

If there is any doubt, it will be resolved in favour of the paying party.

The effect is that costs that are disproportionate may be disallowed or reduced even if they were reasonably incurred and reasonable in amount.

**Figure 11.1** Assessment of costs: standard basis

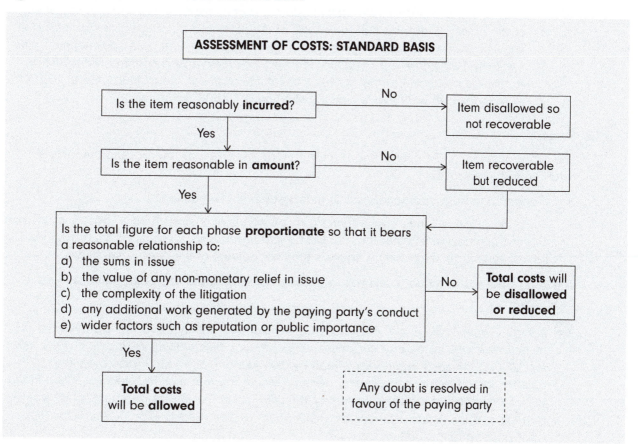

### 11.6.3 Approach to determining costs on the standard basis

When the court is asked to assess the amount of costs payable by an unsuccessful party, the costs judge will adopt a structured approach.

#### 11.6.3.1 Stage 1

The first stage requires the judge to go through the bill on a line by line basis, scrutinising each point in turn. Any items deemed to be unreasonably incurred or unreasonable in amount will be disallowed.

⭐ *Example*

*ULaws LLP represent Halliday Consultants & Co (Halliday) in their claim against Digby Surveyors Ltd (Digby) for professional negligence in relation to a survey carried out prior to their purchase of an office block. Halliday succeed in their claim and Digby are ordered to pay damages and costs on the standard basis. As the parties have not been able to reach agreement, ULaws LLP file a Notice of Commencement and the detailed assessment procedure is set in motion. The judge studies Halliday's bill and rules as follows:*

- *The fees of Expert A, who prepared a report for Halliday to advise on their claim before proceedings were issued, are totally disallowed on the basis that this expense was unreasonably incurred. The judge is not implying that Halliday did anything wrong (and indeed, it is sensible to assess the merits of the case at an early stage), but the report is unreasonable in the costs' context because the court did not give permission for Halliday to rely upon this expert.*

- *The costs of Expert B who drafted a report and gave evidence at trial for Halliday are reduced from £30,000 to £23,000. The judge is satisfied that the item was reasonable to incur as the court gave permission for Halliday to rely upon this expert. However, after taking into account the factors listed in Part 44 (above), particularly the value of the money in dispute, the complexity of the issue and the degree of specialised knowledge involved, the judge decided the fee was too high. This does not mean the expert will only receive £23,000 for their work as they have a contract with Halliday for the full amount; it simply means that Halliday will only be able to recover £23,000 from Digby and will have to pay the shortfall of £7,000 themselves.*

#### 11.6.3.2 Stage 2

The proportionality of the overall figure must then be assessed by reference to the factors listed in Part 44 (above).

- If deemed to be proportionate, no further assessment is required.

- If not, the judge will then scrutinise various categories of cost, such as disclosure or factual evidence, to decide whether they should be further reduced. Once any such reductions have been made, the resulting figure is the final amount of the costs assessment.

The court's powers to reduce costs regarded as disproportionate has been demonstrated in case law.

🔵 *In May v Wavell, Claim No. A02CL398, Central London County Court, the parties were in dispute over a private noise nuisance claim. Although the substantive litigation was settled for £25,000, the costs originally claimed by the claimant, Brian May (previously the guitarist for the rock group Queen), were £200,000. The judge considered each item in the bill and decided to reduce it by some £100,000. Thereafter the proportionality test was applied and this led to a further reduction in the overall costs to £35,000 (although they went back up to £75,000 on appeal).*

Despite being an extreme example, this case does highlight the forceful approach that the courts are taking to costs.

### 11.6.4 The indemnity basis

Costs on the indemnity basis are awarded as a penalty, usually to reflect the court's displeasure with the manner in which a party has behaved either pre-action and/or during proceedings. Costs on this basis must be:

(a) reasonably incurred; and

(b) reasonable in amount.

Any benefit of the doubt is given to the receiving party.

### ✪ Example

*In a dispute over the fishing rights of a lake in Northumberland, Greywater Fisheries Ltd (Greywater) succeed in their claim against Cheviot Landowners Ltd (Cheviot). They are awarded costs on an indemnity basis due to their opponent's conduct throughout the proceedings. When assessing costs, the judge determines that it was reasonable for the receiving party (Greywater) to instruct a particular expert but doubts the expert's fee of £14,000 was reasonable. In this situation, the benefit of the doubt is given to the receiving party and so Greywater will be able to recover the full amount of £14,000 from Cheviot.*

**Figure 11.2** Assessment of costs: indemnity basis

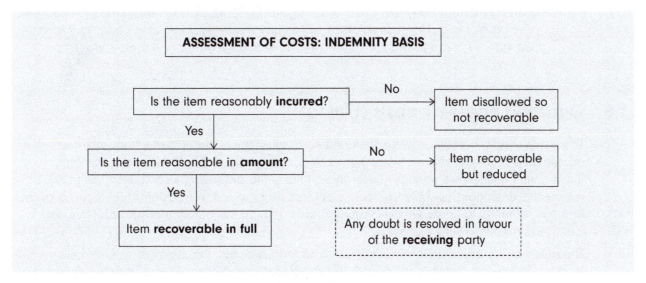

There are two key differences between the bases.

- When assessing on the standard basis, the court will only allow those costs that are proportionate to the matters in issue. There is no test of proportionality on the indemnity basis.

- Any doubts are resolved in favour of the receiving party on the indemnity basis, and the paying party on the standard basis.

## 11.7 Non-party costs

Winning at trial or obtaining a settlement does not always result in success particularly if it becomes apparent that the losing party is unable to pay the costs. Fortunately, the court has a discretionary power to make an order that a non-party meets the costs and this is governed by Part 46. However, although the funding of litigation by third parties is becoming more common, such an order is still exceptional and the court would have to be satisfied that the non-party was the real party interested in the litigation or that they were responsible for bringing the proceedings. External litigation funders such as family, friends or people who have given to a fund-raising campaign and who have no interest in the outcome will not be at risk of such an order; in contrast, third party funders in a more formal context may well be.

Before an order can be made, the third party must be added as a party to the proceedings and may attend the hearing when the court determines the issue of costs. Note there is no requirement to make a finding that the non-party acted improperly before making an order.

⭐ *Example*

(a) *Elgin Cars Ltd (Elgin) obtain a judgment for £65,000 against Birmingham Gears Ltd (BGL) for the supply of faulty gear mechanisms, which they used in the manufacture of their vehicles. Immediately after the trial, BGL go into liquidation leaving no assets with which to meet the costs order. Elgin apply for a non-party costs order against Henrik Larsen, the father of the managing director of the company, and provide evidence in support that Henrik personally funded the defence of the proceedings. The application is refused as Henrik had no interest in the outcome (other than on a personal level).* → not formal.

(b) *Litigation Funders Plc (LFP) commercially funded the claimant, Malvern Technology Ltd, in their unsuccessful claim against the defendant. An application is made by the defendant for a non-party costs order against LFP, which is joined to the proceedings. The court has a discretion to order LFP to pay the defendant's costs and, in this case, despite LFP's representations, they are ordered to pay half of the defendant's costs.*

## 11.8 Qualified one-way costs shifting

There are certain occasions where different costs rules apply under a mechanism known as qualified one-way costs shifting (QOCS). A claimant who makes an unsuccessful claim for personal injuries will normally be ordered to pay the defendant's costs. However, QOCS means the defendant will only be able to enforce that order if permission of the court is given, and this is limited to cases where the judge finds that, on the balance of probabilities, the claim was fundamentally dishonest.

The effect of the provision is inherently unfair in that, although the claimant will not be required to pay the defendant's costs if the claim fails, the defendant must pay the claimant's costs in the usual way if the claim succeeds. However the impact is limited as, at present, QOCS only applies to personal injury claims where the defendant is often backed by an insurance company.

⭐ *Example* 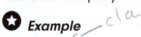 c/a

*Mitchell is injured in a road traffic collision. He wants to issue proceedings against Sally who is insured with Worldwide Insurance Plc (Worldwide) but is currently unemployed. Mitchell's solicitor explains that if he succeeds in the claim, Worldwide will most probably be ordered to pay his legal costs. However, qualified one-way costs shifting means that, even if he loses, Mitchell will not have to pay Worldwide's costs. The only way he will forfeit this protection is if Worldwide can prove that Mitchell's claim is fundamentally dishonest. Reassured by this, Mitchell decides to proceed with the litigation.*

## 11.9 Security for costs

The time and expense involved in dealing with prospective and actual litigation are often considerable. However, the claimant does at least have some control over this as they make the decision whether to proceed or not. In contrast, the defendant has the litigation imposed upon them. Even if the claim is defeated and the defendant obtains an order for their costs, they will never recover the full amount. Even worse, the claimant may be unable or unwilling to pay the costs order, leaving the defendant with the unenviable choice between bearing their own costs or investing further time and money in trying to enforce the order. The provisions in Part 25 on security for costs provide some assistance for defendants who have concerns in this regard.

### 11.9.1 The order

The court has the discretionary power to make an order for security for costs if:

(a) it is satisfied, having regard to all the circumstances of the case, it is just to make such an order; and

(b) one or more of the conditions in Part 25 applies.

### 11.9.2 The conditions *See update*

The defendant has a number of conditions at their disposal with the most commonly used being:

#### 11.9.2.1 Claimant based outside the European Union

The defendant may apply for an order for security for costs where the claimant – whether it be an individual or a company – is resident outside the EU. For individuals this is where they normally and habitually reside; whereas for companies it is where their central control and management are located. This condition recognises the difficulties a defendant may have in enforcing a costs order outside the EU.

#### 11.9.2.2 Claimant is an impecunious company

The defendant must establish there is reason to believe the claimant will be unable to pay the defendant's costs if ordered to do so. Evidence of the company's financial assets and the likely total costs of the litigation will be essential.

#### 11.9.2.3 Claimant has taken steps to make enforcement difficult

For this condition to be satisfied, the defendant must demonstrate that the claimant has taken steps in relation to their assets such that, if they lose the case and a costs order is made against them, the order will be difficult to enforce. The court will consider the effect of any such action and not the motivation. Thus, an order can be made even if, for example, the claimant is relocating to Saudi Arabia to take up a new employment opportunity. However, a failure to disclose assets may be sufficient to establish this requirement. On a separate note, in circumstances such as this, an application for a freezing injunction may also be appropriate.

### 11.9.3 Justness

The court must also be satisfied that it is just to make the order and the following factors are considered important.

(a) *The strength of the claim and the defence*: the less likely the defendant is to win at trial, the less justified they are in seeking security.

(b) *The claimant's ability to provide security*: where the claimant has a reasonable prospect of success, the courts will be reluctant to make an order for security with which they cannot comply as the effect will be to stifle the claim.

(c) *The causes of the claimant's impecuniosity*: the claimant may be able to persuade the court that their poor finances are caused by or contributed to by the defendant's behaviour.

(d) *Property within the jurisdiction*: where the application is made against a claimant resident outside the EU, the court is unlikely to grant security if they have sufficient assets within the jurisdiction that would be available to meet the defendant's costs.

(e) *The timing of the application*: the order should be applied for as soon as practicable.

### 11.9.4 Procedure

As with all interim applications, the defendant should write to the claimant first and ask for security to be provided voluntarily. If not, the defendant should submit a notice of application to the court with a witness statement in support. The evidence must establish that a condition exists, persuade the court it is just to exercise its discretion in favour of the defendant and justify the amount sought.

If the order is granted, it will specify the amount of the security, the date by which the claimant must provide it and the form it will take. Most commonly, the claimant is required to make a payment into court.

## 11.10 Offers to settle and costs

The parties are encouraged to negotiate to settle the claim before the litigation starts and, if unsuccessful, to continue to review the case throughout to seek agreement.

- Where a settlement is reached prior to the issue of proceedings, the prospective claimant will not be entitled to recover their legal costs unless this has been agreed.

- If settlements are reached after litigation has commenced, the terms should be recorded in a consent order or a Tomlin order (see **Chapter 4**) to ensure that enforcement proceedings may be issued to recover any monies due under the agreement, including costs.

## 11.11 Part 36 offers

A party may make an offer to settle in any way they choose and the court will take this into account when deciding the issue of costs. However, if an offer is made under Part 36, there are significant penalties attached if the relevant party makes the 'wrong' decision and rejects an offer that the court subsequently deems to be suitable. This puts real pressure on the opponent to accept an offer made in accordance with the provisions of Part 36, and on their solicitors to give appropriate advice.

### 11.11.1 Form and content

A Part 36 offer will be referred to as such and, to be valid, must comply with the relevant formalities. The offer must:

(a) be in writing;

(b) make clear it is made pursuant to Part 36;

(c) specify a period of not less than 21 days during which, if the offer is accepted, the defendant will pay the claimant's costs (known as 'the relevant period'); and

(d) state whether it relates to the whole of the claim or to part of it, and whether it takes into account any counterclaim.

In practice, most offers will state that acceptance is required within 21 days, so the offeree has three weeks to decide what to do. Because this is the norm, references are made in this chapter to Day 21 and Day 22 to assist in calculating the effect of a Part 36 offer. However, it is important to be aware that a longer period may be specified and a different time limit imposed.

The offer is made when it is served on the other party and the rules of deemed service will apply here. It is inclusive of interest until the relevant period expires.

A Part 36 offer is treated as 'without prejudice save as to costs'. As a consequence, the trial judge will not be made aware of the offer until the case has been decided, both liability and quantum. Only when the issue of costs falls to be dealt with will any relevant offer be produced to the judge.

### 11.11.2 The effect of acceptance

A Part 36 offer may be accepted at any time unless notice has been given of its withdrawal, making the relevant period of 21 days somewhat redundant. However, there may be adverse costs consequences of late acceptance so it is preferable to keep within the deadline.

#### 11.11.2.1 Acceptance within relevant period

If the defendant makes an offer and this is accepted by the claimant within the relevant period, the sum must be paid to the claimant within 14 days and, if not, the claimant can enter judgment. The claimant is also entitled to their costs of the proceedings up to the date on which the notice of acceptance is served on the defendant. If the parties cannot agree costs, a judge will assess them on the standard basis.

If the claimant makes a Part 36 offer that is accepted by the defendant within 21 days, the consequences are the same. The claimant will be entitled to their costs up to the date of acceptance on the standard basis.

#### 11.11.2.2 Late acceptance

If the claimant accepts a defendant's offer after the relevant period has expired and the parties cannot agree costs, the court will normally order that:

(a) the defendant pays the claimant's costs up to the date on which the relevant period expired; and

(b) the claimant pays the defendant's costs thereafter until the date of acceptance.

However, if the defendant accepts the claimant's offer late, the defendant will usually be ordered to pay the claimant's costs of the proceedings up to the date of acceptance.

In all these scenarios, the proceedings will be stayed (paused) to allow for the sum offered and the costs to be paid.

**Figure 11.3** summarises the implications of acceptance of a Part 36 offer by either of the parties.

**Figure 11.3**   Consequences of acceptance of Part 36 offer

| DEFENDANT SERVES PART 36 OFFER ON CLAIMANT | CLAIMANT SERVES PART 36 OFFER ON DEFENDANT |
|---|---|
| • C accepts the offer<br>• Proceedings are stayed<br>• D pays money to C within 14 days | • D accepts the offer<br>• Proceedings are stayed<br>• D pays money to C within 14 days |
| **Acceptance within relevant period (21 days of service of offer)**<br><br>• D pays C's costs up to the date of acceptance on the standard basis | **Acceptance within relevant period (21 days of service of offer)**<br><br>• D pays C's costs up to the date of acceptance on the standard basis |
| **'Late' acceptance (outside relevant period)**<br><br>• D pays C's costs up to the date of expiry of the relevant period on the standard basis; and then<br>• C pays D's costs up to the date of acceptance on the standard basis | **'Late' acceptance (outside relevant period)**<br><br>• D pays C's costs up to the date of acceptance on the standard basis |

*[handwritten annotations: "the gap", "can effectively accept at the relevant time. any more detrimental time. if C is late"]*

### 11.11.3   The effect of non-acceptance

If the offer is not accepted, the proceedings will continue. However, depending upon who made the offer and whether it is beaten at trial, there may be significant consequences in terms of the damages, interest and costs awarded. A decision to refuse what subsequently turns out to be a good offer can prove very expensive indeed. The justification for this tough approach is that the party who made the error of judgment has caused their opponent additional costs and wasted their time, as well as that of the court, by not accepting an offer that they should have.

Because of this, the penalties will be imposed from the day after the relevant 21 day period for acceptance expires (namely, from Day 22) and will apply unless the court rules that it would be unjust to do so.

#### 11.11.3.1 Justness under Part 36

In deciding whether to make an order to impose penalties for non-acceptance of a Part 36 offer, the judge will take into account all the circumstances of the case including the terms of the Part 36 offer, when it was made and in particular how close to the trial, what information was available to the parties at the time, their conduct and whether it was a genuine attempt to settle the proceedings. So when is it just to make an order under Part 36?

✓ An order will be made in the vast majority of cases and it will be the exception not to do so. It is irrelevant by how small an amount the offer is beaten.

✗ It may be unjust where the offeror has not provided sufficient disclosure to allow the offeree to make an informed decision; or, for example, the Part 36 offer expired only days before the trial and crucial allegations that had not been pleaded were raised in the opening of the case.

### 11.11.4 Part 36 consequences at trial of a claimant's offer

If the claimant makes a Part 36 offer, there are three possible outcomes. They could:

(a) win at trial and be awarded a sum that equals or beats their own offer;

(b) win the case but obtain a judgment that is less than their own offer; or

(c) lose at trial.

Each of these will be considered in turn.

#### 11.11.4.1 The claimant wins at trial and equals or beats their own offer

In the words of the CPR, the claimant has obtained a judgment which is at least as advantageous as their Part 36 offer. In this situation, the claimant will do very well indeed as, in addition to being awarded damages by the court, the penalties that may be enforced upon the defendant are potentially draconian. The sanctions, considered below, will be imposed in every case unless it is unjust to do so.

**Additional amount (usually a percentage of the damages)**

As the defendant has lost at trial, they will be ordered to pay damages and interest due under the contract or statute in the usual way (the sum awarded). However, the defendant will also be required to pay an additional amount – effectively 'extra' damages.

(a) For damages of up to £500,000, the defendant must pay an additional amount of 10% of the sum awarded.

(b) For damages in excess of £500,000 and up to £1 million, 10% of the first £500,000 is payable and thereafter, 5% up to a maximum of £75,000.

Where the remedy awarded is non-monetary, the term 'sum awarded' refers to the costs.

⭐ *Example*

*Klein Wholesalers Ltd (KWL) are claiming £1.1 million in damages against Freight Services Ltd (Freight) for failing to deliver a consignment of valuable goods. KWL make a Part 36 offer to settle of £900,000, which Freight refuse. The litigation proceeds and KWL succeed at trial. The judge awards £950,000 in damages and interest as claimed in the particulars of claim and so KWL (the claimant) has beaten their own Part 36 offer. They will receive an additional sum calculated as follows:*

*£500,000 x 10% = £50,000*

*         +*

*£450,000 x 5% = £22,500*

*_____*

*Additional sum = £72,500*

*_____*

*Freight are ordered to pay £72,500 on top of the initial figure of £950,000 giving a total of £1,022,500.*

The remaining penalties take effect from Day 22, the day after the relevant 21 day period for the defendant to accept the claimant's Part 36 offer expires.

**Enhanced interest on damages**

From Day 22 onwards, the percentage rate of interest that is charged on the damages awarded increases to a rate not exceeding 10% above the base rate – higher than the usual rate claimed in most proceedings (see **Chapter 5**).

To understand the full implications, it is necessary to identify certain key dates.

*Example*

*Continuing with the case of KWL and Freight, the breach of contract and loss occurred on 10 February when the goods were not delivered. The claimant made their Part 36 offer on 26 October. As this is a commercial case, interest was claimed at 1% over base rate in the particulars of claim. Interest at this rate is awarded from the date of loss up to and including Day 21 (16 November) when the relevant period for Freight to accept KWL's Part 36 offer expired.*

*From Day 22 onwards, so from 17 November to the date of judgment, enhanced interest totalling no more than 10% above the base rate is payable. This is a significantly higher percentage.*

### Costs on an indemnity basis

As the defendant has been unsuccessful, the usual order would be for them to pay the claimant's costs on the standard basis from the date they were incurred up to and including the trial and judgment. However, the effect of Part 36 is that the defendant is ordered to pay those costs on the indemnity basis from Day 22 onwards. This will result in the claimant being able to recover more of their costs.

### Interest on indemnity costs

The final penalty imposed is that interest is awarded on those indemnity costs and this may be as high as 10% above the base rate. This is in contrast with the general rule that interest is not payable on costs incurred before judgment. Again, the sanction runs from Day 22.

 *Example*

*In the case of KWL and Freight, the judge orders Freight to pay the claimant's costs on the standard basis from the date KWL instructed solicitors up until Day 21 (16 November). From Day 22 (17 November) onwards, the costs are awarded on the indemnity basis together with enhanced interest. Although this may be up to a maximum of 10% above the base rate, the court decides on a rate of 4% above base rate.*

### Summary

Set out below is a summary of the penalties that apply under Part 36 in those cases where the claimant equals or beats their own offer. As these are potentially draconian, involving many thousands of pounds, the defendant should consider any such offer very carefully indeed.

**Figure 11.4**   Effect of claimant equalling or beating own Part 36 offer at trial

> **CLAIMANT WINS AT TRIAL AND EQUALS OR
> BEATS THEIR OWN PART 36 OFFER**

> C is awarded:
> * **damages** plus
> * for damages up to £500,000 an additional 10% and
> * for damages of between £500,000 and £1 million an additional 5%
> * up to a maximum of £75,000

+

> **Up to Day 21:**
> * interest on the damages from the date of loss as claimed in the particulars of claim
> * costs on the standard basis from the date C incurred them

+

> **From Day 22 to judgment:**
> * interest on the damages at a maximum of 10% above base rate
> * costs on an indemnity basis
> * interest on the costs at a maximum of 10% above base rate

11.11.4.2 The claimant wins at trial but does not beat their own offer

The second possible outcome if the case proceeds to trial is that the claimant succeeds in their claim but is awarded damages that are lower than their own Part 36 offer. In this instance, no extra penalty is imposed on either party. This is because neither did anything 'wrong'. The claimant was right to make an offer but pitched it too high whereas the defendant was correct to turn it down for the same reason.

⭐ *Example*

*In the case of KWL and Freight, the claimant makes a Part 36 offer of £900,000. At trial, KWL are successful in their claim but are awarded £750,000 in damages. The judge orders Freight to pay interest on the damages as claimed in the particulars of claim and costs on a standard basis.*

Part 36 has no effect.

11.11.4.3 The claimant loses at trial

The final outcome is that the claimant is unsuccessful at trial. As a consequence, the claimant will not be awarded damages at all and will be ordered to pay the defendant's costs on a standard basis in the usual way. Once again, Part 36 has no effect.

In summary, there are no penalties if the claimant makes a Part 36 offer even if it becomes apparent that it was ill-judged. However, if the offer is either equalled or beaten, the sanctions for the defendant are severe.

**11.11.5   Part 36 consequences at trial of a defendant's offer**

It is open to either party to make a Part 36 offer and doing so can be just as effective for a defendant, with the particular advantage being the certainty of the outcome. As with the claimant, there are three possible scenarios to consider. The claimant:

(a) wins at trial and beats the defendant's Part 36 offer;

(b) wins at trial but fails to beat the defendant's Part 36 offer; and

(c) loses at trial.

As with any Part 36 offer, the prospect of being penalised in costs, should the offer be rejected unreasonably, acts as an incentive to accept. This is punitive as a claimant who succeeds in their litigation would not normally be expected to pay any of their opponent's costs.

### 11.11.5.1 The claimant wins at trial and beats the defendant's Part 36 offer

If the claimant obtains a judgment that is (to quote Part 36) more advantageous than the defendant's Part 36 offer, it is clear they were justified in their refusal because it was too low. In these circumstances the defendant will be ordered to pay:

- the amount of the judgment plus interest as claimed in the particulars of claim; and

- the claimant's costs on the standard basis.

Part 36 has no effect.

### 11.11.5.2 The claimant wins at trial but fails to beat the defendant's Part 36 offer

What if the claimant fails to obtain a judgment that is more advantageous than the defendant's Part 36 offer; in other words, the damages awarded are either equal to or less than the offer? In this instance, the court will, unless it is unjust to do so, make an order that punishes the claimant financially for continuing with the claim when (in hindsight) they should have accepted the offer. By failing to do so they have, since the relevant period expired, wasted the time and money of both the defendant and court.

Ordinarily, a claimant who succeeds at trial would expect the court to order the defendant to pay their costs for the entire proceedings. However, in the scenario where the claimant fails to beat the defendant's offer, the court takes a different approach. The effect of Part 36 is:

(a) the defendant pays the claimant's costs on the standard basis from when those costs were incurred until the relevant period expired (Day 21);

(b) thereafter, the claimant pays the defendant's costs on the standard basis from the date of the expiry of the relevant period (Day 22) until judgment; plus

(c) interest on those costs (a commercial rate of 1% or 2% above base rate has generally been adopted).

This is commonly called a 'split costs' order because the costs are divided between the parties with the split occurring at the expiry of the relevant period of 21 days.

⭐ *Example*

*Rhian instructs solicitors in relation to a claim for misrepresentation on 12 January. Proceedings are issued on 17 March and the defendant, Luton Garages Ltd (Luton), makes a Part 36 offer of £20,000 on 2 May. Rhian's solicitors explain to her that if she accepts within the relevant period, Luton will pay her costs. She is also made aware that she can accept the offer at any time thereafter unless it is withdrawn. However, Rhian decides to continue with the litigation as she is advised that she has a strong case and is likely to receive at least £25,000 in damages. The trial takes place on 27 October.*

*Rhian succeeds in her claim but fails to beat the defendant's Part 36 offer as she is only awarded £18,000 in damages. The effect on costs will be:*

- *Luton is ordered to pay Rhian's costs on the standard basis from 12 January (the date from when her costs were incurred) up to 23 May (the date of expiry of the relevant period of 21 days after the defendant's Part 36 offer).*

- *Then, despite having won her claim, Rhian is ordered to pay Luton's costs on the standard basis from 24 May (Day 22) until judgment. As this includes the trial on 27 October, the costs are likely to be significant. She will also have to pay interest on those costs and the court orders this at 1% above base rate.*

*In addition, Rhian will be liable for her own costs from Day 22.*

The Part 36 consequences which apply in this situation are summarised below.

**Figure 11.5**   Effect of claimant failing to beat defendant's Part 36 offer at trial

> **CLAIMANT WINS AT TRIAL BUT DOES NOT BEAT THE DEFENDANT'S PART 36 OFFER**
>
> C is awarded:
> - **damages** and
> - **interest** from the date of loss as claimed in the particulars of claim
>
> +
>
> **Up to Day 21:**
> - D pays C's costs on the standard basis from the date when C incurred them
>
> +
>
> **From Day 22 to judgment:**
> - C pays D's costs on the standard basis and
> - interest on those costs usually at 1% or 2% above base rate

### 11.11.5.3 The claimant loses at trial

What if the claimant fails to establish liability so they are not awarded any damages at all? This would be a financial disaster as far as the claimant is concerned because they turned down the money offered by the defendant. The general rule as to costs would apply and the claimant, as the losing party, would be ordered to pay the winner's (the defendant's) costs. However, to penalise the claimant for not accepting the defendant's Part 36 offer, they would also be ordered to pay interest on those costs from Day 22 until judgment – usually at 1% or 2% above base rate.

It is apparent that, although a penalty is imposed on the claimant for their error of judgment, this is not as significant as those which the defendant could face.

## Summary

- The general rule on costs is that the unsuccessful party pays the successful party's costs, although the judge has discretion to make a different order, perhaps to show disapproval of a party's conduct.
- The judge will also determine the amount of costs that are recoverable, unless the costs are fixed by the CPR.

- Costs will be summarily assessed at the end of hearings for interim applications and most fast track trials. In other cases, there will be a detailed assessment of costs involving fully particularised bills of costs, formal objections and responses and a determination by a judge, which may be at an oral hearing.

- There are two bases of assessment, both of which require costs to be reasonably incurred and reasonable in amount. The standard basis is the most commonly used and will only allow costs that are proportionate to the matter. Any doubts are resolved in favour of the paying party. In contrast, if costs are awarded on the indemnity basis, there is no reference to proportionality and any doubts are resolved in favour of the receiving party.

- A non-party may be liable for costs in exceptional circumstances.

- A claimant may be protected from liability for a defendant's costs under qualified one-way costs shifting but only in personal injury cases.

- A defendant who has concerns as to whether the claimant will be unable or unwilling to satisfy a costs order against them may apply for an order for security for costs.

- Both parties can make offers to settle including offers under Part 36. If the offer is accepted it must be paid by the defendant to the claimant within 14 days of acceptance, failing which the claimant can enter judgment.

- If a claimant makes a Part 36 offer that is not accepted by the defendant but which the claimant equals or beats at trial, severe sanctions will be imposed on the defendant. However, Part 36 has no effect if the claimant wins but is awarded a lesser sum or if they lose the claim.

- If a defendant makes a Part 36 offer that is rejected by the claimant and which the claimant fails to beat at trial, a 'split costs' order will be made. If the claimant loses, penalty interest is payable on costs, but Part 36 has no effect if the claimant wins and beats the defendant's offer.

## Sample questions

### Question 1

A claimant is considering issuing proceedings in the County Court against the defendant for loss of profits estimated at £25,000. Before taking the matter further, the claimant wants advice from their solicitor about the costs implications and how these will be dealt with by the court. The solicitor writes to the claimant explaining these.

**Which of the following statements contained in the letter of advice is correct?**

A   If the case proceeds on the fast track most of the costs are fixed by the CPR.

B   If the case proceeds on the multi-track costs are usually subject to summary assessment.

C   Each party will generally bear their own costs in making or responding to interim applications on the way to trial.

D   In most instances, costs will be ordered on the standard basis so that they must be reasonable to the matters in issue.

E   If costs are ordered on an indemnity basis any doubt is resolved in favour of the receiving party.

## Answer

Option E is correct.

Option A is wrong as although, for example, the costs of the advocate preparing and attending the trial are subject to the fixed costs regime of the CPR, most costs are not. Option B is wrong because the costs of multi-track litigation are generally subject to detailed assessment. However, the costs associated with interim applications are often addressed on a summary basis by reference to the usual principle that the unsuccessful party is responsible for the successful party's costs – option C accordingly is wrong.

Option D is wrong. Costs on the standard basis are recoverable if they are proportionate to the matters in issue – not 'reasonable'.

## Question 2

A company's business is dependent upon a few major contracts, including one with the local Council. As a result of a disagreement, the Council breaks off the relationship. The company sues, alleging that the Council was not entitled to terminate the contract. The Council applies for a security for costs order on the basis that the company will be unable to pay its costs if the Council wins at trial after the company admits it is in financial difficulties.

**Which of the following statements best describes what might happen during the security for costs application?**

A   The court cannot take into account the strength of the claim or the defence. Such matters must be left for determination at trial.

B   The Council should provide evidence in support of its application, such as the company's accounts and poor credit ratings.

C   The court cannot take into account any argument that it would not be just to make an order because the company's financial difficulties are as a result of the Council's wrongful termination.

D   If the court is satisfied that one of the required conditions applies and that it is just to do so, it must make an order for security for costs.

E   Even if the application is successful, the Council will have to bear its own costs in making that application. The purpose of the application is to provide security for future costs, not to quantify past costs.

## Answer

Option B is correct. The application is likely to be made on the grounds that the claimant is an impecunious company. In such cases, the defendant should produce evidence of the company's poor financial standing (such as the company's accounts and poor credit ratings).

Option A is wrong. The strength of the claim and the defence are matters that the court may take into account (although it is true that the court will want to avoid a situation in which the merits have to be considered in any detail).

Option C is wrong. An application for security for costs may fail where the claimant is able to persuade the court that its shortage of money has been caused by or contributed to by the defendant's behaviour (for example, in terminating a contract and not paying the agreed contract price when there was no legal basis for doing so).

Option D is wrong because the court's power to make an order for security for costs is discretionary rather than mandatory. Option E is also wrong. The usual costs position on any interim application is still relevant when making or opposing an application for security for costs, namely the loser pays the winner's costs.

### Question 3

A claimant makes a Part 36 offer of £40,000 on 1 March to the defendant to settle their dispute. The offer expires on 22 March (Day 21). The defendant rejects the offer and the matter proceeds to trial. After considering the evidence, the judge finds in the claimant's favour and damages are awarded against the defendant in the sum of £45,000.

**Which of the following is a consequence that will apply under Part 36?**

A    Unless it is unjust to do so, interest will be payable on the claimant's costs from 23 March onwards at a rate of 1% above base rate.

B    Unless it is unjust to do so, interest will be payable by the defendant on the damages awarded at a rate of up to 10% above base rate from the date of cause of action.

C    Unless it is unjust to do so, a split costs order will be made so the defendant is ordered to pay the costs up to 22 March and the claimant pays the costs from 23 March up to and including the trial.

D    Unless it is unjust to do so, the defendant will pay the claimant's costs on the standard basis up to 22 March and thereafter, from 23 March, on the indemnity basis.

E    Unless it is unjust to do so, an additional amount of £2250 will be payable by the defendant to the claimant.

### Answer

Option D is correct. Where the claimant secures a judgment which is at least as advantageous as the claimant's own Part 36 offer (as here), one of the consequences of the defendant not accepting the offer is that it will become liable to pay the claimant's costs on the indemnity basis from Day 22 onwards, unless it is unjust to do so.

Option A is wrong. Although it is correct to state that one consequence of the claimant securing a more advantageous judgment is that the defendant will be liable to pay interest on the claimant's costs from Day 22 onwards, that interest is payable at a rate of up to 10% above base rate.

Option B is also wrong because the penalty interest of up to 10% above base rate does not run from the date of cause of action, but from Day 22. Option C does not apply to this scenario. A split costs order would be relevant if the defendant had made a Part 36 offer which the claimant failed to beat. Furthermore, the additional amount payable on the damages is 10% for the first £500,000 awarded, and so the correct figure is £4500 and not £2250 as stated in Option E. This is only equivalent to an additional amount of 5% of the damages.

# 12 Enforcement of Money Judgments

## SQE1 syllabus

By the end of this chapter you will be able to apply relevant core legal principles and rules appropriately and effectively, at the level of a competent newly qualified solicitor in practice, to realistic client-based and ethical problems and situations in relation to **enforcement of money judgments** as follows:

- oral examination (order to obtain information)
- methods of enforcement
- procedure and mechanisms for effecting valid enforcement in another jurisdiction

Note that for SQE1, candidates are not usually required to recall specific case names, or cite statutory or regulatory authorities and these are provided for illustrative purposes only.

## Learning outcomes

The learning outcomes for this chapter are:

- To appreciate how to investigate a judgment debtor's means.
- To evaluate when different types of enforcement methods should be used and how to conduct them.
- To understand how to enforce a judgment outside England and Wales.

## 12.1 Introduction

The conclusion of the trial is not always the end of the proceedings. Having obtained a judgment, the opponent should pay the monies due without any further action being necessary, but this does not always happen. This may be for a variety of reasons, from a lack of the means to pay to simple avoidance. Because the court does not automatically enforce the judgment, it is up to the successful party to pursue their opponent for the money. The winning party, referred to as the judgment creditor, will have to consider the best method of enforcing payment.

The question of enforcement should be considered before proceedings are even commenced; indeed, there is little point in obtaining a judgment against a party who clearly cannot pay as this would simply be 'throwing good money after bad'. Appropriate investigations into the whereabouts and assets of the opponent should be undertaken at an early stage.

## 12.2 Investigating the judgment debtor's means

To determine the best method of enforcing the judgment, it may be necessary to obtain more information about the judgment debtor's financial circumstances. There are two possibilities:

(a) instruct an enquiry agent; and

(b) apply to the court for an order to obtain information from the debtor.

Although an enquiry agent may succeed in locating assets that the debtor seeks to hide and may be a quicker way forward, this approach does incur expense. The second option, which is covered by Part 71 and was previously referred to as an oral examination, is considered next.

### 12.2.1 Order to obtain information

An order to obtain information from a judgment debtor is a court order requiring the debtor to attend before an officer of the court to be questioned on oath about their finances or those of a company of which they are an officer. The procedure is as follows:

(a) The judgment creditor files a notice of application at court setting out details of the name and address of the debtor, the judgment the creditor is seeking to enforce and the amount owed. Any specific documents that the creditor wants produced at the hearing should be listed.

(b) The order is normally personally served on the debtor who can, within seven days, request payment of their reasonable travelling expenses to and from the court.

(c) The hearing will usually take place in the County Court hearing centre for the area where the debtor resides or carries on business.

(d) The examination is conducted by an officer of the court, or a judge if requested by the creditor.

(e) Standard questions are asked, although the creditor may also request additional ones. The officer will make a written record of the responses given by the debtor, who will be invited to read and sign it at the end of the hearing.

(f) If the debtor fails to attend court, the judge may make a committal order against them, which is usually suspended provided the debtor complies with the order.

## 12.3 Methods of enforcement

The judgment creditor can, if they wish and can afford to do so, use one or more of several different means of enforcement, with the four most common being summarised below:

**Figure 12.1** Methods of enforcement

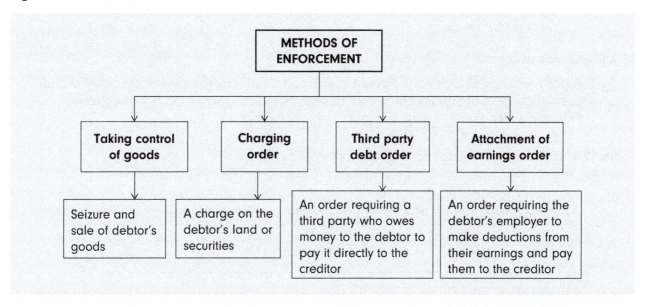

The solicitor must decide, in light of information obtained about the judgment debtor, which method of enforcement is most suitable. However, there are some restrictions that limit the choice; for example, when an attachment of earnings order is in force, permission of the court is required to take control of the debtor's goods.

## 12.4 Taking control of goods

This method of enforcement is governed by Part 83 and is used where the amount owed may be recovered by seizing the debtor's possessions of an equivalent value. The items are then sold by public auction.

- *Who?*

    In the High Court, the task is carried out by a High Court Enforcement Officer (HCEO) and in the County Court, by enforcement officers (often referred to as bailiffs).

- *Powers?*

    Enforcement officers cannot force entry into a debtor's home, but they can use reasonable force to enter business premises if they believe the debtor's goods are inside.

- *What may be seized?*

    The usual contents of a home or business premises including motor cars, computers and banknotes, but also less common ones for instance boats and securities such as share certificates.

- *What is exempt?*

    The so-called 'necessary items exemption' only applies to individuals and not to a judgment debtor that is a partnership, limited company and so on. If applicable, items such as clothes, bedding, furniture and household equipment, which are reasonably required for the basic needs of the debtor and their family, cannot be taken. Neither can work tools, computers, vehicles and other equipment that are necessary to the debtor personally for work or study, subject to a maximum aggregate value of £1,350. In addition, goods that belong solely to another, such as a spouse or other family member, or those subject to hire or hire-purchase agreements may not be removed. Any disputes concerning a co-owner's entitlement to a share of the proceeds of sale will be resolved by the court.

### 12.4.1 Choice of court

A party who has obtained a judgment in the High Court may issue a writ of control in that court, regardless of the amount to be enforced. However, where a party has obtained judgment in the County Court, different provisions apply as follows:

**Table 12.1** Enforcement of judgments: County or High Court?

| Judgment sum | Court in which to enforce judgment | Document required | Who enforces |
|---|---|---|---|
| Less than £600 | County Court | Warrant of control | Enforcement officer (bailiff) |
| £600 or more but less than £5,000 | Either the County or the High Court. If the High Court is chosen, the judgment must be transferred from the County to the High Court. | Warrant or writ of control as appropriate to the court | The enforcement agent applicable to the court |
| £5,000 or more | High Court (except for proceedings under the Consumer Credit Act 1974) | Writ of control | High Court Enforcement Officer |

### 12.4.2 Procedure

The procedure differs slightly depending upon the court in which the judgment is to be enforced.

*High Court*

(a) The judgment creditor delivers a praecipe (request) and two copies of a writ of control to the court office, together with the judgment.

(b) The court seals the writ and returns one copy to the creditor.

(c) The creditor then forwards this to the HCEO for the county where the debtor resides or carries on business, for the writ to be executed.

*County Court*

(a) The creditor files the form of request for a warrant of control at the County Court hearing centre that serves the address where the goods are to be seized.

(b) The warrant is executed by the enforcement officer for the district where the debtor resides or carries on business.

When executing the writ or warrant of control, the enforcement officers usually immediately either remove goods or take control of them. However, if the debtor needs time to pay, they may enter into a controlled goods agreement under which the debtor acknowledges that the enforcement agent has taken control of the goods and, further, that they will not remove or dispose of them before the debt is paid. The effect is that the goods remain on the premises for a few days to allow the debtor one final opportunity to pay.

If payment is still not received, the goods seized will be sold at a public auction and the amount required to pay the judgment, including costs, will be deducted from the money raised, with any surplus being returned to the debtor (and any co-owner).

### 12.4.3 Advantages and disadvantages

Although often effective, there are limits to the powers of HCEOs and enforcement officers. As a general rule, they cannot force entry into a debtor's home and a savvy debtor may simply refuse them entry. However, they are able to use reasonable force to break into business premises if there is no living accommodation attached and the debtor's goods are believed to be inside – particularly helpful when enforcing against a commercial debtor.

There are certain advantages of enforcement in the High Court, one of which is that HCEOs are usually paid on their results – based on the amount collected – and so it is generally perceived that they are more effective in achieving a successful conclusion. Also, in the High Court, interest continues to accrue on the debt. However, in many cases, the logistical difficulties involved (for example, cars can be hidden in garages), the costs of this method of enforcement and the relatively low re-sale value of the goods seized mean that the judgment creditor does not obtain all the monies due to them.

## 12.5 Charging orders

Under Part 73, it is possible for a charging order to be made either on land or on securities, such as stocks and shares. The effect is that the creditor is placed in a similar position to a mortgagee. The charging order will sit on the asset until such time as it is worth the creditor pursuing the matter further and applying for an order for sale. However, this may involve a considerable wait until, for example, the land has increased in value such that there is sufficient equity in the property to cover the judgment debt.

### 12.5.1 Charging order on land

In addition to being able to apply to the court for an order charging the debtor's land with the amount due under a judgment, a charging order can also be made in respect of land the debtor owns jointly with another person. In this instance, the order is a charge upon the debtor's beneficial interest, rather than upon the land itself. Once a charging order has been made, it should be registered at the Land Registry or (if unregistered) at the Land Charges Department.

At this point, although the creditor has security for the debt, they still do not have their money. To obtain this, the creditor would have to apply to the court for an order for sale of the land charged and the judgment will then be satisfied out of the proceeds of sale.

### 12.5.2 Procedure

Where the debt is more than £5,000, the application for a charging order can be made either in the County or the High Court. However, if it is made to the County Court, the application must be submitted to the County Court Money Claims Centre.

There are three stages to the procedure.

Stage 1: interim charging order ← FC.

- The creditor must file an application notice including details of the judgment debt, the land over which the charging order is sought, and the names and addresses of any other person affected such as a party with a prior charge over the property. The creditor must also file a draft interim charging order (ICO).

- The application will usually be dealt with by a court officer without a hearing, who will either make the ICO or refer the matter to a judge for further consideration.

- The ICO, the application notice and any documents filed in support must be served by the creditor on the debtor within 21 days.

- The debtor then has 14 days to request that the court officer's decision be reviewed by a judge.

Stage 2: final charging order

- If any person objects to the making of a final charging order (FCO), they must file and serve written evidence stating the grounds of objection within 28 days of service of the ICO.

- If an objection is received, the court will transfer the application to the debtor's home court for a hearing.

- At the hearing the court can make a FCO, discharge the ICO or direct a trial of any issues in dispute between the parties.

Stage 3: order for sale

- If the interim order is made final, the creditor has a charge on the debtor's land, which can be enforced by an order for sale of the property. However, in order to do so, fresh proceedings must be commenced.

### 12.5.3 Advantages and disadvantages

A charging order is a useful means of securing payment against those debtors who lack liquid (available) assets and where other forms of enforcement would not recover the debt. The main advantages are that, although it does not necessarily result in prompt payment, a charging order does secure the judgment debt. Furthermore, it may encourage the debtor to make efforts towards settling the debt, particularly as interest will continue to accrue (unless the debt falls under the Consumer Credit Act 1974).

However, a charging order will not always be effective. It is not appropriate where there are significant other prior charges or mortgages over the property so that there may be no or insufficient equity available to enforce against, or where the debtor has no beneficial interest over it. Even if granted, payment may not be received for many years if an application for an order for sale is unsuccessful, perhaps because there are other people in the house such as children, who will be severely affected by a sale. Nevertheless, it may be the only way forward if there are no other assets against which the creditor can enforce and it is preferable to wait for the monies owed rather than lose them entirely.

### 12.5.4 Charging order on securities

A creditor may also obtain a charging order on a debtor's beneficial interest in certain specified securities including UK government stock, shares and unit trusts. The order will normally provide for the charge to extend to any interest or dividend payable. The procedure is similar to that for obtaining a charging order on land.

## 12.6  Third party debt orders

The debtor may be owed money by a third party, for example:

- bank or building accounts that are in credit; and

- trade debts due to a business.

In these circumstances, the court can make an order under Part 72 requiring the third party to pay the creditor sufficient of the monies to satisfy the judgment debt and costs. This is known as a third party debt order.

The debt must belong to the judgment debtor solely and beneficially.

### ⭐ Example

*Nafeesa owes £8,500 to Hair Stuff Ltd (HSL) for equipment purchased for her beauty salon. Judgment is obtained against her and HSL seek an order to obtain information. Nafeesa admits that she has an account with £5,300 in Barcloyds Bank but HSL cannot enforce against this, as it is in joint names with her husband. She also discloses that she is owed £2,200 by Happy Days Ltd for a corporate event. HSL apply for a third party debt order to compel Happy Days Ltd to pay the debt to them rather than to Nafeesa.*

### 12.6.1  Procedure

An application for a third party debt order must be issued in the court that made the order being enforced, unless the proceedings have (subsequently) been transferred to a different court. The procedure is as follows:

(a) The creditor applies to court without notice to the debtor, providing details such as the name and address of the branch where the money is held and the account number.

(b) The judge will make an interim order, which has the effect of freezing the bank account or funds held by the third party. At this point, no money is paid to the creditor but a hearing will be listed no less than 28 days later.

(c) At the hearing, the court will consider any objections and, unless there is a good reason not to do so, the order will be made final. This requires the third party to pay the money to the creditor.

### ⭐ Example

*Continuing with the scenario above, Nafeesa attends the hearing and objects to the making of the third party debt order over the £2,200 owed to her by Happy Days Ltd. She provides evidence that it will cause her and her young children real hardship. She is already behind on her rent payments, the landlord is threatening to evict her family and she is having to access food banks to survive. In the circumstances, the judge decides not to make the order final.*

### 12.6.2  Advantages and disadvantages

The main benefit of this method of enforcement is the element of surprise as the debtor will not be aware of the application until after the order has been made. By this time, their bank account or funds held by a third party will already have been frozen. However, an informed debtor is likely to be aware of this as a possibility and may move the funds as soon as a judgment is made (if not before). If the account is not in credit on the day when the order is served, it is ineffective. Furthermore, to be successful, the bank account must be held in the sole name of the debtor and, if in joint names, the application will fail.

## 12.7 Attachment of earnings

An attachment of earnings order is an order that compels the debtor's employer to make regular deductions from the debtor's earnings and pay them into court. For this method of enforcement, the debtor must be employed.

⭐ *Example*

> *HSL apply for an attachment of earnings order against Nafeesa. The application fails because Nafeesa is self-employed.*

### 12.7.1 Procedure

Applications for an attachment of the debtor's earnings must be made to the County Court as the High Court has no power to make these orders. As a consequence, if the judgment has been obtained in the High Court, the proceedings will have to be transferred to the County Court before this method of enforcement can be used.

The procedure is set out in Part 89.

(a) The creditor applies to the County Court Money Claims Centre.

(b) The court informs the debtor of the application and requires them either to pay the sum due, or to file a statement of means giving details of their income and outgoings.

(c) On receipt of the form, a court officer will make an attachment of earnings order, fixing the repayment rate by applying certain guidelines. Only if there is insufficient information to do so will the matter be referred to a judge. The order will specify the *normal deduction rate* and the *protected earnings rate*. The latter is the amount that the court considers is reasonable for the debtor to live on, so if their earnings for a particular week are equal to or less than this figure, the creditor will receive nothing that week.

(d) The order will be sent to the parties and to the debtor's employer, with instructions to deduct the amount ordered from the debtor's pay and forward it to the court. The employer is entitled to deduct a small additional sum in respect of their administrative costs.

(e) If either party objects to the order that has been made, they can apply for the matter to be reconsidered by the district judge at a hearing.

### 12.7.2 Advantages and disadvantages

Attachment of earnings orders are an effective means of obtaining payment of a judgment debt provided the debtor remains in work and is not self-employed. However, if the debtor loses their job, the payments will cease and if they move employment, the creditor will have to repeat the process. In addition, the court may order a very low value instalment so the judgment will take a considerable time to satisfy.

## 12.8 Enforcement in another jurisdiction

Whether an English judgment can be enforced abroad and, if so, the method used will depend upon the nature of the judgment and the country concerned. In some countries, a simplified process is available but, if not, the party will have to decide whether to issue fresh proceedings abroad or to give up entirely.

The situation is complicated by the number of different systems in place.

### 12.8.1 Scotland and Northern Ireland

Enforcing a judgment in the home countries is relatively quick and straightforward and is governed by the CPR. Part 74 requires a creditor to:

(a) obtain a certificate confirming the date of the judgment, the sum awarded and details of interest and costs; and

(b) make an application to the court in Scotland or Northern Ireland, supported by evidence, to register the judgment within six months.

If the application is successful, the judgment will be registered and may be enforced using local methods.

### 12.8.2 Within the European Union  *See update*

The Brussels Regulation (recast) 1215/2012 provides a simplified mechanism for the enforcement of judgments in European Union Member States. Foreign judgments may be registered with the local court and, thereafter, enforced in the same manner as a judgment of that country. An almost identical outcome is achieved for nations such as Norway, Iceland and Switzerland using the Lugano Convention.

The creditor presents a copy of the judgment together with a completed standard form certificate at the enforcing court. Although the debtor could apply for refusal of recognition of the judgment, this will not be the norm. The creditor will then proceed with their chosen method of enforcement, which will vary from country to country.

The Withdrawal Agreement between the European Union and the United Kingdom preserves this position for judgments given in proceedings instituted before 31 December 2020. The position for proceedings commenced on or after 1 January 2021 depends on what (if any) deal is reached. If none, the creditor's ability to enforce an English judgment will be determined by the national law of the European State where enforcement is sought. Certainly additional time and costs will be expended and some Member States do not have rules allowing for the recognition and enforcement of judgments from non-EU states.

### 12.8.3 The Commonwealth

A company may have dealings with a variety of Commonwealth states including Australia, Pakistan and Jersey. Enforcement is possible under the Administration of Justice Act 1920 for High Court judgments and the Foreign Judgments (Reciprocal Enforcement) Act 1933 for judgments of the County Court. The judgment must be final and registered within 12 months for the 1920 Act but the creditor has six years for matters that fall within the 1933 Act. Failure to do so means the creditor loses their right to enforce outside of the jurisdiction.

### 12.8.4 Other countries

There are many countries that are not covered by the above systems with the USA, Japan and China being the most important examples. In these countries, the creditor will usually have to issue fresh proceedings and instruct local lawyers to pursue their claims.

### 12.8.5 Practical considerations

Where a claim involves a foreign element, the claimant should consider carefully how realistic their chances of enforcing the judgment are before commencing proceedings. If enforcement is likely to require new proceedings to be issued, it may be sensible to start the claim in that country rather than in the English courts.

## Summary

- The question of enforcement should be considered before proceedings are issued to avoid wasting time and money on a debtor who cannot or will not pay.

- If further details are required on a debtor's finances, the creditor can apply to the court for an order to obtain information.

- The creditor should consider the most cost-efficient way of enforcing the judgment.

- If the debtor has assets with some value, the creditor can apply for an order to take control of those goods, bearing in mind that some may be exempt from seizure.

- A charging order may be made over any interest the judgment debtor has in land or certain specified securities.

- A third party debt order may be made against a bank account or building society account that is in the sole name of the judgment debtor, or a trade debt owed solely to the debtor.

- If the debtor is employed, an attachment of earnings order may be an effective method of enforcement.

- The procedure for enforcing an English judgment in a foreign country depends on where enforcement is required. In many cases, arrangements are in place to assist but, if not, the law of the State where the judgment is to be enforced will apply.

## Sample questions

### Question 1

The claimant has obtained judgment for £147,000 against the defendant. The defendant disputes that he has the means to pay the judgment debt and points out that he lives in rented accommodation and has no regular income. The claimant has received information from a friend that the defendant has significant assets including properties, which he owns in a nearby town.

**Which of the following best describes the action that the claimant should take?**

A   The claimant should write to the defendant requesting that he provide details of his income, expenses, assets and liabilities.

B   The claimant should instruct an enquiry agent to seek further details about the defendant's finances.

C   The claimant should apply for an order to obtain information from the defendant relying upon the court officer to ask standard questions.

D   The claimant should apply for an order to obtain information from the defendant and submit additional questions.

E   The claimant should instruct an enquiry agent to seek further details about the defendant's finances and then apply to the court for an order to obtain information, including additional questions.

## Answer

Option E is correct. Although the claimant could write to the defendant asking for details of his finances, given the debtor has already stated he does not have the means to pay, it is unlikely he will respond properly – hence, option A is wrong. The claimant should consider applying to the court for an order to obtain information as there are sanctions if the defendant fails to comply. However, as the defendant appears to be hiding assets, he may not answer the questions fully or truthfully; thus, although options C and D are correct, they may not be the most effective approach.

The best way forward is option E because the claimant will be able to find out specific details about the defendant's finances, enabling them to tailor questions appropriately when they apply for an order to obtain information. As the judgment is for a significant sum of money, it would be worth the claimant taking both steps before proceeding to enforcement. Option B is not wrong, but is not as complete as option E.

## Question 2

A creditor wishes to enforce their judgment against the debtor (a limited company). After carrying out enquiries, the creditor establishes that the debtor has a number of assets. They own a factory premises and the plant and machinery, but rent offices nearby. The debtor has a bank account that is overdrawn, but a significant amount of money is owed by a customer for a trade debt. An expensive motor car driven by the managing director was recently purchased by her for her own personal use.

**Which of the assets could the creditor enforce against?**

A   The creditor could enforce against the factory premises, the plant and machinery and the trade debt.

B   The creditor could enforce against the factory premises, the trade debt and the motor car.

C   The creditor could enforce against the plant and machinery, the rented offices and the overdrawn bank account.

D   The creditor could enforce against the plant and machinery, the trade debt and the motor car.

E   The creditor could enforce against the factory premises, the plant and machinery, the trade debt and the motor car.

## Answer

Option A is correct. The debtor owns the factory premises and the plant and machinery so both of these assets are available for enforcement, as is the trade debt because these monies are owed to the debtor. However, the debtor only rents the offices, so these cannot be enforced against and nor can the motor car as it is owned by the managing director personally. There are no monies in the overdrawn bank account so this asset is not available to pay the debt either. All of the other answers either include assets that cannot be enforced against or miss those that can.

## Question 3

The judgment debtor, who is self-employed, has the following assets: a house, which she owns but which is subject to a mortgage equivalent to the value, a warehouse, which she rents and where she stores valuable stock that she purchased for her business, and a building society account in which she has £100.

**Which asset is likely to prove the most effective for the creditor to enforce against?**

A   The creditor should apply for a charging order against the house.

B   The creditor should apply for a taking control of goods order for the warehouse.

C   The creditor should apply for an attachment of earnings order.

D   The creditor should apply for a taking control of goods order for the stock.

E   The creditor should apply for a third party debt order over the building society account.

**Answer**

Option D is correct as the stock is described as 'valuable'. Although the creditor could apply for a charging order over the house, the facts state that there is no equity in the property (option A, therefore, is not the best answer). The warehouse is rented so cannot be enforced against – hence, option B is wrong.

Option C is wrong because the creditor is self-employed and attachment of earnings orders only apply to those who are employed. Option E is not the best answer as, while a third party debt order could be obtained over the building society account, the small amount of money means that it is not the most effective asset to enforce against.

# Index